# THE *Painting* AND THE *Piano*

## An Improbable Story of Survival and Love

### JOHN LIPSCOMB AND ADRIANNE LUGO

D1456774

Health Communications, Inc.
Deerfield Beach, Florida

*www.hcibooks.com*

Library of Congress Cataloging-in-Publication Data
is available through the Library of Congress

© 2017 John Lipscomb and Adrianne Lugo

ISBN-13: 978-07573-1992-1 (Paperback)
ISBN-10: 07573-1992-0 (Paperback)
ISBN-13: 978-07573-1993-8 (ePub)
ISBN-10: 07573-1993-9 (ePub)

HCI, its logos, and marks are trademarks of Health Communications, Inc.

Publisher: Health Communications, Inc.
        3201 S.W. 15th Street
        Deerfield Beach, FL 33442–8190

*Cover and interior design by Lawna Patterson Oldfield*

Adrianne wishes to thank her parents, Will and Bea Cahn, for giving her a loving and caring foundation. May they rest in peace. As well as her brothers and sister-in-law for their support, contributions and love. Adrianne also wishes to thank her sister for always trying to protect her. Most importantly, she wishes to thank her three daughters, Alex, Sam and Frankie.

Johnny wishes to thank his mother, Eloise Cella, may she rest in peace. As well as his father, John Lipscomb, his brother and sisters for their support, contributions and love.

*If you want to make God laugh,*
*tell him your plans*

—Unknown

# CONTENTS

# PROLOGUE

# WE CAN NEVER LET GO OF OUR MOTHERS

*There's a phrase, "the elephant in the living room,"
which purports to describe what it's like to live with a
drug addict, an alcoholic, an abuser. People outside such
relationships will sometimes ask, "How could you let such a
business go on for so many years? Didn't you see the
elephant in the living room?" And it's so hard for anyone
living in a more normal situation to understand the
answer that comes closest to the truth; "I'm sorry, but it was
there when I moved in. I didn't know it was an elephant;
I thought it was part of the furniture." There comes
an aha-moment for some folks—the lucky ones—
when they suddenly recognize the difference.*

—Stephen King

*M*y dad was driving from Missouri to New Braunfels, Texas, to visit his stepdaughter Chandler, when he lost consciousness and crashed into the side of a building. He was lucky. Even still, he was so close to death in the emergency room that a nurse called me to ask, Are you in a position to make end-of-life care decisions for your father?

I felt my chest tighten as her question made me truly aware of the reality of Dad's situation. *My dad is surrounded by incredibly competent people, and not that long ago he wouldn't have let me walk his dog on my own,* I said, *but for some reason he's made me executor of his estate.*

*Do you want us to put a red bracelet on him?*

*What's that?*

*It's a Do Not Resuscitate bracelet.*

*Oh.*

*If his heart or breathing stops we'll let him go. Another term for it is Allow Natural Death.*

The old man was quite a bit smarter than I gave him credit for. He knew I couldn't even kill a fly.

For several days I sat by his bedside and watched as he slowly came back from the brink. I was glad to spend that time with him, but I was lonely for Adrianne. Although I called her when I could, I felt uneasy being away from her. The world spins a little faster when she isn't close.

But since that phone call from the ER nurse, things have improved. Dad has gone from near-death to marginally better, and within a few days he was holding forth from his hospital bed as if he was at his own dinner table with a long series of orders and demands. Listening to him, I wondered where the red DNR bracelet was when we needed it.

Now my stepsister Chandler and I sit with Dad as the low light of late afternoon fades into the deep, bright blue of twilight that the painter Maxfield Parrish so often used. Dad's speech slows and sentences trail off with a wave of his sallow, thin hand, as if he is trying to send us off on an errand without the effort of another word. Waves of pain ripple and crest behind his eyes.

*Dad, give yourself another bump of morphine.*

He tilts his head toward the morphine pump and follows the thin pipette running into his IV. *Give me some water and I'll push the button.*

I hand him the button and he pushes it twice. His jaw slackens as the medicine moves through his body, and his eyes droop. My mind follows him as he fades. He is not the strong independent man I've known my whole life, and I am scared to lose him.

It all feels so different from thirty years ago, when I stood at mom's bedside in an ICU in St. Louis, waiting for her to die. For a woman born into affluence, who'd held such promise early in life, the loneliness of her death was testament to how far she'd fallen.

Adrianne's birth mother died alone as well, but she'll tell that story.

*I think dad's pretty much out for the night,* I say to Chandler.

We walk to the car and Chandler climbs into the passenger seat. I ease the car into the cool, Texas spring evening.

We are bathed by a halo of streetlight but, high above, the inky sky is suffused by shimmering starlight.

*How're you doing, Johnny?* Chandler asks.

I drive slowly along a wide boulevard that runs past quiet neighborhoods. Almost by instinct I head toward Cheeves, an attractive little steak house and café we've been to a few times already.

*It's tough to see Dad like this.*

She looks at me. *You seem a bit lost inside your own head.*

*I'm sorry . . . It's hard not to think about Mom.*

*I remember.* She looks out the window. *She was a difficult woman.*

*Yeah, she was.* I tighten my grasp on the steering wheel. I don't like talking about Mom. *Adrianne's was probably worse.*

*I don't really know anything about Adrianne's mom.*

My face feels warm. *It's kind of embarrassing to me that you don't know more about Adrianne.*

Chandler turns toward me. *Why's that?*

*I remember how close we used to be when we were kids, after you and your mom moved into the house, and I'm sorry we've lost that a little bit.*

*Me too,* she says.

It has been a long way back to the world of the living for me. Every now and again there are reminders—lost connections, painful trespasses—that bring back how I used to be.

I glance at Chandler. Her eyes are soft, weary looking. *That's okay Johnny. You're here now.*

*Adrianne had it worse than me.* I tell her a bit about the circumstances of Adrianne's birth and how that affected her childhood and the rest of her life.

Chandler shifts in her seat. *You know, I was at a restaurant with Dad recently . . .*

I love her father and have always affectionately called him Uncle Jules. He's a gentleman in the finest Texas tradition, and a noted psychiatrist.

*. . . and we're drinking wine, waiting for our food, when he starts talking about his work. He's getting a good head of steam going when I say, 'Dad that's all well and good, but what's the key to psychiatry?'*

*Of course, he immediately launches into a discourse of the current understanding of the workings of the mind and one thing and another—all of it laced with the usual psychobabble—which is interesting, but I've heard it all a million times.*

*So I break in again and say, 'Dad, how have you helped so many people? Can you sum it up in one sentence?'*

A faint smile crosses her lips.

*I thought I'd stumped him because it took him a few beats, but then he gets that grin of his—you know, almost demure—and says, 'When I meet with a new patient the first question I ask him or her is, Tell me about your mother. Well, they'll start with that and wander off about their spouse or kids or boss and so on and I'll say, That's interesting, but tell me about your mother.'*

*I don't get it,* I say.

Chandler laughs. *I didn't either so I say, 'Dad, what the heck does all that mean?' And he says, 'If I know the relationship a child has with his or her mother, then I can help that person.'*

*Did you ask him why?*

*No, not really. But he did say that one of the core elements to our humanity is the mother-child bond. If that bond is removed or damaged it's like taking gravity away. All of a sudden that child's left spinning.*

*I don't think you can blame everything on the mother.* I turn the car onto Temple's modest main street of shops and restaurants.

*No, of course not.* She smiles at me. *I'd hate to think what that would mean for my own kids. But maybe it's a big reason why you spent so much of your life spinning.*

*Adrianne went through it too.*

*I can imagine . . . well, I can't imagine what it was like for her, it must have been horrible to be so young and go through that, but I can see her, such a little girl, trapped in a nightmare.*

I pull the car into a parking spot across from the restaurant. Other than the sound of a woman laughing as she walks by with her man, it is quiet.

I look at Chandler. *It's the beginning and end of our story . . .*

*What do you mean?*

*What your father said. It was a lot to survive, and that we actually found each other . . .*

*She's not from your world, is she?*

*No. Long Island and a ratty little apartment in Brooklyn is a long way from that.*

I lean back in my seat and rub my eyes. I miss Adrianne more than ever.

*All of it, our story, is a series of improbable mercies.*

# Chapter One

# ADRIANNE

*I* was born addicted to heroin.

But my story doesn't start there. It starts with my earliest memories of my family.

Long Island flows through my parents' veins. It shows in their manner, their clothes—so chic in all of their disco-era glory—the way they wear their hair, and most particularly in the way they speak. It's *tawlk* not *talk, mothuh* not *mother, cawfee* never *coffee,* and *Lawn Guyland* rather than *Long Island.*

Their conversations are staccato-like, respectful, and playful. Often, Dad interrupts Mom to correct a mixed metaphor or improper idiom.

*Ady Maidy*—their nickname for me—*I know you promise you're gonna waulk and feed a dawg if we get one, but I'll tell ya, it's the truth of puddin'* . . .

*You mean proof,* Dad says.

*Wha?*

*Proof, proof is in the puddin'.*

*What'd I say?*

*You said, 'Truth of puddin'.'*

*Oh for goodness sake . . . you know what I meant . . .*

Our home is filled with love and laughter and the play of three kids: my older brothers Harry and Jeffrey, and me. We're Jewish, but not really religious.

Mom or Dad tuck me in each night before bed with a story and often Mom sings, *Ah baby, you're my Ady Maidy, I love you so* . . . They check under the bed and in the closet for scary things before turning off the light and leaving the door cracked just a bit.

Saturday mornings I wake up early and jump into bed with them. *Oof, Ady Maidy,* Dad says as I land on him, *I'm gonna find your tickle spot.* My four-year-old body falls apart giggling.

*Come give ya mothuh a hug, Ady Maidy.* I wiggle from Dad to slip into Mom's arms.

Mom gets up and makes breakfast while Dad runs out to the Honey Bun, our favorite bakery. He always makes sure to get me a jelly donut. After breakfast and yard work, Dad often takes me to Times Square Store, a long-gone, *Lawn Guyland* department store.

*Ady Maidy, where we goin'?*

*Toys?*

*Yes ma'am. Get what ya want, as long as it's reasonable.*

He loved to spoil me rotten.

Mom and Dad enjoyed theater. On some Saturday nights, even when I was a little girl, we would go into Manhattan to see a show. My first was *Annie*, but we also saw *Oklahoma*, *The Sound of Music*, and others. I loved them, especially hearing the songs that permeated our home sung for us in a beautiful theater.

But most Saturday nights Mom and Dad would go out while Grandma watched me. I would squish into the couch and play rummy with her until it was time for *The Lawrence Welk Show*. *To bed Ady Maidy*, she'd say, but I'd beg her to let me stay up just a little bit later so I could watch the bubbles. She would say okay and I'd curl into her lap to watch. When the bubbles were over, she'd put me to bed.

I loved our home. It was a split-level that from the outside looked like the house in *The Brady Bunch*. However, the inside was something different. The first thing you'd see when you walked through the door was a large stained-glass mirror that hung on the wall between the entryway and the kitchen, which was straight ahead. In front of the wall was a little ornamental rock garden with a few imitation plants and a gilded Greek statue of a woman playing a lyre.

To the left, a short hallway brought you to the living room. To the right were stairs going up to the bedrooms. My brother Jeffrey, eleven years older than me, had a reel-to-reel tape player. I could hear it playing through the wall between our rooms: Sinatra, Dean Martin, Elvis . . . I fell asleep listening to it. Mom said that my first word was *Beatles*.

Most of my friends thought we were rich, but we weren't. It just seemed that way. We lived on a corner lot and the front yard looked professionally landscaped, but that was just my dad. He was good at things like that and always had his hands busy on all kinds of projects. He had a train set in the basement that he tinkered with for hours. He'd let me sit on his lap and tap the little electric lever to make the trains go.

One time he built a model of a historic sailboat that took him forever to finish. He put it on a ledge on the wall in our living room, but it broke when Harry threw a pillow and hit it. That was the only time I saw my dad spank anybody.

In our front yard there used to be a huge weeping willow. During the summer I could play under it, almost hidden by its long, languid branches. Late one summer a hurricane ravaged it, leaving it a toppled mess. Mom cried, but I couldn't understand why.

*Because it was part of our family,* she said.

She was a sensitive woman with the heart of an artist, even if she seemed like a *Lawn Guyland* housewife on the outside. When she wasn't cleaning or tending to me or Harry, she was knitting, crocheting, or painting.

My favorite of her paintings hung on a wall in our living room. It's a turn-of-the-century scene of an older woman needlepointing a delicate, white length of fabric as a girl watches. The light is soft, the colors muted. The woman sits upright as the girl, in a clean white dress, white knee socks and black Mary Janes, leans toward her. Both gaze tenderly at the small, framed circle of fabric in the woman's hands.

When Mom read or knitted she sat serenely in a sofa under that painting. When I saw her, I would totter to her and she'd put her knitting or book down as I climbed into her lap. Looking up at the painting, the gentleness of the moment, I always wanted to be the little girl.

*Is that me?* I'd ask.

*Of course Ady Maidy. Who else could it be?*

A few years later, I would hide behind that sofa to avoid something horrible.

*Mom and Dad on vacation*

In my longest-held memories events unfold in images, like photo slides falling from a carousel into a projector. It's mid-July of 1967. The light of summer is diffuse and particularly bright, the sky a deep azure blue. I'm playing beneath the willow; the weather is warm, but the shade is cool.

*Ady Maidy, come in and have some lunch.*

I'm almost five and kindergarten starts in the fall.

Mom sits across from me and rests her clasped hands on the Formica tabletop. Her eyes are soft, but the corners of her lips are drawn together.

*Adrianne, there's something I need to tell you.* She rarely uses my name. *You know your dad and I love you very much?*

*I think so.*

*We do . . . very much.* Mom's wearing a deep red sleeveless cotton blouse. She slides one hand from the other and gently scratches in small circles around a freckle on her forearm. *But I need to tell you something.* Gone is the shortened *Ya*, replaced by a much slower, more deliberate *You*.

*Okay.* The peanut butter and bread feel thick in my mouth.

Mom's eyes are moist. *You're a lucky girl. Do you know that?*

*I think so.*

*Well, you are for many reasons, but also because you have two parents.*

*Yeah, you and Daddy . . .* A slick of peanut butter coats the ridges of my mouth. I lick it, but only manage to smear more across my upper lip. Mom reaches for a cloth napkin and folds it in half. She licks a corner of the napkin and wipes the mess away.

*No . . . I mean, you have two other parents, other than Mommy and Daddy.*

*Do all kids have more parents?* I place the partially eaten sandwich on my plate.

*No, just the lucky ones.* Mom puts the napkin down. She scratches behind an ear then turns the napkin in her fingers.

*Do Harry and Jeffrey have more parents too?*

Mom clears her throat, *Harry does, but Jeffrey doesn't.*

*Why doesn't Jeffrey?* This idea of more parents, more of a good thing, is intriguing.

Mom's lips stiffen and her cheeks puff just a little, as if she's trying to hold the words in so she can consider each one. *You're our child. Sometimes mommies and daddies make a baby and sometimes, if they're good, a baby comes to them. We were very lucky to have you come to us.*

She looks down at my plate. *Don't you want some more of your sandwich, honey?*

*No, my tummy hurts.*

*I'm sorry—*

*What do my other parents look like?*

*I don't know. We've never met them.*

I bite my lower lip. *Are they nice?*

Mom drops her eyes to look at the napkin as she twists it with her fingers. *Well, since you're such a wonderful little girl I imagine they are.*

*I bet she's pretty.* I cross my legs under my chair. The vinyl seat cover rubs against the back of my thighs. *How come I haven't met them?*

Mom pauses to scratch her nose. She spots a tiny ant on the tabletop and pinches it between her fingers. *I don't know.*

*Do they love me like you and Daddy love me?*

She continues twisting the napkin. *I don't know honey. I've never met them, but I know they want to meet you.*

*How do you know that?*

*We got a call saying they did. Do you want to meet them?*

*I don't know. Mommy, my tummy hurts.*

*Do you want to lie down?*

*No, I want to go play.*

*Okay, Ady Maidy.*

I walk out of the kitchen feeling like I don't know anything about parents. If a little girl like me can have two sets of parents, what else is there?

I play for a little while under the willow tree. My best friend Jill, she lives across the street, sees me and comes over. We lose ourselves in our imaginations and slowly my stomach starts to feel better.

The next image to drop into the projector is of me sitting on a vinyl seat in a Long Island Railroad car with Mom and Dad.

It's August 6th, my fifth birthday, and we're going to Manhattan to meet my other parents.

The train moves quickly between stations. I want to be excited, but I'm more nervous than anything else. Dad is looking out the window as Mom reads. He keeps flicking his lower lip out past his top front teeth so that it pops out from under his mustache.

*What're you smiling at Ady Maidy?* His eyes are wrinkly and puffy.

*You look like a fish breathing,* I say.

*Eh?*

*When your lip flaps out, you look like a gold fish.* I pucker my lips and open and close them like a fish. They make a soft *pwop* sound.

Dad smiles. His eyes squint, making the wrinkles underneath scrunch up. *You look like a fish too,* he says then puckers his lips, *Pwop . . . pwop . . . pwop . . . pwop . . .*

*Will I have to play with them?* I ask.

Dad shrugs. *I don't know what they want to do. Maybe look at you like a monkey in the zoo.* The corners of his mouth curl slightly.

*Seriously Daddy—*

*They'll get to meet you. Maybe they just want to talk to you.*

*About what?*

He turns his head to look out the window then down at his hands, which are folded in his lap. *I don't know, Ady. The whole thing's a mystery to me.*

Another image drops from the carousel.

I'm in an office in Manhattan. There's a large mirror embedded in one wall. The furniture is small, a table and two chairs built especially for children. There are a few toys, but none of them are very interesting.

The room is bare and cold, even though it's mid-summer in Manhattan.

*Honey, we have to go, but we'll be back soon, okay?* Mom says.

*Where are you going?* I feel fidgety and kick at the kiddie chair next to me.

*Just for a little walk, not too far.*

My tummy hurts and I don't want to be there.

*Okay, Ady Maidy?* Dad asks.

*We'll be back in a jip,* Mom adds.

*Jiff,* Dad says.

*Wha?*

*Jiff! We'll be back in a jiff.*

*Good grief. She knows what I mean, don't you honey?*

Mom and Dad look at the woman who brought us to this room. I don't remember her name, maybe it was Ms. Abramsky, but she's wearing beige polyester pants and a sky blue short-sleeved blouse with a ruffle running along either side of the buttons.

Her arms are folded across her belly. *It'll be okay. Your mom and dad will be here in a minute.*

I look at my parents. *Mom and Dad are right here.*

Mom's eyes are sharp, head tilted, arms across her chest, purse grasped tightly in her right hand. Dad's eyes are soft, moist. His hands are in his pockets.

*I guess I mean Mr. and Mrs. Schoenowitz,* Ms. Abramsky says.

*Can we step out into the hall?* Mom asks.

*Yes Mrs. Cahn,* replies Ms. Abramsky.

*Will, why don't you stay with Ady,* Mom says to Dad. She and Ms. Abramsky step into the hall. The door shuts solidly behind them.

I couldn't hear what they said, nor do I think I wanted to, but when I was older Mom rehashed the conversations she'd had with the agency.

*Everything was fine until I called to say we wanted to adopt Adrianne,* Mom remembered saying.

*I know,* responded Ms. Abramsky.

*When we first came into this agency we were very clear that we were looking for a baby girl that we could adopt—*

*I wasn't here then—*

*I know that, but it should be in the file because when we were called we were told that you had a little girl from drug-addicted parents and that it would be a long-term foster parenting opportunity that probably would turn into an adoption.*

*At that time the mother was in jail and the father was nowhere to be found,* said Ms. Abramsky.

*Right . . . and all the time your agency is telling us, 'Don't worry, everything is fine—'*

*And it was. When you asked about adopting Adrianne we had to try and contact the biological parents, which we did—*

*Uh huh—*

*—When Adrianne was born Mrs. Schoenowitz voluntarily put Adrianne into foster care, so we had to try to speak to both Mr. and Mrs. Schoenowitz—*

*So that's why we're here now—*

*—and they wanted to meet Adrianne.*

*What about adopting Adrianne? Is that still in the picture?*

*Mrs. Cahn, we're a foster agency and in no way an adoption agency. We have certain guidelines.*

*Does one of those guidelines include telling Mrs. Schoenowitz she has the right to take Adrianne back?*

It took a long time for Mom to get an answer to that question.

For two weeks I'd wondered what my other parents would be like.

I knew that some parents could be cruel, but not in my world. In my world, Mom and Dad loved me and I loved them. I wasn't nearly old enough for the disillusionment and conflicts of adolescence. I had bragged to friends that I had two extra parents, as if it was a reward for being a good child. I still believed in Santa Claus and that only good things happen to good people.

But sitting quietly with Dad in a cold, bare room with a large mirror, it all feels too real. I don't want it. It's my birthday and I want to leave, but I know I can't.

My stomach hurts so much.

The door squeaks open. Mom and Ms. Abramsky walk in.

*The Schoenowitzes are here,* Mom says. *We have to go.*

*Ady Maidy, we'll be back in a bit,* Dad says. *We're going for a walk, but not far, okay? Then we'll have our birthday city day, okay?*

*Okay,* I say looking up at them. *What do I do?*

*Wait here, honey, and they'll come in,* says Ms. Abramsky.

Dad scratches at the side of his nose. *It'll be okay. See ya soon.*

Mom and Dad walk out. I remember Dad taking one last look back at me, his eyes moist.

Ms. Abramsky leans out the door and watches my parents walk down the hall, then turns to me. *I'll be back in just two seconds, okay?*

*Okay.*

She steps out into the hall, leaving the door open. I hear her open another door and say, *Okay.*

Ms. Abramsky walks back in. Her head is turned and she is speaking to someone behind her.

Herb Schoenowitz comes through the door. He's tall and lean, but round shouldered to the point of being stooped. His skin is unsettlingly pale for summer. His hair is brown, close-cropped and swept back from the top of his forehead. His eyes blink quickly, as if he'd just walked into bright light and his mouth curls at either end, forming a slight Cheshire Cat-like smile. He's wearing a paisley tie, black slacks, and a white, short-sleeve Oxford shirt. To my memory, his demeanor is that of an agnostic dressed for church.

Behind Herb is Elaine. She's a squat, heavy-set woman with blunt features, wearing a sleeveless floral dress. Thick, black plastic sunglasses dangle from the dress' collar. Her eyes are dark, glassy looking; they lack any warmth. Her arms are scarred by track marks from shooting heroin. Her legs are mottled by abscess scars and blackened from phlebitis caused by years of heroin use. Her eyes wander the room.

Elaine is a hideous and scary looking woman. My stomach hurts so much, I feel like I need to throw up.

The two of them stand near the door, Ms. Abramsky slightly to the side; Herb scratches at his right arm; his head seems to nod slowly forward and back. Elaine's shoulders slouch toward the floor as if the weight of the handbag she holds in front of her is pulling them down. Her head nods slightly, too.

I was too young to know it then, but the nodding was the result of methadone.

*Adrianne,* says Ms. Abramsky, gesturing toward them like a game show host to a dishwasher, *this is Herb and Elaine; they're your birth parents.*

Elaine's mouth is flat, eyes cool. Herb's Cheshire grin widens as his eyebrows seem to pull his entire face upward.

*Happy birthday Adrianne,* Herb says. Elaine looks at him like he's an idiot.

*Mom and Dad on vacation*

# Chapter Two

# JOHNNY

I was conceived in drink, gestated in alcohol, and born into a party *The Great Gatsby* would've approved of.

As with all babies born in the late 1950s to Ladue families—Ladue is to St. Louis what Scarsdale is to New York City or Beverly Hills to Los Angeles—my birth was heralded by a week-long party. In the one photo I have just after my birth, mother reclines in a hospital bed, legs crossed as if she were in a chaise longue at the club. There's a sadness in her eyes, but her lips, slightly parted and with a fresh coat of red lipstick, give her a contented look.

She's wearing a white chiffon peignoir and her auburn hair is cut à la Audrey Hepburn circa *Roman Holiday*. Her right hand drapes lazily over one leg; her left raises a vodka tonic to the camera.

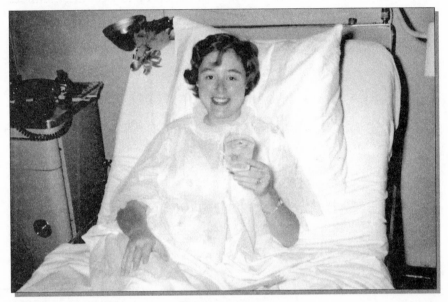

*Just after my birth*

I was probably only a couple of hours old when it was taken.

No doubt Dad was behind the camera, snapping away with one hand while balancing a drink and a lit Winston in the other. Other photos I've seen highlight the usual coterie of Ladue friends—powerful, old money, elegant—smoking, drinking and toasting the new parents.

I'll make my appearance in later photos, but this one stands out. It's closest to the single, lifelong image I have of Mom: reclined, wrapped in a bathrobe, and drinking. She's never smiling. In her eyes is the persistent sadness that haunts me to this day. Every aspect of her, of this memory, betrays the extremity of her drinking.

Not everyone who knew her thought of her this way. Aunt Mae Cella always saw Mom as her beautiful little niece; she could do almost no wrong. And then, Mom's friends only saw her as the debutante, the refined socialite, a graduate of Smith College from one of the best and wealthiest families of Ladue.

*Oh Johnny Lipscomb, your mother is such a love,* I remember one woman saying during a party at our house. I was probably only about five or six, maybe younger. She leaned toward me, giving a high-pitched squeal as her drink spilled over its rim. *Oops, oh my, sorry, El*—short for Eloise, what Mom's closest friends called her—*I spilled . . .*

In another photo, taken June of '57, Mom and Dad sit in the "L" of a leather bench-seat tucked into a corner of one of the clubs they used to haunt; I'm not sure which one. Dad wears a tuxedo with a white jacket while Mom is every bit the socialite in her cotton evening dress. Dad smiles, eyes wide. Mom's lips are softly parted, eyes demure.

When I think of my parents, or at least my childhood memory of them together, they are dressed to the nines, ready to go out. In the foyer of our house gather lifelong friends, scions of powerful, old money families. In Ladue they made up a small, insular group of elites. Everything they needed to know about a person was learned by asking where they went to school. They didn't mean college, but which prep school: St. Louis Country Day School (boys) or its sister, Mary Institute (girls).

We all went to the same private schools, belonged to the same clubs, and frequented the same parties thrown by the moneyed high society of St. Louis. Membership was defined by pedigree as much as by money. I remember hearing that our country club had turned down August Anheuser Busch, Jr., grandson of the founder of Anheuser-Busch and owner of the St.

*Mom and Dad before I was born, 1957*

Louis Cardinals[1]. He lacked the proper birthright. Later he started his own country club, and later still our club finally did let him in.

*Hey Johnny Lipscomb,* Dad said to me one night as he and Mom eased their way out of the house with friends. *You remember Uncle Donny and Mr. McDonnell, don't you?*

Uncle Donny was the son of the founder of Ralston Purina and later its CEO, while Mr. McDonnell was the son of a founder of the aircraft manufacturer McDonnell Douglas.

*Yes sir,* I said, rocking back on my heels. At four or five years old, I was very shy around Dad and his friends.

*You remember how to say hello, right?*

*Yes sir. Hello, Uncle Donny,* I proffered my hand for him to shake. *Hello Mr. McDonnell.*

---

1. He started his own country club, but after a number of years our country club finally did let him in.

Uncle Donny smiled. *Nice to see you Johnny Lipscomb.* Then he looked at Dad. *You ready, Lippo?*

*Just a minute, Don.* Dad grabbed his coat and turned. *Johnny, be a good boy and don't run Lizzy ragged tonight, all right?*

*Yes sir.* I took a step back toward my usual spot near Lizzy.

Mom was a presence in our house, but Lizzy was the center of my life and the heart and soul of our home. My earliest memories of my parents, of which there are scant few, revolve mostly around them leaving or, in the case of Mom, simply being unavailable.

*Johnny-Jump-Up*

Lizzy is different.

If I close my eyes and think back I see myself as a very young boy walking hand in hand with Lizzy along the narrow semi-private drive we lived on.

Shaped like a lollipop with a twisting pipe cleaner stem, Oakleigh Lane was lined by cottonwood, dogwood, maple, and oak trees. Our feet crunched on loose gravel, which in later years routinely remained embedded in my scuffed and bloody knees after some heroic bike crash. During spring, floating in the air around us, were bits of white fuzz drifting down from cottonwoods and whirligig seed pods set loose by maples. A shallow creek wound lazily along and around the road with small bridges passing over it every so often.

Bordering Oakleigh Lane were more roomy houses with long meandering driveways. They were home to some of the wealthiest and most powerful people in St. Louis and in the country. Dad's friend John McDonnell, Chairman of McDonnell-Douglas and philanthropist, was our neighbor and a close family friend. A few houses down lived William Masters and Virginia Johnson, the famed sex researchers better known as Masters and Johnson.

A short walk through a thin woods lived Dr. William Danforth, chancellor of Washington University and Uncle Donny's brother. Uncle Donny lived only two lanes from us. The Pulitzers, of the Pulitzer Prize, lived nearby as well. Their son Bobby was one of our troop of boys playing, rampaging and roaming in and among the woods near our home.

With a couple of other families we owned an old fire engine that we parked behind the house. Dad drove it in town parades with us kids hanging off it and waving, but mostly it was a warren for our gang of kids.

Beyond the garage was the badminton court and near that, the gardens. I remember watching Jasper work in the gardens and yard and helping him every so often. He was a sweet, massive man with very dark skin. Once, I watched him pull a six-inch-round tree right out of the ground. At the back of the yard was the creek where Jasper and I burned leaves in the fall and my friends and I would spend so many hours playing.

Our other neighbors, who lived either on Oakleigh Lane or a short distance through the woods, were doctors, lawyers, corporate leaders, and national politicians. Essentially, anyone who met the *de facto* test of affluence and culture, which included speaking without the typical St. Louis/Missouri accent of *warsh* for *wash*, *Missoura* for *Missouri*, *bat-tree* for *battery*, and *Innerstate Farty-Far* for *Interstate 44*.

In Ladue we were impeccable in our dress and taught with something of an iron will, if not fist, to use very proper English. With the same rigid discipline we were also taught to conduct ourselves in front of adults with a form of manners and respect that is probably no longer practiced anywhere outside of the military.

It all seemed so normal: nannies, country clubs, private schools, the titles and wealth of our parents and their friends, manners to excess, Lacoste shirts with the telltale green alligator logo, coat and tie for school, and an aloof seclusion from the rest of St. Louis.

Within this world apart, my childhood revolved around Lizzy. I took my first steps within her vigilant reach. Hers was the first face I saw nearly every morning. She dressed me, gave me breakfast, and stood with me to wait for the school bus to kindergarten, then first and second grade. When I was old enough to play on my own in the yard and woods or down by the creek, she'd call out for supper and wait by the kitchen door, smiling. *John David, I knew it was you comin' 'cause I could see your blond hair bouncing in my direction. Now go wash the world off your hands and face.* Mostly I was John David; sometimes, when she felt affectionate, I was *Master John*, and at times *Boy*, as in, *Boy, I am going to beat the tan out of yo' hide.*

She was a tall, thin woman, probably no more than ninety pounds, raised in Alabama. She could frost your spine with just a few words, but most of the time she had a slow, almost languid demeanor. She carried herself elegantly, even though I rarely saw her wear anything other than a thin white uniform.

She never did anything without a small clot of snuff pouched in her lower lip. She also mumbled from sunrise to sunset, emitting a rumbling, incessant tremor that caused the small bump of snuff in her lip to bounce slightly.

Throaty sounds such as, *Eh hmm, oh yes, mmm hmmm, Lohd have mercy,* were used like conjunctions between each thought as it made its way from her mouth. When I was little I nearly lived under Lizzy's apron strings, so my childhood was punctuated by *Mmm hmmm, his mouth overloaded his butt . . . Lohd, Miz Lipscomb make me go round my elbow ta get to my thumb . . . oh yes, there ain't much meat on that bone, now is there? . . . Eh hmm, put yo wishes in one hand and manure in another and which one gonna fill up first? . . .*

Her room was next to mine in the back of the house and each night I took comfort in hearing her slow, rhythmic walk up the back steps from the kitchen. In one hand she'd have a can of Budweiser; we were all practically weaned on the stuff. In the other, she held a round, silver tin of snuff between her thumb and middle finger, so she could flick the tin with her wrist. She did this in a way that caused her pointer finger to slap the top of the tin to pack the finely ground contents, like black ground coffee, to one side. The slapping of the tin kept time with the thud of each of her hard-soled shoes hitting the next wooden step.

She'd stop mumbling long enough to lean into my room and say, *Master John, time you were asleep,* then go into her room and sit with her beer and snuff, mumbling to her small black-and-white TV. In the summer of 1969, when I was ten years old, I remember watching the first moon landing with her on that old TV. The whole while she mumbled, *C'ain't be . . . Snowball's chance in hell they's really on the moon . . . Just you watch, whole damn thin's made up . . .*

Every now and again she'd break wind, then stop her mumbling long enough to look at me and say, *Lohd have mercy, John David. You went and lost yo' manners.*

Throughout the day she'd periodically stick her head out the kitchen door mumbling about something, look around to see if anyone was watching, and spit a long stream of tobacco juice into the bushes. It was a thing of beauty.

*What the hell was that?* one kid asked after witnessing Lizzy's purging.

*Just Lizzy,* I answered.

When I was about nine years old, I asked my dad where Lizzy came from.

*Alabama,* he said. *I believe her parents were cotton pickers and she's mentioned something about having picked cotton herself.*

*She must've started when she was a kid,* I said.

*Why do you say that?*

*I don't think she can read because the other day she meant to put insect repellent on Joshua's arms, but used oven cleaner instead.*

*She couldn't read the label?*

*I thought it might just be Lizzy being Lizzy, but I guess not.*

Another time I asked Lizzy about what her life had been like in Alabama. She didn't say much, but did tell me about chasing rabbits. *When one'd bolt from where it was hidin' we'd go after it until we caught it or it got away, which wasn't very often. Sometimes theys little heart'd give out and die,* she said. *We'd snatch 'em up by the ears and that'd be what we ate that night.*

By the time I was eight or nine, I'd already learned to shoot a gun and hunt for rabbits and birds in the woods around our house as well as on my uncle's farm a few hours from Ladue. Until I heard Lizzy talk about chasing rabbits it had never occurred to me that someone would do that.

*Why didn't you just shoot them?* I asked.

*No gun, Master Johnny.*

Her life was always a mystery to me. I knew she had a family, and that even though she lived with us most of the time, she had a home that she would go back to from time to time for one or two nights. I never saw her house or met her kids. I didn't really think to ask. She was the woman who got me up in the morning, got me dressed and off to school. She was the woman who walked me down Oakleigh Lane, the person who cooked dinner—always fried and usually pork chops—the overseer of baths and then, after we said goodnight to Mom and Dad, if they were home, the person who put us to bed each night.

She lived with us and was part of the family, or at least the part of the family that took care of my sister, brother and me.

From the bits and pieces she told me of her past I managed to put together that World War II opened the opportunity for her to leave Alabama and the cotton fields behind. The war created a tide of migration across the rural South, which carried Lizzy to the St. Louis Army Ammunition Plant, a sprawling complex of buildings on the outskirts of the city.

Lizzy worked there through the Second World War, the Korean War, and into the late 1950s. Her children were born and then, I assume, grew up and left for their own lives. Lizzy's eyesight deteriorated, probably from the chemicals she worked with, and in about 1957 or '58 her employer said she was too old to continue.

With his first child on the way, my dad felt the need to hire a nanny, as was customary in Ladue. It was probably also a demand of Mom's. I imagine Lizzy arriving at our house with her face framed by thick, heavy looking horn-rim glasses, her black hair greased and pulled straight in a severe ponytail. And all of her ninety pounds and strong features—in her youth she must have been a beautiful woman—taut and determined to work for this young, white, affluent couple. She must have figured that if she could handle high explosives for nearly twenty years, she could handle the off-spring of these two.

She started as my nanny, then the job grew to include Lisa in 1961 and Joshua in 1964. Over the years she took over all of the responsibilities for our home, in something of the same manner as a frog will sit in a pot of cool water as more and more heat is added to it. She never seemed fazed and despite her years of work, her energy was undiminished.

She tended to and cared for three energetic smalls, kept the house orderly, cooked, arranged rides for us (despite her many talents, Lizzy didn't drive), and acted as the social secretary for not only us kids, but Mom and Dad too. Lizzy was also our disciplinarian.

One day she heard me being unkind to one of my playmates. She snatched the broom that seemed to never be out of reach, smacked it on the counter and pointed it at me. *John David, keep it up and I will beat the pure divine tar out of you.*

*Yes ma'am,* I said.

Turning away from me she mumbled, *Mm hmm, shakin' like he's tryin' to pass a peach pit.* I think she was smiling.

Most of the time all we got was the warning, but if I kept it up she'd chase me around waving the broom: *John David, I am gonna tan yo hide!* She generally caught me and gave me the business. Generally speaking, I probably deserved it.

Larger infractions meant Dad was going to hear about it when he got home. Dad was a man of his time. He's who you think of when you think of the standard 1950s guy: an authoritative, sincere man who looked you directly in the eye when he spoke to you. He was tall, good looking, strong, athletic, and always had our respect. The best way I can describe him is to say that when he put his hand on your shoulder, it was a warm, stern feeling.

When he called your name you went straight off, not because you were afraid, but because you respected him and the authority he had over your life. You did what you were told and minded your manners: stood for a lady entering or leaving a room, minded your elders, used proper table manners, spoke clearly, and never forgot your place.

He was fun, too. He was the guy who'd let you ride on top of the car along the dirt roads at our cousins' place in the country. He did back flips into the river. He set up football and baseball games and taught us how to fish, shoot and hunt.

Dad was usually respectful, with only one exception: when speaking among friends he could be racially insensitive. Even as a young boy I knew the power of certain words, especially those around race, and his speaking in this manner didn't square with the polite dignity with which he treated Lizzy or any other person of color. Some may excuse it as being a different age, but it never felt like an authentic piece of him.

One evening, on a night Lizzy was with her family, the phone in the front hall rang. It wasn't too late for me to be up, but Mom had long been put in bed. Dad answered, *What, Lizzy?* He listened for a bit. *I'll be along within the hour,* he said and gently put the phone down. I watched him look up the stairs, pause, then pick up the receiver, *I'm sorry to bother, but could you come over and watch the kids? Lizzy stabbed someone.*

Later I found out that a friend of Lizzy's grandson had tried to rape her, so she stabbed him with a large kitchen knife. He didn't die, but things being what they were, Lizzy was arrested. That night Dad drove into St. Louis to bail her out of jail. The next day he spoke to his lawyer and was referred to a topnotch defense attorney whom he hired to represent Lizzy. I suppose he did a good job because the issue never went to court.

That was Dad, loyal and respectful. I don't think he ever said more than a few words about what happened to Lizzy, in my or anyone else's presence.

Growing up with Lizzy watching over the house, I knew that she would have killed for us, too.

When I was about eight years old, Mom challenged Lizzy to a running race down Oakleigh Lane.

*I don't know Mizz Lipscomb,* Lizzy said, holding her arms across her belly.

*Oh come on Lizzy.* Mom unintentionally listed to one side and she held a long, slim cigarette between her fingers. *I used to be a pretty good athlete back in my school days.*

Lizzy looked sidelong at me. *Why don't you race John David?*

My stomach tightened. I didn't want to race Mom and I didn't want to see her race Lizzy, especially out on the street where people could see.

*Oh Lizzy, I know I can beat him,* Mom said, taking a drag from her cigarette. *Come on, give me a good race.*

*I'm too old to race a young woman like you,* Lizzy said.

*Now Lizzy, you're just making up excuses. Go on, the starting line can be the end of the driveway. Johnny, you say 'Ready, Set, Go.'*

Lizzy tightened her arms around her belly. *Where we gonna run to?*

Mom took one more drag, dropped her cigarette into the grass along the side of our driveway, and pointed to the McDonnell's driveway, about thirty yards away. Then she kicked her high-heeled shoes off into the grass—as usual she was dressed as if on her way to a cocktail party—and walked to the end of the driveway.

Lizzy shook her head and followed her, hands still crossed across her belly. The feet of Mom's pantyhose picked up little bits of loose gravel so that she wiggled and tipped a bit as she walked.

*Now come on Lizzy, you've got to try,* Mom said. The pixie cut of her youth had given way to a more mature shoulder length bob, held back from her face by a red silk hair band. Her body was also no longer as lithe as in the photo from my birth: legs a bit stouter, waist a bit wider, and the first hints of pudge showing around her neck when she tilted her head forward.

Lizzy mumbled something. Though her white uniform fit loosely over her thin frame, her arms, neck and legs were toned, sinewy. Her shoulders were broad and strong, waist thin.

*Start us off Johnny,* Mom said.

When I dropped my hand and said *Go!* Mom lurched forward, stepped on a sharp bit of gravel, and took a skip step, *God damn it—"*

Lizzy shot forward easily, almost gracefully. Nearly as soon as the race began it was over. I don't think Mom even made it to the McDonnell's driveway before giving up.

*Well done Lizzy,* Mom said.

*Thank you Mizz Lipscomb.*

I stood at the end of our driveway not sure what to do. As Lizzy neared I could hear her mumble, *Liquor does all her thinking, um hmm.* Then she looked at me. *Time for lunch, John David.*

*Go on Johnny,* Mom said, picking up her shoes. Then she walked up to the house and back to the couch in the formal den, a distinct room from the kids' den, where she sat, drink in one hand, lit cigarette in the other, phone cupped to one ear.

If, as Adrianne said, memories are like slides in a projector's carousel, the race with Lizzy is one of only a few childhood images of Mom in my carousel. The earliest is of me spilling out of mom's wood-paneled station wagon into our driveway because she forgot to strap me in and close the door properly.

*Damn it Johnny,* she says, stopping the car. *Good lohd boy, are you hurt?* I hear the heavy sound of her high heels clacking on the cement and then the thud of her hip bumping against the back of the car as she comes round to pick me up and put me back in. She is angry as she hits the gas, jerking the car forward and setting the two of us off on whatever errand she needs to run.

The next slide. I'm still very young and it's supper. Dad is there, so is Lisa and Mom, but not yet Joshua. I leave the table and reach for a crystal blue bird from the top of an antique buffet. Mom rushes from her chair and I don't think her feet touch the ground before she is upon me. She slaps my hand so hard the sound of it—and the howl I let out—causes Lizzy to come from the kitchen.

The next slide. A storm is whipping up. Lightning flashes in the distance and thunder rumbles over the house. Then we hear Mom's heavy footsteps. For a small-framed, five-foot-three woman she has a very hard walk. Grandfather Cella (Mom's dad) once said, *She has small, fast feet and when you hear them come along—clunk, clunk, clunk—you know it's an 'I'm-carrying-a-big-stick-and-you-better-be-ready' move.*

*Come with me Joshua,* she says. *We're going to cure you of your fear of lightning.* Mom weaves toward Joshua, who is maybe three or four years old, and grabs him by the hand. She leads him out through the kitchen door into the back yard, past the apple and mulberry trees and large garden. Every so often Joshua tries to pull away, but her grip is tight and she yanks him closer. They reach the badminton court, which has a hard, cement-like surface. Bracketed by lights, and bisected by a tall net, it looks like a small tennis court.

Mom pulls Joshua to the middle of the court and he tries one last time to pull away. She jerks him back toward her. Wind swirls and whips around them. Bolts of lightning break the darkening sky and thunder rumbles through the house. Mom is bent over, encouraging Joshua, but his face is buried in her side. I am watching all of this through the window.

Heavy rain sweeps up the yard and large drops spatter against the window, making it impossible to see clearly. They've become two blurry forms, Mom in a light pink cocktail dress and Joshua in navy blue shorts and a white Lacoste shirt.

Soon I see them walking, or perhaps running, to the house. The kitchen door opens. *Storms come and go, Joshua,* Mom says, looking down at him, water dripping off them both, the outline of her body clearly visible through the wet fabric of her dress. *You just go inside when they do and don't fuss or cry over it, you hear?*

The two of them leave the kitchen. Before long, Mom is back on her couch wearing another summer dress, hair dried and brushed, drink in one hand, long, thin cigarette in the other, chatting on the phone. Joshua's in his room.

Another slide drops and we're at Busch's Grove, our favorite restaurant and a clubby staple of Ladue. It's probably 1965 or 1966. There is a *Mad Men-esque* quality to it. Wood-paneled walls, elegant tables set at regular intervals, and a men's only bar mark this as a place where one might run into the likes of the ever-so-suave Xavier Cugat or Dean Martin making the rounds.

The owner, a well-dressed man who knows his is *the* spot for the pride of St. Louis, welcomes us in. Waiters nod at Dad. Mom, a bit wobbly, stops to say hi to some friend. We follow the maître d' to our table, excited, wearing our best clothes, going through the rituals of a night out at Busch's Grove with Mom and Dad.

Mom and Dad have already had cocktails, and drinks are ordered as soon as they sit. They laugh, every now and again nodding at couples passing or seated nearby. Drinks arrive: scotch for Dad, vodka martini for Mom. Dad lights a Winston and Mom tugs on a refined, lady-like cigarette. Dad sits ramrod straight. Mom slouches languidly, her cigarette dangling from her thin fingers.

*What're you going to have, Johnny-Jump-Up,* Dad says, smiling at me.

Food is ordered: prime rib for Mom and Dad, burgers for the kids. Then a second round of drinks. Mom and Dad talk and laugh. The room is filled with movement. Every so often loud, deep laughter bursts from the men's bar. Our dinner arrives.

Mom is even more wobbly. Dad smiles as he cuts into his rare prime rib. He looks up; Mom shoots a look at another table and laughs loudly. I take a bite from what seems to be an impossibly huge burger. Mom falls backward out of her chair. She is choking and cannot breathe. Dad stands, stiff, unsure what to do. The room becomes church-quiet. People look, murmur. Dad rushes to Mom and sits her back up. She is suffocating, fighting for air. A man pushes Dad aside. It's a doctor who lives near our house. He and his wife are friends with Mom and Dad. He reaches around Mom's gut from behind, clasps his hands, and pulls hard. Once, then again, and a chewed piece of meat tumbles from Mom's mouth.

*Thank God you were here,* Dad says. Mom is quiet, sheepish. We are all quiet. A few *well dones* come from tables. Soon everyone is seated again and chatting, except for us. We eat our meals quickly and quietly. Mom finishes her drink, and then we leave.

The next slide is more a collage of grandiosity than a single image. *Nod your head forward,* Mom says to Lisa. *Then hold either side of your skirt like this.* She raises her skirt slightly. *Now place your right foot slightly behind your left and bend like this.* Lisa does as Mom says. *This is what you'll have to do when we meet the Queen of England someday.*

*Don't let anyone take your photo!* she'd say if we were flying anywhere, either commercial or private. *We don't want to have what happened to the Lindbergh baby.*

Unbelievably, she managed to find her way onto the game show *Jeopardy!*

*I'm a Smith girl after all,* I heard her say over the phone. We sat in the living room of friends to watch her taped episode. She got creamed, but she was there.

Then there was the daily dressing up and endless phone calls while drinking on the couch. It was her pre-Internet virtual world of life as a socialite. Chummy gossip, talk of the club, and status as defined by her place in the social pecking order, which, with her wealth and genteel appeal, was never in doubt even as she lived life with a drink in one hand and cigarette in the other.

This is how I remember Mom the most when I was a kid: seated on the couch in the den, smoking, drinking, chatting. It's not so much a memory as it is a general feeling of where Mom was in my life. Lizzy played lead while Mom was a peripheral character. She could be menacing, embarrassing, and sometimes present if not loving, but mostly she was distant, in the background, to be avoided if possible.

Some of this was her preferred posture—*Mom is couched,* is what we would come to call it in later years—but some of it was the parenting philosophy of my time: *Get the hell out of the house . . . be back by six, ya hear?* We did.

We went everywhere and everyone was our friend. The woods, the creek, and neighborhoods were ours and each house was a home to us with an open fridge. During the stifling heat of summer it was, *Help yourselves to pop and popsicles boys, but then get the hell out of here.* We could walk to the country club and spend afternoons at the pool. We wandered the woods with first our BB guns, then our pellet guns, hunting rabbits, birds and squirrel. We were free, kid free, which is the best kind of freedom, without any of the helicopter parenting of today. We raced bikes without helmets, chewed Indian gum from the creek, hollered and made noise, ran on legs that never tired . . . *Do what you are going to do and don't get into trouble.*

By the end of the day the gang of us kids would as likely find our way to our house as that of a friend's. Dad would pull up in his large Oldsmobile Toronado, trim lines, maroon, power everything. It was a dignified, muscular-looking car that seemed to be gliding along the road even when parked in the driveway.

We'd hear the engine shut off and, a moment later, the front door would open and Dad would be standing in the foyer yelling, *From the number of bikes I nearly ran over I assume there must be about ten of you all here. Time to get on home.* Kids would emerge from the nooks and corners of the house and slip out to their own homes, moms, and dads.

His keys would clink as they landed in the small dish on the antique table in the foyer. He'd loosen his tie and leave his coat hanging over the spiraled volute-end of the banister. Tired—as with all of his friends he worked hard—he'd find Mom in her drinking perch and as often as not he would have to put her to bed for the night. Alone, he'd sit in the den with his own drink and cigarette.

In the background Lizzy, a lump of snuff swelling her lower lip, would mumble her way through frying something wonderful for dinner—*She ain't worth the salt in her bread.* Dinner was casual, the kitchen table or TV trays in the den, and quiet conversation with Dad, *How's school, what's so-and-so up to?* and stories from our day. Lizzy's puttering and mumbling, interrupted occasionally by a stream of tobacco juice spit into the bushes, would go on and on.

Before too long Dad would announce it was time for bed. A polite goodnight and I'd be off; Lisa and Joshua already asleep. Teeth brushed, hands and face washed, I'd lie in bed daydreaming until I heard Lizzy's solid shoes on the steps and she'd come to my room, *Go to sleep Master Johnny, you got another day tomorrow*... followed by the creak of her door, the latch sliding home, the click of her black-and-white TV, and the soft murmur of a show harmonizing with the low echo of her mumbling.

It was a happy life, where everywhere we went was fun and good. Oakleigh was that kind of lane, and it was a much different era. It never occurred to me to wonder why Mom was never part of it, never around or available. My needs were amply met. I was happy.

If I'd paid more attention I probably would have noticed the nature and intensity of Mom and Dad's arguments evolve. Maybe I'd have seen the meaning of the cigarette burns in the carpet around the couch. I'd have seen how Dad's leather desktop was burned from cigarettes fallen from an ash tray and stained by Mom's sweating highball glass. I'd have witnessed Dad's desperation, doing all he could to keep our lives together, which meant taking over Joshua's carpool for school, doing the grocery shopping, cooking on Lizzy's nights off, and, sadly, mixing Mom's cocktails when he was available, to soften her increasingly sharp edges. I'd have seen Mom's devolution from society girl to drunk to utter mess, where there wasn't enough left of her to salvage by the time Dad got home from work. His only moments with Mom during his workweek were marked by her slurred incoherence, a fresh burn mark on the desk, carpet or couch, and incisive, caustic taunts as he led her to bed.

But I didn't notice. I was just a kid, nine years old. I was euphoric to be off on my own each day and content to be firmly within the reach of Lizzy each night. So on that day in late spring when Dad called Lisa, Joshua and me into the living room, I had no idea why.

When you walk into our home you enter into the foyer. The stairway to the upstairs is ahead of you. To the left is the dining room where under the carpet, near the head of the table, is a buzzer to summon servants. We had no staff, just Lizzy and Jasper, so we rarely ate in the formal dining room. Of course, Dad was always late at work and Mom inaccessible so there was rarely any need for formality.

From the foyer, the living room is off to the right. Walking into the living room there is a flowered sofa to the left. To the other side of the sofa is a large, colonial fireplace with a large portrait of Mom hung above it. As you face the fireplace there is a set of bay windows to the right that face out over the driveway and small hill where in the winter we built sled runs. As the weather warms, jonquils and daffodils mark the beginning of spring.

To the left of the couch is another set of windows looking out over the drive around the garage and large parking area behind.

The most distinctive item in that living room was an olive-colored antique piano set near the bay windows. Stenciled around the piano's body was a series of fluted Grecian vases linked by ivy vines and ornamental Chantilly. A sheaf of meticulously arranged family photos stood on the piano's lid. Placed at an angle before the keys was a linen-upholstered bench.

Mom was sitting on the couch, remarkable for its floral upholstery and lack of cigarette burns and stains. Lisa was six years old and Joshua only three. I was a lanky, energetic boy. We sat next to Mom while Dad stood, looking anxious.

*Before you guys hear it from someone else, your mom and I are getting divorced.* There was a force of will behind his voice and he spoke as if he was delivering hard news to the people of his company.

Mom's eyes widened at Dad's blunt words. She looked wounded. Lisa was still, her eyes soft, unmoving. Joshua looked lost. My eyes drifted down to my clasped hands.

Mom brushed the front of her skirt. Her legs were set at an angle, tight together, and her hands returned to their genteel position in her lap, right on top of left. *This is what your father wants,* she said.

*Eloise*—Dad began, but then said nothing.

I'd heard the word *divorce* before, but it was an abstraction. It was something that had happened to one of my friends, and was often spoken of by adults in the same hushed tones as gossiping about someone's cancer. It was a failing. A social faux pas. A sign that someone in that house was not right, because marriages didn't end. They were consecrated by God, society, and the cultural norms of the time.

Divorce was the mark of something bad and I felt it in my gut. I wondered what could be so wrong that *divorce* had to happen. Why did anything have to change? Why did the order of our lives, my life, have to be undone by a word, *divorce*? Did I do this?

*I'll be moving into an apartment and you kids will be here with your mother,* Dad said, explaining the details of divorce with the same grim determination as announcing layoffs to employees. I sat quietly and listened.

Each word confirmed the one true fact of what divorce meant: life as I'd known it was irretrievably breaking. My body sank as the reality of Dad's leaving, the loss of family, security, normalcy, penetrated deeper into me. It was a pitiless revelation that life was alterable and its vagaries were beyond my control and were now, more than ever, in the hands of my mother. My heart raced and my legs and arms felt weak, tired.

Dad finished and Mom looked at Joshua, Lisa and me, *We're going to Florida.* Then to Dad, *We need a break, from you.*

I walked away from the living room to get ready to leave. My head was down. I heard Lizzy mumbling in the kitchen, *Lohd, lohd, lohd.* Maybe she knew what I couldn't possibly foresee: life was about to get so much worse.

# Chapter Three

# ADRIANNE:
# A VULNERABLE CHILD

*Adrianne, you were happy, a happy-go-lucky kid.*
*You loved being the little girl treated like a princess in*
*our family. Then Herb and Elaine came into our lives and*
*there wasn't anything you or anyone could do.*
*Whenever you saw them, there was a sadness to you.*
*I used to distract you; help you get back to being*
*that happy-go-lucky little girl, remember?*
*That was my job and why I was*
*put on this earth.*

—Harry Cahn, Adrianne's brother

laine Schoenowitz, my biological mother, wanted to give birth to me at the Polyclinic Hospital in the Hell's Kitchen section of Manhattan. It's an elegant, art deco building famous for treating Marilyn Monroe. It's also the site of Rudolph Valentino's death.

Not long after going into labor, Elaine started to hemorrhage. With her life and my life at risk, she made it into Polyclinic, but it didn't take long for a doctor to notice track marks running up and down her arms. *We don't treat junkies here,* he said. They put her in a cab and sent her to Bellevue.

Somehow we both managed to survive and on August 6, 1962, I came into the world.

Not long after that, Elaine went to jail for either theft or forgery or prostitution. It's hard to know because by this point in her life incarceration was a constant state of being.

Herb was in Florida. His mother and sister lived there, but I have no idea what Herb was doing.

With the snipping of the umbilical cord I was cut off from my first supplier of oxygen, nutrition, and heroin, which led to the hell of withdrawal: tremors, diarrhea, vomiting, rapid breathing, fever, restlessness, and unceasing, high-pitched crying.

I was treated for heroin addiction at Bellevue, then a social worker brought me to the Jewish Child Care Association in lower Manhattan, a few blocks from the Brooklyn Bridge. To my family, it would be *the agency*.

Not long after my arrival, the people who would become my mom and dad walked into the agency. *We're looking for a little girl who is adoptable,* they said.

Elaine was in jail and the agency had no idea where Herb was. That's why the agency told Mom and Dad, *We have just the little girl for you.*

Of course, riding the train home after meeting Herb and Elaine for the first time, I don't know this part of my story. It's my fifth birthday and my body rocks with the swaying train as it makes its way home to Wantagh, about a third of the way up the Atlantic side of Long Island.

A bedroom community to New York City since the 1950s, Wantagh, as with most of Long Island, has Levittown-like tracts of houses forming small, tight neighborhoods. These neighborhoods fade into ice cream stands, beach shops, and small family-owned restaurants serving the hordes of New Yorkers leaving the city for the summer tourist mecca that is Jones Beach.

Thankfully, we don't live near the water. Our house is on a quiet, tree-lined street in the northern section of town. The houses are so close it's almost impossible not to know what the neighbors are up to. On warm, summer evenings there's the smell of charcoal and sounds of families in their backyards with friends.

As the train nears Wantagh, Mom and Dad are quiet.

I'm resting my head in Mom's lap. She's stroking my hair. The sun dips toward the horizon, framing Dad in a halo of golden light.

*Mom?*

*Yes Ady Maidy.*

*I don't think I want to see Elaine and Herb again.*

*Okay sweetie, but I'm not sure I can promise that.*

*Why not?*

*It's complicated.*

*Why?*

*It just is.*

Complicated means I can't say no. It means Mom and Dad can't say no. It means Herb and Elaine have a measure of leverage that grants them the right to intrude in our lives.

At the end of that first visit Ms. Abramsky, the agency's social worker, said *Herb and Elaine want more visits.*

Mom's eyes widened, *They want what?*

*They can come out of nowhere and ask this?* Dad asked before Ms. Abramsky could respond.

*What if we just say no?* Mom asked.

*You're foster parents; look, all they've asked for is an occasional visit. We'll start here at the agency where we can supervise them. We'll see how it goes from there, but you really don't have to worry.*

*What if they ask for her back?"* Dad worried.

*They're making moves like they do,* Mom added.

*Don't worry. It'll never happen.*

Mom refers to herself as a realist, but she is a born pessimist. To her way of thinking: if something can go wrong it will, so prepare for it. Dad is a born dreamer, though he would describe himself as an optimist. His way of thinking is: if something goes wrong, don't worry. It'll be all right in the end.

Neither of them believed Ms. Abramsky. They also knew they had to agree to more visits. As Mom said to me on the train, *It's complicated.*

Over the next year we go to the city every so often, where we wait for Elaine and Herb to show up at the agency. They are always late, sometimes three hours or more.

Herb brings me gifts, such as a stuffed animal or a toy, which are intended for a girl younger than me. I wonder if Herb even knows how old I am. Then we go into the playroom where there are toys and a large mirror. Herb tries to engage and connect with me. Elaine is uninterested.

Herb's interest wanes after about fifteen or twenty minutes and he settles into a chair to watch me play. I try to lose myself in a pretend world, but I'm distracted by Herb's slack eyes watching me.

After an hour Ms. Abramsky comes in and says, *Time's up.*

*Already?* Herb says with a sudden smile. All of his features appear to rise or fall with his eyebrows.

*Well, that was nice,* Elaine says.

Herb and Elaine pick themselves up and say goodbye to me. There is no hug. It's more like coworkers going home at the end of a shift, though Herb maintains his foolish, bright-eyed smile.

*I'll be in with your parents in a minute,* says Ms. Abramsky.

A little bit later, Mom and Dad come in and off we go, maybe to a museum or out for lunch. Then we're home and life resumes its normal pace and rhythms.

*Did you see their heads?* Dad asks Mom after one of the first visits.

*You mean the nodding?*

*Yeah, they looked like a couple of bobble-heads,* Dad says.

*And why are they always late?* Mom asks.

*I dunno.*

*Better never than late.*

*You mean better late than never.*

*No, I don't! I mean never; I wish they'd never show up and we didn't have to do this ridiculousness.*

*Me too,* Dad says. His eyes look worried.

I agree with Mom, better never than late.

In the fall of 1968, Mom tells me Elaine and Herb will come to our house for the next visit.

*Why? We don't ever do anything.* I'm six years old and tired of these periodic disruptions.

Mom's eyes wander to the handful of first grade reading, spelling and math worksheets spread on the kitchen table between us. *At least we won't have to go into the city and the agency.*

*I don't care.*

*I know.*

*Please, please don't make me.*

*I don't want to, Ady—*

*Then why are you?*

Mom looks down at the table. *It's complicated.*

I sweep my hands across the table and the papers scatter. *That's all you ever say.*

*Ady, I don't know what else to say. If it were up to me you'd never have to go.*

I rest my head in my hands, *I don't want to do this anymore.*

*I know seeing your other parents is—*

*No.* Tears bubble and spill from my eyes. *I hate school. It's stupid.*

Kindergarten had been fun. I loved being with other kids, especially girls my age, and I liked the games and running around. First grade was different. There was more sitting still and listening. Instead of playing, I struggled to read *Dick and Jane*-like books or work through spelling and math primers. My body always felt wiggly and my mind wandered. I daydreamed, or something popped into my head and before I knew it I was telling it to the girl or boy next to me. With a frown the teacher would tell me I was the last person who should be talking.

On Fridays we did a spelling quiz and if we got eight or more out of ten correct, the teacher pasted a gold star next to our name on a chart. I rarely got more than a couple correct so I was the only kid without a gold star, which made me feel dumb. Everyone else had at least a couple by late fall, and some got one nearly every week.

Through first grade and into second, I had trouble writing my own name.

*Don't you worry Ady Maidy, you'll lick it; you can do anything my little doll,* Dad said.

Mom rolled her eyes, *Some people just have to learn the hard way.*

*What?* Dad said, pinching at his persistently baggy eyes. *That's not what you mean.*

*What do you mean?*

*When people learn something the hard way it's because they do something dumb and it bites them back.*

*Well, I know what I mean—*

*But nobody else does,* he smiled.

*—Adrianne is going to have to work harder than most anybody else because learning is tougher for her, that's what I mean.*

*Okay.* Then looking at me, *You're a smart one Ady Maidy. You'll do well, I know you will.*

In my mind's eye, Herb and Elaine's visits to our home run like an aged reel of home movies spliced together. The opening scene is of me sitting on a landscaped ledge in front of the house waiting for them to show. More often than not, they don't. When they do, they are hours late.

A splice bounces through the projector. Herb and Elaine pull up in an aged and beat-up Oldsmobile. Herb rises up out of the car and stretches the full length of his lanky body while waving at me. Elaine crouches out from the car, but is unable to fully straighten her stooped shoulders and plump body.

They both look tired, though Herb is happy to see me. Elaine's expression rarely displays any emotion other than life-weariness. Oval, black Jackie Kennedy-like sunglasses cover her eyes.

Herb is sweating and wipes his brow with a handkerchief. Elaine's wearing black polyester pants and blouse with a sheer white cover. It's summer and she's wearing short sleeves; I can see track marks pockmarking her arms. Herb's arms are also scarred.

Both are dependent on methadone, which makes their heads tilt on the axis of their necks.

I hold Mom's hand and hover by her side.

*Hi Will, Bea, how are you,* Herb says, holding out his hand.

*We're good, Herb. How are you, Elaine?* Dad grasps Herb's hand.

Elaine holds her white leather purse loosely with both hands. Her low eyebrows and pointed glare betray her state of mind.

*Traffic must have been horrible?* Mom asks. She squeezes my hand in regular intervals. *To be so late, again.*

*No, not too bad, Bea,* Herb says, unaware that Mom is making a point rather than asking a question.

*Herb can be a little slow out of the house,* Elaine says.

*Oh, well you have to drive carefully with that car of yours—*

*Okay,* Dad says before Mom sharpens her point. *Come on in. Adrianne's been waiting.*

Herb and Elaine walk in and Mom offers them something to drink. Both say yes and Elaine follows Mom into the kitchen while Herb kneels down to say hello to me.

*Hey Adrianne, how are you?* he says, smiling.

*I'm okay.*

*Herb, why don't you come on into the living room,* Dad says.

We walk through the entry into the living room and Herb eases into Dad's chair where he usually sits to watch TV or read the newspaper. Dad pauses for a moment then sits on the couch. I sit next to Dad, underneath Mom's painting of the child and her grandmother. The comfort of the girl and older woman are a stark contrast to the tension between Dad and Herb.

In the kitchen, I hear mom making Lemonade and Elaine's voice following her around the kitchen. Elaine talks about her life as if it was a series of tragedies heaped upon her by a faceless, malevolent being.

*Life's taken a few turns,* Elaine says.

*It must have,* Mom says.

*What do you mean?*

*To be, you know, in this situation.*

*Right, well, it's not easy with a guy like Herb.*

Mom looks at Elaine, unsure what to say.

*He's like a child, you know? He can't take care of himself.*

*You must cross quite a bear with him.* Dad isn't available to fix Mom's idiom.

*Right, he's quite the cross to bear.* Elaine studies Mom and crosses her arms. *Why I ended up with him, I don't know. I was a natural beauty, you know.*

*I can see it.*

Elaine puts her sunglasses in her purse. Her eyes are narrow and sleepy looking. *My dad used to own a very popular nightclub in Florida; Dean Martin asked me out once.*

*Oh,* Mom says.

In the living room Herb wipes sweat from his brow and talks about his job at the methadone clinic. *It's a sad thing,* Herb says, *I'll tell ya Will, seeing these guys, women too, coming in messed up by heroin. I thank God I'm no longer on the schmeck.*

*Schmeck?* Dad asks.

*Yeah,* says Herb, his head bobbing, a wisp of a smile on his lips, *Yiddish for smack.* Herb lets out a wheezy laugh.

*Oh,* says Dad.

Mom walks in with the drinks, Elaine right behind her. Elaine stops and looks at Herb. *Nice place you have here; small, but nice.*

*Thank you,* Mom says. *We make do.*

Elaine wanders back to the entryway and looks up the stairs. *Do you mind?* Without waiting for an answer she starts up them. Mom puts her hands on her hips and lips pressed together, eyes wide, looks at Dad.

*Too bad she's so shy,* says Herb with a wan smile. Mom and Dad look at him.

*I guess I'll go fold laundry,* Mom says, heading up the stairs.

Elaine walks to Jeffrey's room and without knocking opens the door and leans against the doorframe.

*Hi Jeffrey.*

*Hi.* Jeffrey pulls off the headphones plugged into his stereo. Each earpiece looks like a large, black half-egg. He's in his room because he doesn't want to see Elaine and Herb.

*How are you, Elaine?* If nothing else, Jeffrey is polite.

*Same old crap, different day.*

*Okay.*

*I used to have a nice stereo like that when I was a kid,* Elaine says. *Mine was a lot nicer than that. My dad bought it for me and he didn't buy anything cheap.*

*That's nice.*

*Yeah, he could be a son of a bitch—he had friends in the mafia, you know—but he liked to spoil me rotten. Did I tell you he owned a big-time nightclub in Florida?*

*A couple times . . .*

*. . . And that he had friends who were famous entertainers?*

*Yes.*

*I was quite beautiful too . . .* she says, drifting off. A slight smile crosses her face, *I got champagne tastes, but I'm livin' on a beer budget. Such is life, right? Could be worse.*

Harry also hides away in his room, terrified that Elaine will bother him. He's older than me—five years older—and like me, he's a foster child. At age ten or eleven, he's less afraid of the idiosyncrasies of Elaine and Herb than he is of the possibility that his own biological parents could reappear at any moment.

He asks Mom and Dad if this will happen, if it's possible. *No Harry,* Mom says. *Your situation is much different. It won't happen to you.*

*Yeah buddy, can't happen, won't happen, don't even think about it. I'm not,* Dad says.

Later, Mom will tell Dad, *We don't know what the story is with Harry's parents.*

*Don't worry Bea. It'll be all right.*

*How can you say that? How can you? The agency told us Ady's parents were long gone, and now look. Do they look long gone to you?*

*It'll be all right.* Dad's mantra.

*'It'll be all right,'* Mom says, folding her arms, *right up until we get a call that they want her back. The agency said to us point bank—*

*Blank.*

*What?*

*Point blank.*

*Whatever. When we asked about adopting Harry they said, 'Don't start anything. Things are going well this way, so don't look for trouble because according to the law we have to look for the father, and what if he wants him?' Remember?*

One day, a man does call. His voice is deep and vacant. *Do you know what happened to my son?*

*No,* Mom says, her voice wavering. *Why would you ask me such a thing?*

*I've heard that you have Elaine's daughter. Do you have her son too?*

*Go ask THAT woman; I have no idea what you're talking about.* She hangs up, hard.

Mom is relieved the call was not for Harry, but it feels too much like a close call. She is afraid that at any moment an errant, unworthy parent or set of parents will appear and take not just one, but two of her beloved children. She hides these feelings, but the tension sometimes bubbles up to the surface.

At Thanksgiving, only a short while after the call, Dad pokes around the kitchen preparing to cook the turkey. Alternately, he talks to himself and Mom with a playful lilt to his voice. *Where did that turkey get to? Bea, where the heck's the turkey? You hide it?*

*It's in the refrigerator,* Mom calls back from her perch on the couch, where she's crocheting.

With his most affected honey-voice, Dad says, *Ady Maidy, I think your mom has hidden the turkey. Where could it be?* Drawers slide open; contents clink and jangle, *Nope, not in here . . .*

*Dear God,* Mom says, putting down her needles and yarn. She pushes herself off the couch and marches into the kitchen. Harry and I hear the refrigerator door open with a jerk, and then the sound of a plastic-wrapped turkey landing on the counter. *Here's the God damned turkey. Don't screw it up.*

After my seventh birthday Elaine and Herb push the agency for visits outside of my family's home. At first they ask for Mom and Dad to bring me to their apartment on Coney Island Avenue in Brooklyn.

*It would only be for a couple hours, maybe once a month,* Ms. Abramsky tells Mom over the phone.

*No,* Mom says.

*I think you should be . . .*

*No,* Mom repeats.

*All right, let me speak with Elaine and Herb.*

The next call from Ms. Abramsky announces that Elaine and Herb will continue coming to Wantagh, but they expect to be able to take me for short outings, an hour or two.

*I don't know,* Mom says, knowing her back's to the wall.

*This isn't something you can negotiate,* Ms. Abramsky says.

*They keep coming back wanting more and more. Who's to say they won't just say they want Adrianne back? This is where they're going, you know?*

*I know it feels like that, but it won't happen, we won't let that happen.*

*You and me, or the agency won't let that happen?*

*The agency. We have no interest in pushing a child to be with anyone we feel is not a fit parent.*

*But that's my point. What I'm saying is Herb wants to say to the world, 'Look, I'm rehabilitated; I'm a regular guy.' I have no idea what SHE wants. That woman barely even speaks to Adrianne when they visit.*

*Maybe they just want to maintain some sort of minimal relationship with their daughter? Is that so hard to believe?*

*They're going to keep asking for more.*

*Well, right now it's an hour or two with Adrianne outside of your home. They're entitled to that.*

*Mmm, hmm,* Mom says and hangs up the phone. Looking at Dad, *We've gotta let them take Ady for outings; like they're the type to pack a picnic basket.*

Dad is sitting on the edge of his easy chair, hands clasped, forearms resting on each leg. *They're gonna want her back,* he says. Gone for a moment is the eternal optimist.

*She says the agency won't allow it.*

*She said that again?*

*Yeah, but you know how bureaucracies are. They talk and tell you one thing and then somebody above them has a brainstorm and it all changes.*

*It'll be all right. If they said that, it'll be all right.* The eternal optimist returns, but his moist eyes and clenched hands betray his unease.

*Do you think they're saying that to Herb and Elaine?* Mom asks. *Do you really think they're saying, 'Don't even think about asking for Adrianne back?' No way, no way they're saying that. That agency is hand feeding each of us what they want us to know and protecting themselves.*

*They have to be on our side. Who would hand Ady over to those people?*

⟩≈⟨

Herb and Elaine are consistently inconsistent. Many times they don't show up, which is one of their better qualities. When they do, they are hours late.

Our excursions are rarely noteworthy. Sometimes we go to the beach. Other times it's to the *Sunrise Diner*. I find myself walking along the boardwalk or sitting across a table from them; Herb asks me how I like school and Elaine stares blankly toward the water or fidgets with her purse. I give Herb credit. His eyebrows work hard to pull the rest of his slumped face up into a smile. He wants to be nice and make a connection with me. He's just terrible at it.

Once, after my eighth birthday, in the late fall, Herb drops me off at the door. Elaine doesn't have the energy or desire to do more than sit and wait in the car.

*How ya doin' Ady Maidy,* Dad says, patting my shoulder as I walk into the house. He looks up at Herb. *Thanks for dropping her off.*

*Of course,* Herb says. He lingers for a moment and there's a beat of silence between him and Dad. *Listen, I've got great news.*

*Yeah?*

*Yeah, we're getting our other daughter back.*

*Other daughter?*

*Bina, her name's Bina, she's about a year-and-a-half older than Adrianne ...*

*Oh.*

*She's been with my mother in Florida, but Elaine and I think we have things pretty well together so we're bringing her home.*

*You are?*

*Yeah, we are; soon, couple of months maybe.*

*Okay, good for you.* Another beat passes between them. *Well, enjoy the rest of the weekend,* Dad says, and closes the door.

Mom's in the kitchen. *What?*

*They have another daughter, Bina, a little older than Ady,* Dad says. *He said they're bringing her back home.*

Mom leans against the counter. *It's only a matter of time until they ask for Ady back, you know?*

*I know.*

*When we got into this foster parenting thing we always said if a parent wants their child back, we'd do it.*

*If they were stable and could provide a good home,* Dad reminds her. *There's no way they are fit to be parents, not to our Ady.*

*I know, but what do we do?*

*I don't know. It'll work out in the end . . .* His words drift off and Dad walks to the basement, where he spends the rest of the evening tinkering with his trains.

*Are you happy?* Herb asks, as we sit in a booth waiting for our food. It's mid-November, 1970.

I don't understand what he means by *happy*. Of course I'm happy with Mom and Dad. I'm eight years old and I love them. There's a jelly donut every Saturday morning, periodic trips to the Times Square Store, listening to Jeffrey's music through the wall, pretending to be pirates with Harry in the basement, and dinners out to our family's favorite restaurant, Kwong Ming.

I remember we went to Kwong Ming for my birthday when I was five or six, but I wasn't happy about it.

*They won't sing Happy Birthday or have a cake,* I sobbed.

*Don't you worry Ady Maidy, they'll have cake and a song.*

Sure enough, our waiter brought a cake to our table after clearing the dishes away. Dad stood with the other waiters and waitresses, all of whom were Chinese, and sang Happy Birthday to me. Mom looked at Dad, seeming proud that she married him, that he was hers.

Now in the booth with Herb and Elaine I think, am I happy? *Yes, I suppose so,* I say. Does Elaine wince, or is memory playing a trick?

*How about now? Do you like being with your mom and dad?*

Does he mean Herb and Elaine or mom and dad? *I guess,* I say.

*Tell me Adrianne, do you like dancing?*

*I suppose so.*

*I mean, like ballet or jazz . . .*

*She's too young for jazz dancing,* Elaine says. The air outside is warm, bright and sunny, but Elaine is wearing her usual black polyester pants, black polyester blouse and white long-sleeve cover.

Herb looks at her. *Well, you know . . .* He juts his arms out, one past Elaine's face, and makes them waggle, to impersonate a ballerina.

*Stop it,* Elaine says, pushing Herb's arm down, but she smiles at him.

*I like to dance,* I say.

*Do you take lessons? Are you in a class?* Herb asks. He's leaning forward, hands clasped and resting on the table.

*No.*

*That's too bad. How about gymnastics?*

*Gymnastics?*

*Yeah, you know, like in the Olympics; that Vera something-or-other who won the gold in Mexico City.*

Elaine's eyes widen. *How do you know that?*

*I pay attention; it's something Bina likes.* Then he looks at me.

*I like it, I guess, but I don't do it, except sometimes in gym we do somersaults or jump rope, and I can do cartwheels.*

*Would you like to join a team, go to a class?*

*I don't know.*

*How 'bout school? Do you get good grades?*

No matter how hard I work and how much help I get from Mom, each subject is all but impenetrable. *No, I don't.*

Herb glances over to Elaine, whose eyes are veiled, sedate looking.

*Why not?* Elaine asks. *I was pretty smart when I was a kid; still am.*

Because I'm not very smart, I think. *I don't know.*

*Do you get enough help from Will and Bea?* Herb asks.

I don't like that Herb and Elaine call Mom and Dad Will and Bea. *Yeah, MY MOM helps me a lot.*

Herb sits back in his seat; eyebrows up. He wipes his brow with a napkin.

Elaine looks at the middle of my forehead, *Well, Bea must not do a very good job if you get bad grades.*

*Yeah,* Herb adds, wiping the back of his neck with the napkin. *You're a smart kid.*

I don't like how Herb's praise makes me feel. I'd be completely lost if not for the two-sides-of-the-same coin nature of Mom and Dad: grounded realism from Mom and eternal optimism that I'm *one smart kiddo* from Dad.

I love being the apple of Dad's eye. Herb doesn't have the right to intrude on that.

The call from Ms. Abramsky comes in the winter of 1971.

*Well, I suppose we knew this was coming,* Mom says into the phone.

*I guess,* says Ms. Abramsky.

From his easy chair, hands clasped, Dad asks, *What is it Bea, what do those people want now?*

Mom covers the phone, *They want Ady back, Herb and Elaine want her back.* She wipes away a tear and speaks into the phone, *How can they do this?*

*I think they just want to try to put their family back together.*

*So they're going to take Adrianne because they wanna prove to the world they're normal people?*

*They say they want their family back together . . .*

*They're not, you know?*

*Not what?*

*Normal. They're not fit to be parents, not to Adrianne. I can see it, feel it. You must know it too? These people aren't fit, they aren't good people.*

*That's not for me to say.*

*But you're not going to let them do this, right?*

*I can't say that either.*

*What happened to 'Don't worry, we won't let it happen, it'll never happen?'*

*We still support you and Will as Adrianne's foster parents . . .*

*But?*

*It's complicated.*

# Chapter Four

## JOHNNY: DEEPENING CHAOS

*I'll tell you what I remember about your mom.*
*She was stunningly gorgeous, but tragically drunk.*
*Now I see you and think, when we have*
*alcoholic parents we can leave and go our separate ways*
*or we become the parent. Johnny, you did*
*what you had to do to survive.*

—Laura Boldt, Johnny's friend since fourth grade

Mom and Dad's wedding wasn't just the celebration of their love, hopes and aspirations. It was also the merger of two of Ladue's wealthiest and most powerful families.

Mom's connection to wealth and privilege traces back to Louis Cella, my great grandfather. He was a self-made millionaire who started his climb as a grain speculator, then expanded into hotels, theaters and other commercial properties in St. Louis and throughout the Midwest and South.

His interests included horseracing and bookmaking, which led him into the racetrack business. He owned tracks in St. Louis, Kentucky and New Orleans, but the jewel in the crown was Oaklawn Park, which was not much more than a dusty dirt ring when he purchased it in 1916. Within two years, Oaklawn would nip at the heels of racing meccas such as Churchill Downs, Saratoga Springs and Belmont Park.

In 1917, Louis decided to build The American Theater—an ornate and elegant Beaux Arts-style arts venue affectionately known as *The American*— that became *the* cultural center of St. Louis.

Unfortunately for Louis, he died in 1918 at age fifty-one before realizing his dreams for Oaklawn. Continuing the Cella legacy fell to his brother Charles.

By the 1930s, Kentucky Derby winners and other nationally known thoroughbreds raced at Oaklawn. It was also the home of the Arkansas Derby and was considered by horseracing's literati to be one of the *grandes dames* of horse racing facilities in the United States.

Everything the Cellas touched turned to gold. Oaklawn and the many other racetracks, hotels, theaters, and commercial properties financed by Charles and then by his son, John G. Cella, flourished. By the start of World War II, the Cella family was the second wealthiest in St. Louis and lived like the Missouri Brahmins they were. They threw so many extravagant parties for the fashionable elite that at one point their yearly budget for Dom Perignon was $600,000.

This is the world Eloise Shearer Cella was born into, and it suited her perfectly. Mom was *the* beautiful, patrician debutante, held safe by inherited affluence like a pearl snug within its protective nacre.

When I was a boy, six or seven, Dad told me this story:

*Your mother was my childhood sweetheart, you know that Johnny? I loved her the first time I saw her, in a photo my friend Kaut White showed me in sixth grade. He kept it in his wallet and when he showed her to me, well, I'd never seen anyone as beautiful as your mother looked in that photo. I asked, 'Who is that?'*

*I don't think Kaut meant for me to take an interest in her because he grabbed the photo back, but he said, 'That's Eloise Shearer Cella.'*

*Looking at that photo, I knew I was in love with whoever this Eloise Shearer Cella was.*

*Kaut never got anywhere with her, but unbelievably enough, her family moved into number 8 Upper Ladue Road. I lived at number 11. One way or another I got to know her and I spent more time at her house than I did at my own. She was funny and sweet, smart, and the most beautiful girl I'd ever known. Anyone'd be lucky to end up with a girl like her.*

It's nice to know they married for love.

Dad was a good looking boy. With his broad smile, bright ginger hair, wide set eyes, and lean, muscular body he looked like the all-American, corn-fed, Midwestern kid. He was born with a sweet disposition, had politeness beaten into him, and loved playing football, basketball and baseball.

He also inherited a ladies shoe empire built by his father.

No one could accuse Vergil Calvin Lipscomb of being the overindulged scion of old money parentage. He came from a family of old school

Appalachian coal miners where hardship, Old Testament discipline, and hard work were the rule. Vergil made his peace with the Old Testament, but never accepted mining and impoverishment as his lot in life.

He was a man of unassailable gumption and shrewdness. As he once told me, *I always knew who I had to grease to get the wheat.* Like a well-honed scythe, Vergil cut a swift path from prospective Depression-era coal miner to founder of Town & Country Shoes in 1942 at age thirty-eight.

He had to sell his house to raise capital to get the company going, but he had ingenuity and an incredible color sense. With World War II gaining steam and leather dedicated to making army boots, helmet chin straps and the like, he developed a range of fashionable shoe styles in fabrics that weren't rationed.

Vergil received patents for his shoe designs and then, after the war, started producing handbags, clutches, berets and other accessories to match the company's shoes. During the mid to late 1940s, Vergil's ideas were major fashion innovations that redefined the high-end market for ladies' shoes.

At its prime, Town & Country was the nation's number two producer of women's shoes, with four factories that pumped out 10,000 pairs of shoes per per day. It was an early tenant in the Empire State Building, counted Nordstrom and Lord & Taylor as among its biggest customers, owned a luxury, dual-prop plane, and held a half-interest in a Lear Jet with a personal pilot for Vergil's travel needs.

When anyone asks about Town & Country Shoes, I tell them their mom probably wore a pair.

Wealth did not satisfy all of Vergil's ambitions. He wanted acceptance into the crème-de-la-crème of the Midwest's social elite and worked to avoid the label *Hillbilly-Riche.*

When he noticed that Dad, Uncle Michael and Aunt Jane were developing rural accents he made the move to Ladue. Once there, he settled his children in the right schools: St. Louis Country Day School (affectionately known in Ladue as Codasco) for the boys and Mary Institute for Jane. He made sure that his family belonged to the proper clubs and were friends with all the right people.

He worked at overcoming his Missouri twang and likely felt hobbled by his marriage to a woman with a name rooted in the rural Midwest: Gussie Greta Pearl Pitchford Lipscomb. When family came to visit, 11 Upper Ladue Road was the only place they had to use a knife and fork to eat chicken. No one, not ever, picked their food up off the plate in Vergil's house. In 1948 Vergil endured the social anxiety of divorcing Gussie Greta. He then married a lovely woman named Bettyjane.

A few years later, Dad graduated from Country Day and with his six peers received a ten-week trip to Europe. They stayed at the Excelsior Hotel and bought either motorcycles or cars (a sleek French Alcyon motorcycle for Dad) with which they traveled through southern France, Italy, and Switzerland. Upon return, Dad left for Cornell University, but was eager to get to work in the family business and after two years of college began work for Town & Country. While still a young man, he assumed the role of president of the company.

With him all this time was Eloise Shearer Cella. On June 15, 1957, they married and two of St. Louis' most influential families became entwined, for better or worse.

The Christmas after my ninth birthday is the usual unavoidable and annual convergence of the families.

Routine traditions punctuate the week leading up to that Christmas. Dad and Lisa and I—Joshua is too young and Mom is a mess—attend the

Christmas chorus show at Rossman, the private grade school that feeds into Codasco. With the final stanza of *Silent Night* I am freed for two weeks of Christmas vacation.

The next day Lizzy, with Josh, Lisa and I tight to her heels, sets up decorations around the house while Mom occupies her perch in the formal den. That evening Dad takes us kids in Mom's wood-paneled Ford Country Squire station wagon to pick up the Christmas tree. We pile into the car, our breath like frosty little clouds as Dad eases down the road to where the Boy Scouts have taken over a small parking lot to raise money selling Christmas trees. We always pick the largest, widest tree and Dad jokes that he may have to cut a hole in the floor to make it fit. Once home, we set the tree up in the living room next to the piano.

After dinner Dad sits in the living room with a scotch and smokes while Lizzy mumbles her way through unpacking our ornaments and Christmas tree lights. Mom is dead to the world and bundled in bed. Lizzy hands us each an ornament and bit by bit the tree comes to life.

Christmas Eve morning there's a coating of snow, so I pull on my snow pants and Lizzy bundles Joshua and Lisa, three and six years old, into snowsuits. I spend an hour or so sledding down the small hill that our driveway winds up while Lisa rolls snow into balls to make a snowman. Joshua is happy to roll in the snow, but begins to cry when Lizzy won't let him sled with me. This is the beginning of his need to do all he can to keep up with me.

In the afternoon Lizzy lets Josh, Lisa and I up into the attic, where there is gold-painted, fine insulation. We pick bits of insulation out and take it downstairs where Lizzy helps us glue it onto Popsicle sticks to give as gifts to the adults.

That evening Dad, Lisa, Joshua and I wait in the foyer at the bottom of the stairs for Mom. Dad has wrestled Joshua into a cute little suit with

*Lizzy and me at Christmas*

suspenders and Lisa into a pink, cotton and lace, long-sleeved dress. Dad and I are in nearly matching suits. Lizzy is at her home to spend Christmas Eve and morning with her family. Mom is upstairs getting dressed.

*El, we need to get there before midnight, ya know?* Dad calls up the stairs. Josh is fidgeting in Dad's arms, my entire body feels itchy, and Lisa is tugging on his suit coat. *Lisa-Pie, please, I can't help you right now.*

*Daddy please,* she whines, *I just want to go.*

*El will you please come down!* Dad snaps.

We hear Mom walk from their room. The carpet dulls her steps until she reaches the long landing at the head of the stairs, then comes the familiar rapid succession of *clunk, clunk, clunk,* the stem of her heel hitting the wood floor hard, followed by the ball of her foot slamming down.

Holding the banister with one hand, empty glass in the other, she descends the stairs, glaring at Dad. She's wearing a light blue satin formal dress that flares at the waist, with blossom and leaf appliqués. When she reaches the last step she lays one hand on the top of the newel post, holds her glass up with the other and strikes an elegant pose.

*Don't I look exquisite?* she says to Lisa and me. She steps down and places the glass on a table for Lizzy to pick up when she returns the next day to cook Christmas dinner. She narrows her reddened eyes and levels them at Dad. *I told you, I'll come down when I'm ready.*

*El . . .* Dad starts to say, but then thinks better of it. *Let's go.*

Dad rushes us out into the night to eat dinner with Luju, Mom's mother. Luju and Lampau divorced at nearly the same time as Vergil and Gussie. A year or so later, Lampau married Geneva and Luju got a capuchin monkey.

When we walk through the front door we are greeted by the full presence that is Luju. Her eyes are demure, like Mom's, but lack the persistent sadness of Mom's. A layer of powder gives her face a milky complexion that focuses one's eyes on her bright red, pursed lips. Luju's black, chiffon dress is snug around her chest and midriff, then falls loosely from her waist. There is, as always, an off-ness to Luju's bearing, an indescribable unease that some small, important detail is amiss.

*Hello Mother,* Mom says, taking off her coat and gloves and handing them to the maid. She steps forward to kiss Luju's cheek and catches a heel.

*Merry Christmas dear.* Luju steps forward with an Old Fashioned in a crystal rocks glass. She catches a heel too, and the two women stumble into one and another and laugh.

*I'm sorry Luju,* Dad says, *El's had a few.*

Mom waves her hand dismissively. *John, give it a rest. It's Christmas.*

*John,* Luju says, *why don't you get your wife and you something? While you're at it, you could freshen my drink too.* Luju raises her glass toward him. All that's left is ice, maraschino cherry and orange peel.

Dad sticks his hands in his pockets and leans back on his heels. He refuses to be undone by Luju and Mom's antics. Then he takes the glass and walks off to make drinks.

There are cousins in the house so Lisa and I wander off to find them and play with Luju's monkey.

When dinner is served—a formal meal with three different meat courses —every adult is deep in their cups. Christmas is open season on alcohol for Mom and Luju but both of them make it through dinner upright. Mom is nothing but smiles as she ignores Dad.

After dessert Dad smokes one last cigarette in the parlor with his in-laws, probably to give his stomach a chance to digest and burn off a bit of the scotch and wine before driving us home. Mom gathers herself up, hugs and kisses Luju, and then steps carefully in her high heels to the car.

We get home at about ten and, within minutes, a few of Mom and Dad's friends show up. One of them is Uncle Bobby, who isn't a real uncle, but Dad's longest-held and best friend. Parking his 1966 Ford Galaxy—a large, four-door car that looks like a cross between Dad's Toronado and Mom's Cadillac—in the front yard, he skids on the snow and the car almost slides back down the hill.

He enters our home with a door-slamming burst of energy and drops his long, black wool coat on the antique wooden bench in the hall. He's a teacher—Harvard educated and classmate of Dad's at Codasco—and I suppose he dresses like a Harvard-educated-English-major-turned-teacher cliché: beige corduroy jacket and matching pants, a white shirt with blue pinstripes holding back a taut, round beer belly. His bloodshot eyes framed by tortoiseshell glasses shine with delight in his red face.

*Lippo!* he says to Dad and the two men grab each other in a vigorous, back slapping hug. Both are tall, but Dad's muscular frame contrasts with Uncle Bobby's lankier physique.

When he sees me his eyes light up. *Johnny-Jump-Up, Merry Christmas boy!* Johnny-Jump-Up is the pet name he gave me when I was a toddler and used to jump into his lap when he visited.

Though there are only a handful of people, the house overflows with loud voices, laughter, and cigarette smoke. Mom is drunk to the point of falling over so it's up to Dad to get Lisa, Josh and me up to bed. I'm tired, excited for the morning, but I miss Lizzy's reassuring steps up the back stairs, her mumbling and the white noise of her TV, even the sound of her spitting tobacco juice into a tin can.

I lie in bed listening to the adults downstairs. They laugh and drink. I can hear tearing cardboard and jangling metal parts: they are pulling toys from their boxes and putting them together. The sound of it makes me excited for the next morning.

Mixed with loud adult voices and laughter is the sound of Uncle Bobby trying to play *The Little Drummer Boy* on the piano. It's nothing more than a confused jumble of sour notes and Uncle Bobby singing, '*Here they hold me*' . . . *no that's not it, God damn it* . . . '*When they hold me*' . . .

*That's not it either Bobby,* Dad calls out, laughing.

*I'll get it you son of a bitch.* More sour notes on the piano, *Something, something,' Pa pum a dum um*' . . . *awwww shit* . . . From there, the song as rendered by Uncle Bobby devolves into a string of obscenities. This is my Christmas Eve lullaby.

The next morning it's cold and clear. No new snow, but there's enough on the ground to make it a white Christmas.

I rush downstairs in my pajamas to the Island of Misfit Toys scattered around the Christmas tree and piano. Most are wrapped, poorly, but those built last night, such as new bikes for Lisa and me, look dangerous. Highball, martini, and rocks glasses litter ceramic Christmas tableaus. The stockings and ashtrays are full.

I'm the first up. Lisa comes downstairs to find me sitting on the carpet looking at the tree. She sits next to me. *When do you suppose we can open a present?* she asks.

*I don't know. When Dad comes down?*

We don't have to wait long for Dad. We hear him come down the back stairs into the kitchen and walk into the living room carrying Joshua. He's wearing PJs under a robe. His eyes are bleary and bloodshot. Dad pulls a pack of cigarettes and a Zippo lighter from a pocket in his robe and lights a cigarette.

*How 'bout it gang? Wanna open a present?* His voice is hoarse.

Later, we dress in our formal clothes again, wait on Mom as usual, and then drive to Vergil's house on Millionaire's Row. Vergil passed away two years ago, but Bettyjane lives there. Nanna, Vergil's first wife, has moved to the tony Detroit suburb Grosse Point to live with Aunt Jane and her family.

Then we return home to open presents. Lizzy is there and has been cleaning, mumbling and working on Christmas dinner since about noon, *All of 'em must a been drunker than Cooter Brown . . . Lohd, what a mess . . . what's fo' dinner? I tell ya what's fo' dinner; goodness, nothin' but goodness, cookin' it all day . . . um hmmm . . . got to cook it right . . . um hmmm . . . there it is, there it is . . .*

With the gifts unwrapped, we play amid discarded wrapping paper. Mom pours her first drink and waits for the slow parade of friends and relatives. The first is Uncle Bobby. We love him and are happy to hear the large engine of his Ford Galaxy power up the driveway. He parks around back and climbs out of his car, red-faced and smiling.

He shuffles toward us, eyes bright, if a bit bleary. *Lippo, let's build these kids a proper sled run,* he says, pointing to the hill etched by our earlier sliding. Soon we are outside with Dad and Uncle Bobby working with snow shovels. I try to help while Joshua bounces and rolls in the snow and Lisa makes snow angels.

Just as it seems the sled run is getting interesting, Uncle Bobby calls out to Dad, *Getting thirsty?*

Dad smacks snow out of his gloves. *I suppose I am. Probably should also make sure Eloise isn't about to burn the house down.*

After we come inside, the parade of friends and relatives begins. They pile out of huge American-made cars and wander into the house. All of the men are broad shouldered and cocky. *Lippo,* they say with muscular hand-shakes, *how are you.*

The women are nonchalant and greet each other with cat-like eyes. *Eloise, you look absolutely beautiful.*

And, of course, from the men there's a chorus of, *Johnny-Jump-Up, did Santa bring what you wanted for Christmas?* followed by a firm handshake. The women tilt slightly on their heels; their prim faces expectant, waiting for some sort of response.

*Yeah, I guess so.* My nickname sounds boyish, diminutive. My face feels warm. *May I be excused?*

*What's that, Johnny?* Dad asks.

*Can I be excused?*

*'May I,'* Mom corrects. *Why don't you get the kids working on something;
a game?* Then, looking up to the guests, *Drink?*

Luju is among the missing but, as in years past, she'll ride with Aunt
Mae. The two sister-in-laws are thick as thieves and share a cultivated sense
of style and fashion emblematic of their era and moneyed status. In their
black cocktail dresses—worn daily and at all hours—heels or white mules by
the club pool, and oversized, gleaming black mink coats paired with black
leather gloves whenever the temperature dips below 55 degrees, each could
be the doppelgänger of the other.

Where they depart is in attitude, bearing and manner. Luju is stiff and
arrogant with a soupçon of pompousness. Aunt Mae is gregarious and, to
me, uniquely lovable.

Single, and happily so, she often picks just me up in her Cadillac to go
out to a fancy club for dinner, or to Howard Johnson's for the best chocolate
cake in town. Sometimes she takes me to plays or concerts at *The American,*
where everyone from the ticket girl to the season ticket holders knows her
as Mae. She has a broad smile a warm, deep laugh, and never stops talking.

Every word and story comes from her in an excited rush and always
begins, *Oh Johnny*—never Johnny-Jump-Up—*you'll never believe this . . .*
She narrates with one hand on the steering wheel, the other punctuating
each sentence, each insight, each moment of humor or disbelief. Her eyes
are bright and features animated. Every so often she playfully nudges my
shoulder and never seems to look at, or even care about, the road. I am the
center of her world. Some evenings she allows me to sit on her lap and steer
the car; the whole while she continues to chatter and laugh, her foot on the
gas as I maneuver the car through Ladue.

Once, walking into the lobby of *The American,* each person we passed
stopped Aunt Mae. It was a whirl of *so-good-to-see-you, my-dear-you-look-lovely*

and excited chatter. In the midst of it she licked her fingers, wiped down my wayward cowlick and, her face inches from mine, whispered, *Life's a banquet, my dear Johnny.*

I smiled. The week before, we'd seen Rosalind Russell in *Auntie Mame.*

Now, with the cousins tended to and adults drinking and filling various parts of the house with chatter and cigarette smoke, I look out the living room's bay window for Aunt Mae. Behind me, Dad, Uncle Mike—Dad's brother—Uncle Bobby and Uncle Charles—Mom's brother—laugh and strain to speak over one another. Dad, Uncle Mike and Uncle Charles are well over six feet tall and physically powerful and imposing men.

Every male in my family is like this. When among the men, I feel unseen and unheard, inadequate and self-conscious.

I turn to look at the three men when their volume increases sharply—they must be arguing about sports or business—then gaze back out the window. *Hey, Aunt Mae and Luju are here.*

I watch Aunt Mae's Cadillac fly up the driveway.

*Dad! Aunt Mae just drove her car down the sled run!*

We rush outside and slip and slide down the hill toward Aunt Mae's car, which is stuffed with presents. Both women wear minks and gloves. Luju has her hands crossed in her lap and looks as if the car will suddenly spin back up the hill and deliver her to the front door.

Aunt Mae rolls the window down and pops her head out smiling and giggling. *Oops!*

Aunt Mae drinks like Auntie Mame, too.

Uncle Bobby helps Aunt Mae out of the car and up to the house while Dad gets in the driver's seat next to Luju. The other men push the car off the snow to the bottom of the driveway and Dad drives it up to the front door.

Mom hugs Aunt Mae at the door, *Oh, Aunt Mae, too funny!*

*She nearly killed us!* Luju says, climbing out of the passenger seat.

*No harm done, lovey,* Aunt Mae snips back at Luju. Turning to Mom, *I think we could use a drink, dear,* and the three matriarchs of our family wobble inside.

By the end of the evening, ashtrays are overflowing, empty liquor bottles fill the garbage can, Uncle Bobby has knocked the Christmas tree over—a tradition of his—Mom's passed out in bed (Dad undressed her) after getting blackout drunk—a tradition of hers—there are more cigarette burns in the carpets, and Lizzy's in the kitchen mumbling away.

This is my life. I have no control over the adults in my life—especially Mom—or my fate. This has been my normal for as long as I can remember.

The following May, Mom and Dad tell us they are divorcing. In the next moment, Mom tells us to pack for a trip to Florida.

I look to Dad for reassurance, but there is nothing there for me. His words and manner feel careless and indifferent, but Mom's drinking weighs on him. He's afraid to lose his childhood sweetheart, the sweetest, most beautiful girl he's ever seen, but she is no longer that girl. She's stunningly gorgeous, but tragically drunk.

I can't imagine Dad's sadness every evening as he all but carries Mom from the formal den to their bedroom.

*Leave me be, John!*

*No El. Enough!*

Mom stabs her finger into Dad's chest, *I don't like you anymore.*

*I'll have to live with that.*

For years he made her drinks to calm her temper, took care of us kids more than any other father I knew, and rarely complained to Mom or asked her to stop drinking. He existed within his pain and fear of losing Mom, hoping that one day there'd be a change, that something different would happen.

No one can live like that forever. Dad started seeing Dr. Herb Rosenbaum, a psychoanalyst, and asked for his help. He told Dr. Rosenbaum—as with everybody, Dad was on a first-name-basis with the doctor—*Herb, I'm doing everything I can to keep the house together, keep our family going, but I can't live like this much longer.*

*Don't you know you're a failure?* Dr. Rosenbaum said.

*What are you talking about?*

*You're a failure at what you're trying to do because it isn't working. All you're doing is enabling her.*

The two of them worked out a plan to admit Mom to Barnes Hospital in St. Louis for a few days. Afterward, she'd transfer to a weeks-long inpatient program in Minnesota. When Dad told Mom she needed to do this for the family, she agreed and went to Barnes, but at the last minute backed out of going to the inpatient program. There wasn't even a slight pause in her drinking.

Desperate, Dad went to Uncle Charles to ask for his help and support in getting Mom to treatment. With Lampau gone, Uncle Charles was in charge of the family's businesses and properties, including Oaklawn, making him one of the wealthiest and powerful men in St. Louis. Not a man to trifle with.

*I'll do what I can, John, but you know Eloise as well as anyone.*

*I do.*

*She won't go easily and there's only so much I can do.*

*I know.*

Dad then went to Luju.

She heard him out, paused, politeness dissolving from her face. *Maybe you should be more attentive to her.*

*I've grown up in your house and spent most of my life doing all I could to ensure her happiness.*

*I don't know, do you think this is necessary? Why do you want to embarrass her and the family like that?*

By then, Luju's drinking was mirroring Mom's, making it questionable whether she saw it as a problem or another point of friendly convergence for mother and daughter. Mom spent a significant amount of time smoking and drinking while on the phone with Luju.

A true businessman, Dad made a good pitch, *It feels a bit much to me too, but her drinking has gone far beyond a bit much. When I look at you, I see a woman of unimpeachable character and control. I see a woman with grace, who is charming and attractive; all the things I used to see in El. For gosh sakes, I married her for these qualities. But the woman I used to know is gone and I know you've seen it, and I know we all want her back.*

Though Luju was a petite woman, she was imposing in her bearing. After hearing Dad's appeal she broadened her shoulders, swelling her décolletage, and raising her body to its full stature. *I won't have her committed against her will and, if asked, I'll say she's gone on an extended vacation to take a break from the demands of keeping a home and raising your children, but you have my support.*

When Dad approached Mom she became apoplectic. *You went to mother, too! You really are the limit John!*

*El, please. You need help—no, no, we need help. Honey, it's not just you, it's us, we need help, okay?*

Mom turned from Dad. An ugly little laugh burst from deep in her throat. *Fine.*

Dad made the arrangements but before a suitcase was packed, Mom backed out. *Go pound sand,* she told Dad.

*El, I will do all I can to support, love and help you if you go, but if you don't go, me staying here isn't helping you and life is unlivable with you. Please, will you do this for us?*

Mom looked him in the eye, *No.*

Dr. Rosenbaum heard the story and said, *It's time for you to get a divorce and a life.*

So that's what Dad did.

As I pack for Florida, Dad packs to move into the Chase Park Plaza. Shortly after Dad leaves the house a taxi pulls up. We gather our things, Mom sluices back the last of her drink, and we're off.

To say the trip to Florida is a disaster would undersell Mom's ability to get blindingly drunk. When the plane lands, her eyes open and she turns to me. *Where the hell are we?*

When we reach the hotel, Mom is incoherent. Two bellhops help her from the cab into the lobby and I sign the register for her. The rest of the week is a recklessly-drunk-alcoholic-mom-attempting-to-manage-three-kids version of spring break. She can't do it and relies on a series of bellhops, concierges, and chambermaids to make sure that we are looked after and that Joshua doesn't wander off and drown in the pool.

Dad knows where we are—we've vacationed at this hotel many times—and does what he can to work with the hotel manager to ensure we're safe. He calls a couple of times to see how we're doing, but on the first call Mom yells, *Go to hell,* and hangs up.

On the second call I answer and try to reassure him: *The hotel people are nice, but Mom is scaring us.*

Dad's consumed with worry and tells Uncle Bobby, *She's so far gone I have no idea how she's keeping them safe, much less fed, or how she's going to get them home. What the hell do I do? Go get them myself?*

He doesn't have to. One morning, Mom announces we're leaving. We pack and by afternoon we're dropped off at home by a taxi. Mom is less drunk than when we'd arrived in Florida. She walks in the door, tells Lizzy to feed us, and goes off to drink, smoke and talk on the phone in the formal den.

Dad comes by when he can to take us out and make sure everything is all right. *Johnny,* he says to me, *when Lizzy isn't around you have to make sure your mother doesn't pass out with a lit cigarette, you hear?*

*I do Dad. Can't you come back? Please?*

*I'm sorry, Johnny. I'd give my life for you kids, but right now I can't.*

Lizzy and I share Mom duty; checking in on her to pick up any lit cigarettes off the floor, couch, or table, then put them out. There are more burn marks on every surface, but nothing's caught fire.

Mom spirals downward. When she's lucid, she's a whirlwind of anger, paranoia and sorrow. She rages: *That bastard . . .* When her anger is spent, she falls to the floor sobbing. *I've lost him, I've lost him...* Incoherence follows, then she passes out.

Saturday night, a month after coming home from Florida, I hear the angry *clack, clack, clack* of her heels marching toward the den. Lizzy is putting Joshua and Lisa to bed. I'm alone in the living room.

I look up and there's Mom wearing black heels, a bathrobe wrapped around her slender, still-elegant body, drink in one hand and cigarette in the other.

*Johnny dear, don't you let them do it.*

*Do what?*

*Take me away. God damn it, don't you let them do it.*

*I won't.* I'd say anything to protect myself from her.

The next day I'm playing outside by the creek with my friends Bill and David. We are the Three Musketeers and do everything together. In my world, Bill's is the perfect family. His dad's a great guy, Mom's stable and at home every day after school, cooks good food, and keeps busy with the PTA. They are as close to normal as I've ever seen. David's Mom died only a few months ago of cancer, so he is cared for by a nanny named Dough, a large black woman who moves about his house like a ship. He and I spend hours in the woods, walking the lane, or at the country club talking. He misses his mom and feels the loss so deeply that he allows himself to cry in front of me. My loss is more ambiguous. She's still alive, but she's not the mom I need. Alcohol is far more important to her than I am.

I worry about Lisa and Joshua, but I leave the house as often as I can to spend time with Bill, David and their families. I'll do anything to be with them, to tuck in with their families at dinner time, to feel the warmth of friendship and family. Friends become my family because they are the only thing that keeps me from completely falling into myself.

With Bill tight behind me, I run up to the top of the bank by the creek and jump toward a large felled maple that went down during a recent thunderstorm. I land on my feet then fall to my knees, and one hand lands in the dirt beneath the tree just as Bill jumps onto it. The maple shifts and rolls onto my hand. I feel the weight of it and pull back. Then I feel the pain.

My hand isn't broken, but it's bloody and hurts like hell. I run up to the house yelling, *Lizzy, Lizzy,* but when I rush in through the kitchen door I can't find her.

*What the hell is it?* Mom calls from the den.

I walk in holding my hand, blood running down my arm. *A tree rolled on it.*

*Wrap a paper towel on it, for God's sake.* Her eyes are glassy and a cigarette bobs in her lips.

Lizzy walks into the den. *Good lohd, Master Johnny.*

*Can you deal with this?* Mom says.

*Come with me.* Lizzy eyes Mom. We walk out toward the kitchen and Lizzy looks down to me. *I saw your blond hair bouncin' in the woods and up the yard coming toward me. You should know I'd come for you. You should always know that.*

Lisa comes into the kitchen and sees my hand, *Johnny, you okay?*

*No, I don't know.*

*You'll live,* says Lizzy.

*Where's Mom?* Lisa asks.

Lizzy looks up at her, *Her den, where else you suppose?*

*Good. She'll make it worse.*

Lizzy wraps a towel around my hand, but there are two deep cuts that need stitches. She calls Dad and he leaves work to take me to the emergency room. Mom doesn't seem to notice him showing up or the two of us leaving.

When we get home Mom is stomping around the house. *Why didn't anyone ask me? I'm his mom and I should take him to the hospital,* she screeches.

*El, there was no way you could take him.*

*Oh, don't you tell me that.*

*You couldn't.*

*You don't have the right to meddle in here, to just walk in here,* Mom says, waving a finger in Dad's face. *You gave that up when you walked out of here.*

*El, I still love you, but . . .*

*Then stop this and come home.* The anger in her face evaporates. Her eyes water and her voice breaks. *I can't do this without you John, I just can't. Please stay.*

*El, go get help and I'll be here when you get back. I promise.*

*Please stay.*

*I can't.* It hurts to see Dad turn and walk through the door.

Mom runs after him and grabs his hand. *No John,* her voice quivers, *I don't want this. I don't want a divorce, to lose you.*

Dad pulls his hand from hers. His eyes are clear as glass, but his chin looks fragile. *El, please don't. Get help. I'll be here when you get back.*

*I can't, I can't. Don't leave.* Mom runs past Dad, tears stream down her cheeks, her body is soft and frail; she throws herself to the ground behind the Toronado.

*El, get up and go inside.*

*No! I won't!*

Behind me I hear Joshua shriek, *Down, down, down . . .*

Lizzy's got hold of him and is carrying his fidgeting body away. *No Master Joshua. No, no.*

Lisa and I stand motionless, eyes wide, mouths open.

*Get up, El.*

*No.*

*Get up.*

*No.*

Dad reaches down and yanks Mom up by her arms. She's all of 110 pounds and looks like a ragdoll as he throws her over his shoulder.

*Put me down, God damn it!*

He carries her past Lisa and me into the house and disappears toward the kitchen.

*Don't you dare,* Mom screeches.

Lizzy rushes out of the kitchen holding Joshua tight to her chest, *This ain't for you Master Joshua.* She takes him upstairs.

*God damn you*, Mom screams, *God damn you.*

Dad emerges from the kitchen. *Johnny!*

*Yes sir.*

*Your mother's tied up in the pantry. Untie her after I've left and she's calmed down, you hear?*

*Yes sir.*

*I'm sorry Johnny, Lisa-Pie.*

Lisa's eyes fill with tears, her wet cheeks burn red. Dad walks past, gets in his car and drives down the driveway. I look at Lisa and she at me.

*We may have to leave Mom tied up for a while,* she says.

*Yeah, I know.*

I don't know who called Luju. Maybe it was Lisa. Maybe Lizzy. Whoever it was, Luju listens. I also don't know how Luju and Uncle Charles do it, but a week later Mom's at the Mayo Clinic and Dad moves back home with us.

*How long is Mom gone for?* Lisa asks.

*Until she's better Lisa-Pie,* Dad says.

Unfortunately, Mom has different plans.

# *Chapter Five*

# ADRIANNE:
# A SPLINTERING CHILD

Judge: *The rights of parents are paramount. This is something you can argue from now until doomsday, but I have to go by the law.*

Lawyer: *Does your Honor recognize there are two tests: The best interests of the child and the fitness of the parents?*

Judge: *No, the best interests of the child is not involved.*

—Exchange in Schoenowitz v. Cahn, April 20, 1972

*T*wo months after Ms. Abramsky's call in January of 1971, Mr. Schatzman, the executive director of the agency, calls.

He is a succinct, precise man whose manner of speaking is distinct in its economy of words. *Hello Mrs. Cahn, the board of the agency has met.*

*Well, this must be important for you to cawl.* When Mom's worried, angry or upset she slips deeper into her *Lawn Guyland* inflection. *Usually, you let Ms. Abramsky cawl with bad news.*

*I feel you deserve to speak with the executive director of the agency.*

*Okay.* Mom places one hand on her hip. Dad calls this her battle stance.

*As I said, the board met and discussed your situation with regard to Elaine and Herb Schoenowitz. Ms. Abramsky told you the agency is supportive of you and Mr. Cahn retaining custody of Adrianne, but that's no longer the case. In our view, and the law's view, we have to respect the rights of Adrianne's biological parents.*

*Just like that?*

*Our deliberation regarding Adrianne's situation was thorough. If you feel we have erred, there is a process for you to make an appeal. I advise you to move quickly. The Schoenowitzes are within their rights to request reunification with Adrianne as soon as the paperwork is approved and processed.*

Mom's body stiffens. *How long is that?*

*Within the next few months.*

*You've made a horrible decision.*

*You are a private citizen and no one can stop you from going into litigation.*

Mom says goodbye and hangs up the phone. She looks at Dad. *Gawd should give that man cansuh.*

Mom and Dad look at each other, but neither says a word. Mom, hands on hips, looks down at her foot, which is tapping. This is her deep thought pose. Without a word she goes to the kitchen to put the kettle on. Dad shakes open the newspaper. His eyes are listless, unable to read or register headlines. This is his deep thought pose.

The optimist and the pessimist are in neutral corners. Thinking, wondering, worrying over what they should do, what each should say to the other.

A few pages turn. A teabag dips into hot water with a little lemon and honey. Dad turns another page and Mom tosses the damp, warm teabag into the trash. She picks up her mug and walks into the living room. She sits on the couch, kitty-corner to Dad in his chair.

*Will,* she says.

*Yes Bea.*

*What do we do?*

*We fight.*

*But this is different . . .*

*Different smifferent.* Dad presses the newspaper onto his lap. *We rocked Ady to sleep and changed every diaper. We soothed every tantrum, sat up with her through every fever and held her tight to calm every fear. We are her parents and she's our child.*

*I've felt all along that we're gambling because I never forgot she isn't my kid.*

*Bea,* he says, sliding to the edge of his chair, *she IS our child.*

*Emotionally she's mine, she's ours, but tawking like we brought her into this world is a wrong analogy.*

*No - it's - not. She - is - ours.*

*Emotionally, she's ours. Please say that.*

*Why?*

*Because I need to know your feet at least touch the ground.*

*Emotionally she feels like she's our kid, and that's enough.*

Mom wipes a tear with the back of her hand. *She's my baby, too.*

*I know. I know you love her too.* Dad runs his hand down his face and sits back in his chair.

*But she's also our foster—*

*Oh Bea, in every way possible we're her parents.*

*In my heart, when we got into foster care, I knew I'm not Ady's biological mother and there may come a day when we have to give her up.*

*We both knew we may have to give up a child, but not our Ady. Not to THOSE people.*

*If I didn't accept reality coming into this,* her bottom lip begins to quiver and she wipes away another tear, *it was the only way I could become a foster mother.*

*You may have gone into this feeling you could give up a child, but you can't.* There's a flame in his eyes. *You can't do it; emotionally, you can't do it now.*

*Don't tell me how I feel. You always tell me how I feel as if you know what I'm thinking. You married me more than twenty years ago, but you still don't know me.*

*Then how do you feel?*

*It would kill me, literally kill me to give Ady up, but this is happening and the truth of the matter is I don't own her. I also think that the agency and the law is against us so maybe it's a stupid idea to spend all our money and put Ady and us through a big fight only to lose.*

Dad pauses for a moment. *Bea, if we don't show our feelings and fight for her, who are we?*

*I don't know.*

Dad presses the newspaper further into his lap. *We raised her and she's part of us, biological or not. If we back away then we aren't running true to who we are, true to form, true to our family.*

*But we're all alone right now. It's just us . . .*

*That's okay. We'll win. I'm sure of it.*

*. . . and a small bank account.*

*We'll borrow the money and it'll all be right. I'm telling you, no judge would give Ady to them.*

*I don't know.*

*Bea, this is what I want and I'm sure we'll win, but you have to be behind it 100 percent.*

*Why do you say that?*

*Say what?*

*Why do you always say things will be all right, like with school or now or anything, when you know it's all hard and painful?*

Dad's innocent, baggy eyes dim. *Because the thought that things may not work out, that school defeats Ady or we lose her, is too painful.*

*Okay.*

*Okay what?*

*This fight is something we have to do.*

Saturday morning I jump into Mom and Dad's bed and spider my fingers up and down one side of Dad's belly. He laughs and tickles me back. Then I hop over to Mom and snuggle in next to her. I'm eight years old and I never get tired of this routine.

*Well, good morning there Ady Maidy,* she says, wrapping her arm around my shoulders. Dad rubs sleep from his eyes.

*Donut?*

Dad gets up, dresses and goes off to the bakery. I stay with Mom and watch her crisp bacon in a frying pan. Jeffrey's in college so Harry is the only of our boys to wander down. He's wearing jeans and a plaid flannel shirt; at age fourteen he looks every bit the teenager. Before long, Dad is home with donuts, we eat, Dad goes downstairs to his trains, Harry disappears to his room, Mom cleans up, and I play with Jill and our other friend, Lynn from down the street. Normal.

Just before noon Mom calls, *Ady can you come to the kitchen?*

When I walk in Mom and Dad are sitting on one side of the Formica kitchen table. Dad's eyes are dull and meditative. Mom looks up, eyes bright, a faint smile.

Mom nods to the chair across from them. *Ady, we need to talk.*

She looks at Dad and Dad leans in toward me, hands clasped on the table. *The thing is Ady, Elaine and Herb want you back.*

*Want me back? What does that mean?*

Dad's fingers tense. *They want you to live with them.*

Mom shifts in her chair, making the vinyl seat cover chirr.

My stomach starts to ache. *I can't live with them if I live with you.*

Mom looks at Dad then me. *You wouldn't live with us anymore.*

My arms and legs feel shaky, like just before you throw up. *You don't want me anymore?*

Dad flattens his hands on the table. *We want you more than I even have words to tell you, Ady Maidy.*

Mom taps her hand on the table top. Her wedding ring clacks on the Formica. *Do you want to live with them?*

Did she ask me that? *No! Please, please don't make me go live with them.*

Dad reaches his hand toward me. *We won't, Ady. We're going to do everything we can so that you stay right here with us.*

*Please help me!* There's a sharp pain stabbing through my stomach. I clutch my arms around my belly. *Whatever you do, don't let them take me! I hate them, I hate them!* Tears stream down my cheeks. My face is hot. My legs and arms tremble.

Mom puts her ring hand on her stomach. *We're gonna hire a lawyer and fight for you, Ady.*

Dad stands and walks around to me. He lifts my quivering body up and sits in my chair with me on his lap. I push my face into the crook of his neck and smell the soft sweetness of his aftershave. He puts a hand on the back of my head and holds me close. I don't want to lose this and I can't imagine living with anyone else, in a different house, family and friends. I'm too young to fully understand love, but not too young to be filled with the love and know it surrounds me.

*Ady, we won't let anybody take you, my little doll,* he says. *I promise.*

I can feel Mom's slight frown. *We'll do our very best Ady. Don't you worry. We'll do our best.*

I start to cry. There's a burning ache at the thought of losing my family, losing Mom and Dad.

Dad starts rocking me. *It's okay,* he says over and over. I tighten my arms around my belly and hide, enfolded in Dad's warm, plump body.

From then on, Mom and Dad do all they can to protect me from the fight, but the genie's out of the bottle. Actually, it's a stomach ache, nausea and insomnia genie. Falling asleep at night requires Mom or Dad sitting on the edge of my bed holding my hand. Stomach aches and small little vomits with no real cause send me to the nurse's office a few times each week. I start crying and my body shakes when I think about what Herb and Elaine want, which sends me to the nurse, too. I'm spending so much time in the nurse's office she no longer asks what's wrong and lets me sit with a bucket between my legs in case I start throwing up.

Elaine and Herb don't show up for the next visit. Meanwhile, Mom and Dad hire a lawyer named Elroy Stark. He's an energetic older gentleman with a cloud of gray hair and veiled, bright blue eyes. One of the things about Long Island is you can tell how wealthy someone is by how far up the island they live. He lives up past Mystic Beach, but not quite to Southampton; wealthy, but not too wealthy to work for Will and Bea Cahn.

Elroy's practice is in lower Manhattan, but for the first appointment Mom and Dad go to his house. He welcomes them at the door and leads them to his office, where he sits behind an imposing desk. Mom and Dad sit at right angles to him.

*Okay,* he says, *what do we got?* Elroy leans back in his chair, hands clasped behind his head, and gazes out at the Atlantic Ocean through a bay window.

Dad tells him the elevator version of our story, but when he says *Elaine Schoenowitz,* Elroy turns and brings his clasped hands down onto the top of his desk.

*Did you say Elaine Schoenowitz?*

*Yes.*

*Large, creepy, drug-addicted woman?*

*Yes.*

*Hmm. This doesn't change anything for me; I'll still get Adrianne back for you.* He pauses and looks off to his right then back at Dad, *but I helped Elaine secure a home for a baby boy of hers some years ago.*

Mom's eyes widen. *Did the father know she was doing this?*

*I don't believe he was in the picture, no.*

*Did money exchange hands?* Mom asks.

*I believe it did.*

(Later, Mom will tell her friends that Elroy helped Elaine sell a baby. *That poor man's baby; the man who cawled asking about the whereabouts of his son.*)

Mom looks at Dad, but both know Elroy's the best lawyer they'll get.

*Okay,* Dad says.

*Good,* Elroy says.

Dad finishes the elevator version and Elroy sits and thinks for a moment, looking out at the ocean.

He tilts his head toward Mom and Dad. *Okay, this is straightforward. The biological parents are a mess and in no way capable of caring for Adrianne, whereas she has a comfortable and loving home with you, right?*

*Yes,* Dad says.

**Good,** he says turning to face Mom and Dad. *The agency's right. The Schoenowitzes can take Adrianne any time after the agency processes the papers. That day, if they're so inclined. What we need to do is gum up the works to slow that process down. We do that by filing an appeal of the agency's decision with the Nassau County court. The court will refer the case to the Department of Social Services, which will hold what's called a Fair Hearing. It's like court, but held by Social Services.*

Mom fidgets in her chair. *Then what?*

*We prove to Social Services in the Fair Hearing that the Schoenowitzes aren't fit parents.*

*And if we lose?*

*Then it goes to a real court as an appeal of the Fair Hearing.*

Mom and Dad look at each other. Dad puts his hands on his knees, *What's this gonna cost?*

*We'll start with eight thousand and go from there.*

Dad writes the check. Mom and Dad's savings no longer exist.

Elroy notifies the agency that he represents Mom and Dad and that they are appealing the board's decision to reunite me with Herb and Elaine. When I hear the word *reunite* it feels so strange, so foreign. We were never united. There is no family to rebuild or return me to. Only the family I have and love now.

The process is slow and creeps along out of my sight. Mom and Dad shield me from phone calls with the lawyer and most other issues related to the case.

It's not enough. I can feel forces beyond my control preparing to converge. It's not that I understand any of it, but the threat of Herb and Elaine taking me from my home hides just over the horizon.

I still can't sleep most nights, but Dad or Mom sit with me. Dad likes to paraphrase John Lennon: *It'll be okay in the end; we just haven't got to the end yet.* Mom is a bit vaguer: *We're doing our best.*

Mom takes me to the doctor for my nausea and stomach aches, which are frequent and painful. I get x-rayed and there are a couple other tests to see if I'm allergic to milk or some other food.

*There's nothing medically wrong with her,* the doctor tells Mom.

*So what do we do?*

*Usually, when we see this with young girls it's anxiety. If there's anything in her life making her anxious, see what you can do to get rid of it.*

Mom looks away from the doctor. *Right. Anything else?*

*Aspirin?*

In the first week of May, Elroy files the appeal of the agency's decision with the court. The court issues notices to Mom and Dad, Herb and Elaine, and the agency, with an initial court date with a district judge on September 7th.

The second weekend of May, Herb and Elaine come to pick me up for one of their visits. The scene at the door is tense.

*When will you have her home?* Mom asks, arms crossed, head tilted back. I'm tucked against Dad's leg. His hand is on my shoulder.

*We'll have our daughter back when we're ready,* Herb says, a sly smile penciled across his face, eyebrows holding his features up.

*Two hours,* Mom says.

*Maybe.*

*Two hours,* Mom repeats.

*We'll see.* Herb holds his hand out to me. *Come on Adrianne, let's go have some fun.*

I ease away from Dad, but don't take Herb's hand and instead lead him to the car where Elaine waits.

Herb and Elaine's heads tilt back and forth like metronomes as they sit across from me at the Sunrise Diner.

*How are things going, Adrianne?*

*Not good.*

The wry smile disappears from Herb's face. Elaine is smoking and there's a small tin ashtray closer to her.

*Why's that?* Herb asks.

*You want to take me away from my family. That's why.*

Elaine smashes the cigarette into the ashtray. *Listen here, damn it.* Her eyes are dirty and bloodshot. *Those bastards at the agency double-crossed me*—she slams one hand on the table top—*by making me sign you away so that woman you call mom could steal you from the hospital!*

Herb's eyebrows lift his face even further, *I think there's a better way to say that.*

*My stomach hurts. Can you take me home?*

When Herb pulls the car up in front of the house I launch out and run inside crying. Mom rushes to the door and slams it as Herb trots up the steps.

School ends and summer vacation begins. The weekends I'm supposed to see Herb and Elaine in June and July, Mom and Dad keep me away from home visiting aunts and uncles. Herb and Elaine complain to the agency, but when the agency calls, Mom says, *It can't be helped.*

On August 6th, I turn nine years old. A week later the agency calls again to complain on behalf of Herb and Elaine. Mom says, *Tawk to our lawyer.*

As predicted by Elroy, the September hearing before Judge Alexander Berman leads to a referral for a Fair Hearing by the Department of Social Services. However, the judge also orders that Herb and Elaine have me one weekend each month beginning in September.

Elroy rises and buttons his blazer at hearing this. *Your Honor, the facts of this case, as described in our appeal, clearly show that the Schoenowitzes are unfit to parent Adrianne.*

Judge Berman scribbles a note, *According to the agency it is within the Schoenowitz's rights to be reunited with their daughter. Isn't it true they've also been reunited with their older daughter?*

Candice Godfrey, a wide, older woman with gray hair, stands. She's the lawyer for the agency and, by default, Elaine and Herb. *Yes, your Honor. The child, Bina Schoenowitz, was reunited with her parents.*

Judge Berman nods and jots down another note. *I'm placing a stay on the agency's decision until the Fair Hearing reaches its conclusion.* He looks up at Elroy. *However, it's unfair to the Schoenowitzes to deny them access to their child.*

And so it goes.

Herb's car squeals to a stop. I step off the ledge and walk to the door to tell Mom and Dad it's time for me to go. I hear one car door slam and then another. Looking behind me, I expect to see Elaine's dark, large form. Instead, it's Bina.

I met Bina a couple weeks before at the agency. The situation was much the same as meeting Herb and Elaine, though a little easier. They brought us to the room with the large, plate-glass mirror and menagerie of toys. All of the toys were meant for much younger kids, but Bina and I nervously fidgeted with them as Herb and Ms. Abramsky tried to help us connect. Elaine sat and twisted her sunglasses around her fingers as she watched.

Bina was nice and we did our best, but it was hard.

*Hey Adrianne,* Herb calls out.

I walk to them midway down the front walk.

Herb waves his hand in front of Bina, *You remember your sister Bina, right?* Pride forces his features to stretch upward with his eyebrows.

Looking at Bina is nothing like looking in a mirror. She's only two years older than I am, but is starting to develop the body of a young woman. She's tall and slender and moves gracefully, like a dancer toward me.

*Hi Adrianne,* she says, brushing a curl of short, brown hair from her eyes. A dimpled smile, both coy and innocent, spreads across her lips. Herb admires her like she's a little statuette.

Next to Bina I feel small and awkward. Cut my hair as short as Bina's and I might be mistaken for a boy.

*Hi, Bina.* I look up at Herb. *Mom and Dad are inside.*

Herb frowns and Bina looks a little confused. This Herb-and-Elaine-as-parents thing is less mysterious to Bina, though I think as difficult. Rather than given up by Elaine at birth, Bina was whisked away by Herb to his mother in Florida, where she grew up with intermittent visits from Herb. Elaine and Herb didn't descend upon her as if from nowhere, as they did with me.

*Ady, is this Bina?* Mom asks from the doorway.

I pause, not sure what to say.

*Yes, it sure is,* Herb says with prideful smile. Mom frowns. *Okay Adrianne,* Herb says. *Grab your stuff. Off we go. Excited?*

*No.*

As we pull up to Elaine and Herb's apartment at Coney Island Avenue in Brooklyn I'm clutching the little floral overnight case that Mom packed for me. The buildings in this part of Brooklyn are squat row houses with a business on the first floor and apartments on the top two.

Herb opens a glass panel door to a steep, narrow staircase. *Welcome home, Adrianne.*

We walk upstairs to their apartment. The door opens into the living room, the kitchen is on one side and flanking the living room are two small bedrooms. Elaine is sitting on the couch smoking. Cigarette burns dot the carpet, furniture, everything.

*Hey kiddo. Nice valise,* she says, and smiles.

The apartment is somewhere between Oscar Madison messy and Felix Unger neat. Cats lie or slink in every nook and corner—each window has one lying on the sill. A dog that looks like a border collie, with long black-and-white hair, lies next to Elaine. Another, a mix of who-knows-what and terrier, curls up on the carpet. Every animal looks up at me, but none shows much interest.

The persistent smell of cigarette smoke almost hides the odor of over-flowing litter boxes and unwashed dog.

*Adrianne, you and Bina will live here.* Herb points to the room to the right, near the kitchen area. In the car, Bina and I started out slowly, but warmed to each other. When Herb points to the room, Bina leads me in and shuts the door.

*It won't be so bad,* she says. I want to cry, but am too scared.

Elaine cooks dinner: stuffed shells with a cream sauce and not bad. We watch TV after dinner and by about eight I'm tired. *Can I go to bed?*

*Sure, Adrianne,* Herb says, after taking a long pull off a cigarette. *You sure you don't want to stay up?*

*Yeah, I'm sure.* As I lie in bed I hear a fight on the street. Two doors down there's a low-slung bar and I'm sure the two fighters are drunk. I pull the covers, which don't smell right, up to my chin. *Please God,* I pray, *I just want to go home. Why can't I just go home?*

The next morning a truck rumbles by, rattling the windows. Sunlight shines in my eyes and each car that drives past seems to have an exhaust problem that makes the floor vibrate. Bina is fast asleep; I have no idea when she went to bed. Through the door I hear a dog stretching, then what sounds like a cat leaping from a counter to the floor.

No one else is awake so I lay in bed staring up at the ceiling wondering what Mom and Dad are doing. Will Dad get me a donut for when I come home?

I don't know how much time passes, but to a nine year old it feels like hours. Finally, Bina stirs and says, *let's go make breakfast.*

*You cook?* I ask.

*Around here I have to.*

Bina doesn't make anything too difficult, toast and jam, but I'm used to Mom doing the cooking. It isn't something kids do.

As we eat Elaine comes out of her bedroom and shuts the door. She's fidgeting with the buttons of a checkered duster that is a size too small. Underneath, her nightgown is dingy and spotted by cigarette burns. She walks to the kitchen and lights a cigarette. *Morning,* she says to no one in particular.

A loud whistle comes from the bedroom. *Go see what the hell he wants,* Elaine says to me.

I walk into their room. Clothes cover a chair and the end of the bed, and have slipped from the bed onto the floor. Nightstands flank the bed, each littered with full ashtrays, toenail clippers, and a couple of books or magazines. Little brown holes dot the bed cover.

*Elaine wants to know what you want,* I say.

Herb looks at me. He's not wearing a shirt and his hands hide beneath the covers. *Coffee, and bring me a cigarette.*

I tell Elaine.

*He won't get out of that damn bed,* she says. *It's ridiculous.*

I bring Herb a cigarette and he looks at it.

*Adrianne, this is one of Elaine's God damn menthol cigarettes. Get me one of mine.*

For the next three hours Herb is either in bed or locked in the bathroom. As Elaine says, *He's doing God knows what in there, but make yourself comfortable; he won't be out for a while.* Elaine eats toast and jam with coffee, then sits on the couch smoking, reading and staring out the window. Outside there is a constant rumble of trucks, vibration of cars, loud people, and the rhythm of the door to the deli below us screeching open, bell ringing, and slamming shut.

No waking Mom and Dad in bed. No tickling and laughing or donut, and no trip to Times Square Store.

Bina and I dress. *What do you want to do?* I ask.

*Let's dress the dogs up.* Bina's eyes brighten and her dimples deepen.

She walks into the living room and looks down to her right, a bright corner near one of the windows. *There's a dog turd,* she says to Elaine.

Elaine looks at it and shrugs. *Herb'll get it.*

Bina drags the collie into our room and shuts the door. Elaine doesn't move.

*I think this young lady is going to the dance tonight,* Bina says, opening a drawer and grabbing a shirtwaist dress with a red top and paisley skirt. The dog is complacent and allows us to pull the dress over his head then brush his long, matted fur.

Herb slinks out of the bedroom to take Bina and me for a walk.

The rest of the day Bina and I play; she's funny and goofy, but Herb and Elaine exist within their own orbits. Then dinner, TV, and I go to bed. The others stay up while I lie there listening to a lullaby of trucks, cars, rattling windows, and drunken men and women using the full range of their voices. I pray: *Please God, let me go home. Why can't I go home?*

Sunday morning I wake to quiet. An infrequent car rattles by, but no trucks making deliveries and no voices of people trying to talk above the din of city life. Bina is asleep and I lie in bed waiting for her to wake up.

I look up at the ceiling, a mosaic of cracks and peeling, yellowed paint. My body feels wiggly, like it needs to move, but I'm afraid to wake Bina up or, worse, wake Elaine.

Bina sits up in bed and the day begins much as it did yesterday with Bina making toast, Elaine surfacing from sleep in her dotted nightgown and checkered duster. Herb whistles . . .

By early afternoon I feel as if I might burst from waiting. Mom and Dad are due to arrive at two, but at one thirty I sit by the window in Bina's room—I can't think of this as my room—looking for their car. At two on the dot I see it pull up to the curb. Mom looks up through her window and Dad leans over her lap, looking to be sure they have the right number.

I grab my floral overnight case and dart for the door.

*Wow kiddo,* Elaine says, standing up, *in a hurry to get out of here?*

Herb comes out of the bedroom and he and Elaine follow me out the door and down the stairs. Mom and Dad stand just on the other side of the glass door, looking confused about how to get in. I burst through.

*Hey there Ady Maidy,* Dad says, as I launch into him.

Mom pets the back of my head, *Ady my love, so glad to see you!*

I pull my face from Dad's belly. His shirt is damp from my tears and my face is hot.

*Well, there she is,* Elaine says behind me.

Mom looks up at Elaine. *I hate to bother, but I have a bladder the size of a walnut and haven't been to the bathroom since we left Wantagh. Do you think . . . ?*

*No.* Elaine says. *There's a bathroom in the garage across the street.*

*See you soon, Adrianne,* Herb calls from behind Elaine.

That night I can't sleep, my stomach hurts so much. At school I can't concentrate and cry if a pin drops. The teacher knows why I'm so brittle and lets me spend time in the nurse's office, sitting on a hard wooden chair, bucket between my legs. This is the one room in the school where everything's adult size. I feel so small.

A day, two days, three, my stomach starts to settle and there are fewer stomach aches, though they won't go away. I sleep, but it's harder to fall asleep than before. Dad holds my hand, Mom reads to me at night. Harry does his best to distract me with games and small projects after school.

Every so often, before bed, Dad takes me to the basement and I sit on his lap as we watch his small, Lionel train move around the track and through the little village and siding he's made for it. His belly is soft against my back and the rhythm of his breathing and the click-click of the train across the tracks calms me.

Wednesday, October 27, 1971, the fight begins in an administrative office of the State of New York Department of Social Services in Brooklyn. It's what one would expect of an early 1970s state government building: humming fluorescent lights, shiny linoleum tiles, uncomfortable plastic chairs, and a folding table where the hearing officer sits.

Elroy, Candice Godfrey, two lawyers and a supervisor for the New York City Department of Social Services, Mr. Schatzman, Mom and Dad, Elaine and Herb, and a few other people sit in chairs facing the table. Behind it sits the hearing officer, Eugenio Roman. He looks as if he's in his late thirties and wears a tan business suit with wide lapels and red-striped tie. His hair is jet black and cut and set so it looks like a helmet. There's a matching mustache that's black and groomed—like a lip helmet—and folds down around the corners of his mouth.

It's not a regular court or court room but it runs the same way, with lawyers presenting testimony and making arguments.

Bina and I are not at the hearing; we sit out in the hall on a hard, wooden bench with Ms. Abramsky. I feel as if I'm going to burst, but Bina is good at distracting us both.

If I were a fly on the other side of the wall, inside the room, I could see Mom looking as if she might explode.

Testifying for the agency is a psychiatrist who'd evaluated me. No surprise, he recommends sending me to live with Herb and Elaine. I didn't agree and, while in his office, I told him so.

Mrs. Godfrey asks if he noticed any emotional issues with me.

*She clearly stated the intensity of her feelings,* he says. *She stated that she did not wish to return to her natural parents, that she would run away, and I believe that she indicated she was, um, that she would kill herself.*

What else would I say?

Elroy paces in front of him. *Were you at all influenced in coming to your conclusion by the fact that both of them have criminal records?*

*I wasn't asked to judge their criminal records. I was asked to judge them as human beings.*

Elroy stops and looks at the psychiatrist. *If I were to prove to you at this hearing that one of the biological parents was charged with and convicted of a crime involving violence, would that change your view?*

*Violence to whom and under what circumstances?*

*Violence to a relative,* Elroy replies.

*I'm not sure of the point of your question . . . My judgments always have to be based upon what I am actually faced with.*

*Did you know about this before you made your recommendation?*

*I did not know it before.*

*Would it have changed your conclusion?*

*Based upon my current examination, no.*

With that answer, Dad exhales loud enough for every head to turn toward him.

Elroy presses the psychiatrist again. *In other words, in the two minutes you have given it thought, you have come to the conclusion you would still recommend the return of this child?*

*I think under the circumstances I would, yes.*

Of course, we have our own psychiatrist.

*Would it serve the best interests of this child to be returned at this time to her biological parents?* Elroy asks her.

*It would seem that there would have to be over-pouring and over-riding positive virtues on the other side to justify removal.*

Not exactly the strong statement we're hoping for, but as we ride the train back to Wantagh later that afternoon Dad says, *I think it went well.*

*Oh, you always say that,* Mom interrupts.

*Hey, I'll tell yah what, that Elroy made their doc look like mincemeat. How could they take Ady from us after that?*

*The pie isn't cooked yet,* Mom says, looking out the window.

The next round takes place almost three weeks later on Monday, November 15, 1971. Bina and I are in the hallway waiting and goofing around. As usual, my stomach hurts and I feel nauseous.

Inside the room is the same set of lawyers, agency representatives, Mom and Dad, and Elaine and Herb. There are also two of my teachers and another psychiatrist hired by Elroy.

When my teachers testify, they are brief and tentative, but tell Mr. Roman that I struggle when returning from Elaine and Herb's. They also describe my parents as attentive and helpful, who do all they can to help me succeed.

Then the psychiatrist steps up to answer questions. Elroy explains the situation then asks the psychiatrist to give his findings. He takes a long time to explain how the threat of tearing me from the only family I've ever known will be traumatic and stunt my emotional growth.

Elroy pinches his upper lip. *In your opinion, would it be to the best interest of the child to be returned and to be taken away from the foster home she is in?*

*Let me put it this way. In the best of circumstances, with two of the most ideal sets of parents, I don't believe it would be in the best interest of the child to be withdrawn from the foster family.*

Mr. Roman interrupts. *Does this mean that the child, Adrianne, should remain with the foster parents in order to properly develop emotionally?*

*I believe this is the only place where she can do that. She is trying to build for herself who she is and what she is and needs as little disruption as possible in order to do it.*

The agency isn't done. They've brought in another psychiatrist. He takes the stand and Mr. Roman asks, *I would like you to consider from a medical point of view the best interests of this child and give me your opinion.*

*I would return her to the biological parents.*

*And, your reason?*

*My reasons, that the parents are ready and able to receive her.*

There's some general discussion, then Elroy gets his shot. *Did you know, for example, that five years ago the father to whom you are returning this child had been convicted of violent crimes?*

*No. What crime?*

*In 1966, a crime of assaulting his mother, of which he was convicted, and the second crime of tearing her apartment to pieces a month or so later, of which he was convicted after trial. Would that change your opinion?*

*No.*

Elroy's body tenses. *And your view is that the child should be returned to these parents?*

*Yes.*

Dad cannot believe what he's seeing and hearing.

Spine ramrod straight, Mom's pessimism stands vindicated. She leans in to Dad, looks straight at Mr. Schatzman. *I don't like that man.*

*I know, I know. It'll be okay.* Dad's mantra feels hollow even to him.

Next on the stand: Herb.

Mrs. Godfrey calls Herb up and starts with her questions. *Now, the Cahn's attorney has been talking about two convictions for a violent act. Will you please tell us what occurred and when it occurred.*

Herb looks at Elaine then describes how he moved to Miami to be near his mother, with the intent of resolving his addiction to heroin. He goes on at some length about his intentions to beat his heroin addiction and come back to New York for me. Often, he looks to Elaine as if for help, but he doesn't answer the question.

Mr. Roman leans forward in his chair and interrupts. *I have not heard mention of a conviction yet of any kind.*

Mrs. Godfrey looks at Mr. Roman. *I will ask him to tell us the story of the process of what happened.*

*Okay.* Mr. Roman sits back.

Again, Herb looks at Elaine. *Therefore, I found myself in a situation wherein I wanted to return to New York.* Herb goes on like this for another few minutes.

Mr. Roman leans forward again. *Can we get to the basics? I don't know where we are in this testimony.*

Mrs. Godfrey pauses. *Mr. Schoenowitz, did you get into a dispute with your mother over Bina?*

*That is correct.*

*Were you convicted or did you plead guilty?*

Elaine mouths something at Herb. *Pleaded guilty.*

*What was the charge against you?*

*To the best of my memory it was assault, only my memory may be wrong.*

*Did you go to prison?*

*I remained incarcerated for maybe two weeks, but again my memory is vague on for how long.*

Elroy looks at Elaine and stands. *I have to object to this. The record says what the sentence was and it contains none of this.*

Elroy, Mrs. Godfrey and Mr. Roman bicker back and forth until Elroy raises his voice. *I would like to make one point to show you how bad this is. He has said very deliberately that he pleaded guilty and in both cases the record says he pleaded not guilty.*

The bickering begins again, but ends with Mrs. Godfrey allowing Elroy to begin his cross-examination of Herb.

Elroy smiles at Herb. *When did you first know you were addicted to heroin?*

*I don't recall the year.* Herb looks at Elaine like a lost actor seeking the next line. Elaine frowns.

*How old were you when you were first addicted?*

*I don't recall now.*

Herb won't pull his eyes from Elaine. Elroy's eyes follow Herb's to Elaine and he smiles at her. *How old are you?*

*I was born in 1932.*

*How old are you?*

*In December.*

Elaine's chair squeaks on the linoleum as she crosses her legs and presses three fingers to her forehead.

*So, how old are you?*

*I have to add that up.*

*Do you need a pencil and paper?*

*Just a moment.* Herb counts in his head and with his fingers, tilts his head toward Elaine. Her lips mime something. *I will be thirty-eight.*

Elroy's smile broadens. *You realize it's 1971?*

*As far as I know, I'll be thirty-eight. My addition may not be correct.*

Elroy takes a moment to let the wheels turn. *These two brushes you had with the law, in both cases you pled guilty?*

*Can you repeat that please?*

*These Florida brushes you had with the law, the two cases you pled guilty?*

*It was a brush with my mother.*

A laugh bursts out of Mom. Dad's eyes water; his face is red from trying not to laugh out loud.

Elroy claps his hands together. *Have you always had this kind of memory, Herbert?*

*I can't remember.*

I hear Dad's belly laugh out in the hallway.

Mr. Roman looks at Herb. His nose crinkles and brow furrows. *I think it's time to call it a day.*

As we walk through the front door the phone rings almost right away. Dad picks it up, *Yeah, yeah, okay,* he looks at me. *Let me just get into the other room.*

One of Elroy's strategies is to bring the media into our story. As more people learn about Elaine and Herb and the agency's decision there will be pressure for the agency to change its mind.

After the first newspaper reporter called Mr. Schatzman, he called our house. *Mrs. Cahn—no longer Bea—do you truly believe it is in Adrianne's best interest to create a media circus around her?*

*People need to know what a horrible decision you've made,* Mom said, hand on hip, full battle stance.

*This isn't going to change our minds.*

Mom frowned. *We'll see.*

She hung the phone up and looked at Dad, who'd rested his newspaper in his lap. *I wish that son of a bitch would get cancer.*

*I know you do,* Dad said, *but as the unofficial public relations manager for this family, keep it to yourself.*

So far there've been stories in the *Long Island Press, Newsday, New York Post,* and *New York Daily News,* as well as on WABC-TV Eyewitness News and WNBC nightly news. With the Fair Hearing, media interest has spiked and Dad spends a few hours that night talking to reporters, as he will after each hearing session. The next day there are headlines like, *Ex-Addict Parents Want Girl, 9, Back; Foster Parents Fight for Girl, 9; Uncertain Future; Battle Begins for Adrianne; Girl Pleads Against Bid by Parents; Foster Dad Raps Agency Tactics; Does Anyone Really Win This Custody Battle?* and *Family Tragedy.*

Of course, I don't see much if any of the coverage. Mom and Dad do a good job of keeping the newspaper stories and reporters away, though they allow a few photos to be taken of me.

As dad talks with a reporter the night after the first day of the hearing, Harry calls me into the kitchen. He's sitting at the table with a deck of cards that he's shuffling between his hands. *Fancy a game of spit?*

This is our favorite card game and I love playing with Harry, even though he's very fast. I know he lets me win every so often so I won't get mad and stop.

*Hey, will you guys keep it down in there?* Dad yells as we laugh and slap cards down on the table trying to be faster than the other.

The day after Herb's testimony, on Tuesday, November 16, 1971, Bina and I are back in the hall sitting on that hard wooden bench.

Today's hearing starts with Mr. Roman throwing Elaine out of the hearing room. *I think that since so far, as I have noted, Mrs. Schoenowitz assisting Mr. Schoenowitz looking to her for answers, I think she should go out of this room for that reason.*

Elroy is a bulldog with Herb. *Do you remember assaulting your mother, beating her up?*

Mrs. Godfrey yells, *I object! The issue isn't what he remembers back in 1966, five years ago. He is now rehabilitated and capable.*

Mr. Roman breaks in. *The issue is whether they are fit parents now.*

*I submit,* Elroy continues, *his fitness is in question by as little a thing as he can't remember his own age and needed a pencil and paper to remember.* He turns to Herb, who looks lost without Elaine. *You don't remember when you first became addicted to drugs?*

Herb stiffens. *You have to repeat that question.*

*Do you remember when you first became addicted to drugs?*

*Remotely.*

*Tell us the year.*

*I don't recall.*

*'Remotely' means something.*

*You said addicted to drugs.*

*What?*

*What drugs?*

*Addicted . . .*

*To what?*

*Now look!*

*I want to specify what particular drug you are inferring that I used.*

*Any drug; heroin and others.*

*My heroin addiction?*

*Yes.*

*When I became addicted to heroin?*

Dad whispers into Mom's ear, *If we're ever going to get outta here, maybe they should let Elaine back in.* Mom smiles.

Elroy throws his hands up. *This has become ridiculous. This man doesn't want to talk.* Looking back at Herb. *Okay, when were you cured of your addiction?*

Herb's eyebrows arch up, the corners of his mouth turn down. *According to the best and most knowledgeable people, there is no cure for addiction to this day.*

For the next twenty minutes Elroy and Herb go back forth over when he became addicted (1955), the number of drugs he's used (Herb is evasive on this point), attempts at sobriety (many), and his relationship with Elaine (rocky, at best). For each, Herb tries to be positive, but he seems confused and the facts stand against him.

Then Elroy asks, *Do you believe you can give Adrianne proper care and tender love and affection?*

*There's no reservation in my mind whatsoever. Better than what she's receiving now.*

*Do you know that Adrianne has stated repeatedly to many people that she prefers to stay where she is and does not want to go back to your home? You know that, don't you?*

*I have heard that from other people.*

*She never said that to you?*

*I have been told about it from yourself, the Cahns and newspaper accounts. She has supposedly spoken of this.*

Mr. Roman interrupts, *What would you do if the decision is for her to return to you and she does not want to?*

*Well,* Herb thinks for a moment, *I never thought anybody would have the audacity to expose her to this situation. I am not . . . I want her. I love her, but I am not, never going to do anything that might affect her growth progress.*

Mr. Roman excuses Herb from the chair and asks him to wait outside the room. Then he asks for Elaine to come back in. An aide goes into the hallway and looks at Ms. Abramsky. *Where's Mrs. Schoenowitz?*

*Dunno. Smoking I think.*

Ten or twenty minutes pass and Elaine walks past with the aide. She's wearing her usual outfit, white and black polyester blouse and pants, and Jackie Kennedy sunglasses.

Mr. Roman asks Herb to wait in the hallway.

Elaine sits in the chair, removes her sunglasses.

Mrs. Godfrey asks a few introductory questions before cutting to the chase. *When did you start using drugs?*

Elaine is demure. *When I was fifteen. That was 1945, the last year of the war . . . I wasn't addicted in '45. I didn't get addicted until 1947, but I was using and I believe my arrest record started around 1947, 1948. In 1955, I was arrested for felonious possession of drugs and sentenced to Bedford state prison. I was drug free when I got out in 1958 and I didn't get re-addicted until about the end of '61, after I got married.*

*Between 1961 and 1965 were you arrested for any cause?*

*Yes.*

*What for?*

*Grand larceny and forgery. I was also arrested for possession of drugs and for prostitution and loitering for that purpose. I think probably half-a-dozen arrests during that time.*

*And you take methadone now?*

*I do; about once or twice a week for the last three years.*

Mrs. Godfrey pauses. *How long has Adrianne been visiting you?*

*About two years.*

*How have the weekend visits gone?*

*Not generally well.*

*What do you mean?*

*I think Adrianne has a great love and affection for her foster parents yet she has also formed a great warmth and affection to us and I think that has torn her greatly, and this is something we have talked about numerous times.*

*How so?*

*Well, she has the best of two situations. She has four adults catering to her and knocking ourselves out to yield to every whim in competition with each other and she is aware of this. She is very bright and sometimes she uses this in the way she wants to.*

Mrs. Godfrey turns Elaine over to Elroy.

He looks at her with an intense, almost glaring stare. *With commendable candor you have listed your criminal record. Now, I ask you, is it possible you overlooked one, two, three or four such items?*

Elaine shifts in her seat. *It is possible I overlooked a dozen, Mr. Stark.*

*Would it be correct to say that your problems with the law started with incarceration at the age of eighteen?*

Mr. Roman interrupts, *Were you incarcerated at eighteen?*

Elaine squirms. *Yes.*

*In what federal penitentiary,* Elroy asks.

*I don't understand. I thought we went into that. What has that got to do with now?*

*Nothing at all except you are forty-two and you were a drug addict at age fifteen, but you didn't say anything about being incarcerated at the age of eighteen.*

*I most certainly did. I'll tell you all about it again, if you want.*

*What jail were you in at the age of eighteen?*

*Lexington Health Services Hospital.*

*How long did you stay there?*

*Several months.*

*What was the charge?*

Elaine shifts her weight. *I told you that already.*

*Not that particular one.*

*It was for violation of the Harrison Act.*

*What is the Harrison Act?*

*Possession of narcotics.*

*How many such prosecutions were there?*

*Numerous.*

*Would you attempt to guess at the number?*

*No I wouldn't.*

*Would you say there were 100?*

*Might be 500.*

Elroy smiles. *Thank you.*

*You're welcome.*

*Mrs. Schoenowitz, when were you married?* Elroy asks.

*October 21, 1960.*

*How many children have you had?*

*Totally?*

*Yes.*

*Four. I have two children by this marriage to Mr. Schoenowitz.*

*The other two were not with Mr. Schoenowitz?*

*That is right.*

Elroy smiles. *Born when?*

*When were they born?*

*Yes.*

*Which one are you speaking of?*

*I am speaking of the two you had in addition to the two we have discussed.*

Elaine shifts her weight again. *Well, one was born 21 years ago, when I was a teenager, and the other one was born in 1964.*

Elroy pauses, turns away, then back to Elaine. *How long were you separated from your husband and on what occasion?*

*I don't recall any.*

*You don't recall that you were ever separated from him from the date you were married to him to today?*

*Not legal separations, no.*

*Please don't spar with me.*

Elaine presses her lips together. *My expertise is not the law Mr. Stark. I think that is yours.*

*A separation means you and he lived in different places. Did that occur during your married life?*

*Only when the law intervened.*

*You mean only when you were incarcerated?*

*Yes, when I have been incarcerated or forced to remain in the city or could not leave the state.*

The next witness is Mr. Schatzman.

Elroy asks about any investigation the agency may have done into the background of Herb and Elaine.

*Mr. Stark, much of the impetus to do this investigation was brought about by you in the sense that the publicity began to break around our area.*

*You mean you wouldn't have investigated?*

*Yes, but much of the impetus is from this.*

*Did you investigate the Schoenowitzes and ascertain their criminal record? Did you know about it long before this date?*

*Our record is scant around the criminal record. There are some facts known. They are in our record.*

*You didn't think that was important or relevant?*

*No, sir, the prime concern was the current and present adjustment . . . May I say one more thing? I think one has to consider well people are capable of change and people do change in all kinds of ways. There is one piece of indication of such a change; there was a time when we had a magnificent relationship with the Cahns and at this point I think our relationship is very strained. So people do change. People's attitudes, people's positions change. I really believe, sir, with all the conviction I can muster up, people can be rehabilitated.*

Elroy says, *Do you believe that part of the reason the relationship is strained is primarily because the Cahns are urging you not to do this in the interest of Adrianne?*

*I would say part of it has to do with you, sir, the fact that you have seen it fit to argue this case.*

*Do you believe the Cahns are doing this for any selfish motive?*

*I asked Mr. Cahn this very question about a week ago and he was at a loss to accept this—*

Dad almost leaps out of his chair. *He's lying!*

Mrs. Godfrey whips her head around to Dad. *I hope, surely hope, Mr. Cahn's statement that Mr. Schatzman is lying is on the record!*

Elroy doesn't budge. *Haven't they said to you on numerous occasions it is the interest of Adrianne, her best interest they are trying to protect?*

*Yes, sir, they have.*

After Mr. Schatzman, Mom and Dad get their turn. Mom talks about how Elaine and Herb never show up on time for visits, how traumatic my visits with them are, my pleading not to let Herb and Elaine take me away, and how it affects my school, sleep and tummy.

If he would let me, I'd tell Mr. Roman about it myself.

Then Dad gets a turn and he tells Mr. Roman about when Herb said he's upset that the agency left me with one family. Herb wanted me moved around every few months so I wouldn't become attached to anyone.

Then Dad says, *There was another time. They didn't request any visits for a period of maybe five or six months. We found out later there was a problem about a death in the family. Mr. Schoenowitz's aunt had committed suicide. I asked Elaine why she didn't call us during that time and she said that the cat kept chewing the telephone wires and they couldn't make calls.*

Elroy asks, *During those five months did they contact Adrianne by telephone or otherwise?*

*No.*

Then Mr. Roman asks Dad, *Do you think they would bring her up properly, morally, religiously, physically?*

*I doubt that. I don't think that a child that is getting training in methadone, speed, the facts of life of heroin, of criminal acts, don't think a child could be brought up morally with all of that. I also think Adrianne should at least have some right to say where she wants to live. She's nine years old, so when do we say a child can express her own opinion?*

And that's how it ended.

For the next five months there is a deafening silence. I'm nine years old. Dad and I spend time in the basement watching the train. Mom combs my hair out in the mornings and puts it in pony tails that sometimes make me feel too little.

One weekend Harry lets me tag along with him and a friend to the movies. We tell Mom and Dad we're seeing *Planet of the Apes*.

*Isn't that scary?* Mom asks.

Harry gives me a glance. *Nah, not too bad.*

*I don't know,* Mom says.

*Awe, let 'em have a little fun,* Dad says. *What could be the harm?*

I love the movie and don't find it scary at all, even a little funny in some parts.

Over all, life at home is much how I want it to be.

The visits to Herb and Elaine's continue. Elaine is unkind and often orders Bina and I to take the dirty laundry in a shopping cart four blocks down Coney Island Avenue to the Laundromat. Herb spends most of his time in the bathroom.

I beg Elaine to let me live with Mom and Dad.

*No,* is all she says.

I'm terrified. My stomach hurts all the time and school is impossible; I'm in fourth grade and falling further behind my classmates. One day I see Ms. Abramsky come into school.

*They're coming to get me!* I scream at the teacher.

She tries to console me, but I fight her off and try to run away. I'm so upset, so scared that they call Mom to come in to pick me up and it takes hours for me to calm down.

On March 17, 1972, the Fair Hearing decision arrives in the mail. It's only two pages and Dad mumbles a few words out loud as he reads, *Pursuant to Section 400 . . . removal of a child . . . the agency did not consider the biological parents unfit . . . she is happy and adjusted during visits with the biological parents . . . the child is becoming increasingly confused . . .*

Dad looks up, eyes wide. *The evidence of the record establishes that the best interests of Adrianne Schoenowitz will be promoted by returning her to her natural parents.*

Dad looks at me. I cover my mouth, which quivers as tears stream from my eyes and my cheeks burn from fear. I am in a state of horror that this could happen. How could anyone take me from Mom and Dad?

Tears bubble from Dad's eyes. *Don't worry Ady. We'll keep fighting. It ain't over yet.*

The appeal doesn't go any better.

This time I get to speak with the judge in his chambers. Right away I tell him I don't want to leave my Mom and Dad. He looks at me and sees I'm crying.

*You know,* he says, *I'm not such a bad man. You don't have to be afraid of me.*

I looked up into his eyes. *Well, you'll be a bad man if you make me leave my home.*

During the hearing before the judge, Elroy argues that the judge must take Elaine and Herb's past crimes and addiction into account. The judge doesn't like hearing that.

*Let me tell you something,* he says. *I take my responsibility very seriously. This is a great burden for me and I'm not going to treat it lightly. So you need not say anything about trying to impress upon me the need for care and concern.*

Then he adds, *I will tell you, frankly, that the courts of this state and the Court of Appeals, particularly, decided clearly and unequivocally that the rights of parents are paramount. This is something that you can argue to doomsday, but I have to go by the law.*

Elroy thinks for a moment. *In other words, Your Honor recognizes there are two tests: The best interests of the child and the fitness of the parents?*

*No. The best interests of the child is not involved. The Court of Appeals has interpreted this very well.*

*It didn't go so well, I guess,* Dad says into the phone when Elroy calls.

*No. Elaine will come to the house tomorrow to pick Adrianne up.*

*Jesus.*

*Yeah.*

*We can't do anything?*

*No. She'll show up in the morning with a social worker from the agency to make sure things go as smooth as possible.*

*Tomorrow? There has to be something we can do?*
*I'm sorry. You can pack a bag for Adrianne and enjoy the time you have.*
*Yeah, right.*

I ask where I'll go to school and what the new school will be like, but neither Mom nor Dad knows. I don't want to leave my friends and my family, and nothing feels right. I'm filled with questions: where will I sleep, will I be able to see Mom and Dad ever, what will my life be like, how will I make new friends, will I have new grandparents or aunts and uncles, what will my life be like? Inside, in my heart and belly, I ache and worry that this will never be over, that I'll never be able to come home.

Mom and Dad do what they can to reassure me, but how do you do that? How does a parent tell their child it will be okay when they know it won't, when they're being pulled from the only home they've ever had, the only mom and dad they've ever known or ever wanted.

I am inconsolable, and I grow increasingly terrified as I watch them pack a few of my things in the small floral suitcase that's become the symbol of all that I don't want.

*We'll get you the rest when we can,* Mom says. Tears course down her cheeks. *I'm sorry Ady. I don't mean to cry.*

*I love you Mom.*

*Love you too.*

Dad gives me a hug. *I can't bear it. God, I just can't bear it.*

That night I crawl into bed with Mom and Dad and feel their warmth near me. I can't imagine any nightmare worse than tomorrow and drift off to sleep to the sound of Dad's soft snoring.

The next day, a crowd of reporters gathers in front of the house. I go sit on the ledge, as I watch them and wait for Elaine.

True to form, she doesn't show up.

The reporters go away. Mom and Dad take us all out to Kwong Ming for dinner.

The next morning the reporters and two TV crews from the city show up and wait. They talk with each other and laugh. Every so often one of them looks over at me on the ledge and seems to feel a little guilty.

Then a dark sedan pulls up. Elaine, sunglasses, polyester pants suit, is sitting in the back. Ms. Abramsky is in the front next to the driver, a man I recognized from the agency.

I run inside, crying. I can't believe this is happening. I run past my floral overnight case and hide behind the sofa. Above me is the painting of the woman embroidering with the child watching, happy, content. I want to escape into it.

My face is hot and wet with tears.

*Ady, I'm sorry,* Mom says, reaching out to me. Behind her Dad's face is as red and hot and wet as mine.

*I can't do this,* he says, and turns away to the kitchen.

Mom frowns as he walks away. *Ady, please my love.*

*No. Never. I'm not going. I'll never go with HER!* I point to Elaine, who's standing a few steps away, next to Ms. Abramsky.

*Let me,* Elaine says, pushing Mom to the side.

*Listen Adrianne, if you really want to come back,* she looks around our living room, *here, I'll let you, but you have to at least give this a try.*

*You'll let me come home?* I sob.

*Yes, Adrianne. I promise you can come home.*

❦

Mom and Dad walk me through the small clutch of media. Elaine never takes her sunglasses off. Ms. Abramsky looks as if someone shot her dog, but she's doing what she has to do, I guess.

From the small gathering of neighbors a woman yells at Elaine, *There's a loving mother*. Elaine doesn't even twitch.

I hug Dad and he whispers in my ear, *It ain't over yet*.

I want to believe Dad, but as I look out at all of the grownups, the reporters leaning toward Mom and Dad hoping for a quote, photographers snapping photos of my tear streaked face, Elaine's face impassive and unmoved behind large sunglasses, Mom and Dad fighting tears that can't be stopped, I know that today he's wrong. It's over for me today because I'm leaving. There is no one who is going to put an end to this, to save me.

Mom squeezes me and brushes a few strands of hair that escaped from my pony tail away from my eyes. *I love you, too. Be good, sweet girl*.

As the taxi pulls away, I hear Mom one last time, *Cawl us!*

The taxi takes us to the agency, where Ms. Abramsky talks with me for a while. Then she says okay, time for you to go with your mom.

*She isn't my mom.*

Elaine grabs my hand and leads me outside. She hails a cab and pushes me in. *JFK airport!*

I'm quiet and angry. Elaine looks at me every so often. I have my arms folded across my chest. Her lips form a half smile, her eyes are hidden behind the sunglasses, then she looks back out the window.

We get out at the airport and Elaine pulls a wad of twenties from her bra to pay the driver. I drag my suitcase behind me as Elaine leads me to a gate. We wait a short while before a stewardess announces the plane is boarding.

Elaine grabs my hand again.

*Where are we going?* I ask her.

*I'm not going anywhere.* She hands the stewardess a single ticket. *You're going to Florida. Bina and your dad are already there.* She lets go of my hand.

*He isn't my dad.*

*Whatever.*

---

DAILY NEWS, WEDNESDAY, JULY 19, 1972            ☆☆☆    5

# Tears and Long Wait, Then Foster Child Is Gone

**By STEWART AIN**

Crying and shouting, "I don't want to go! I don't want to go!" 9-year-old Adrianne Schoenowitz yesterday was coaxed into the white sedan that had come to take her away from her foster parents, the William Cahns, of Wantagh, who have cared for her since infancy.

As she slid across the back seat to sit next to her natural mother, Mrs. Herbert Schoenowitz, of Brooklyn, who told her: "Your mommy is not going to hurt you—nobody is going to hurt you."

The year-long legal struggle by the Schoenowitzes to regain custody of their child had ended on Monday with the refusal by Judge Stanley H. Fuld, chief judge of the State Court of Appeals, to stay lower court decisions ordering Adrianne returned to the Schoenowitzes, both of whom are rehabilitated drug addicts.

**Nearly Hour and Half Late**

Mrs. Schoenowitz and two representatives of the foster agency, the Jewish Child Care Center of New York, arrived at the Cahn home at 10:50 a.m. yesterday, nearly an hour and a half late.

At one point during the wait, Mrs. Cahn and Adrianne broke into tears as they clung to each other on the front lawn of their suburban, split-level home.

A group of 20 women joined the Cahns, waiting for Mrs. Schoenowitz to arrive. Among them was Mrs. Pearl Polk, whose 3-year-old Chinese-American foster daughter had been returned to her natural mother last October.

"One of the first lessons of a mother is to be on time," Mrs. Polk told Mrs. Cahn. "Make them come back again tomorrow."

"How many times can you die?" Mrs. Cahn replied.

As Adrianne stepped into the car, Mrs. Schoenowitz, crying, said she felt "lousy."

"I can't stand seeing her (Adrianne) so unhappy. This is a terrible thing all around. But what am I supposed to do—say here, here's my daughter,

I'll forget all about her? What am I fighting to get my life in order for?"

She said she planned to put Adrianne on a plane to Miami Beach this morning to join her husband and older daughter, Tav, 11, who are vacationing in the resort.

Just before Mrs. Schoenowitz drove away, she tried to comfort Adrianne, who was cowering in the corner

of the Cahn's home. Cahn said later that Mrs. Schoenowitz assured Adrianne that she would be able to visit the Cahns again.

As the car carrying Adrianne pulled away, Cahn comforted his wife who cried uncontrollably: "Oh my baby! I can't stand it. What am I going to do with her room? What as I going to do with her things? It's like a nightmare—is it happening to me?"

Foster parents William and Beatrice Cahn comfort a tearful Adrianne Schoenowitz in Wantagh, L.I.

NEWS photo by Dennis Caruso

# Newsday

### THE LONG ISLAND NEWSPAPER

*10 CENTS*
*WEDNESDAY*
*JULY 19, 1972*

## Tear-Filled Farewell

The final act in the battle for the custody of 9-year-old Adrianne Schoenowitz was played out yesterday at the home of Beatrice and William Cahn in Wantagh, Adrianne's home for the past eight years. Mrs. Cahn comforted her nearly hysterical foster daughter, right. Then Elaine Schoenowitz, the girl's natural mother and a reformed drug addict, arrived to reclaim her daughter. Adrianne drove away with her mother, above, and sobbed: "I don't want to go. Can't I stay?" Page 4.

Newsday Photos by Dick L. Potteus

# Chapter Six

## Johnny: Just Make It All Stop

*"Johnny never talked about his mom.*
*Not to me, not to George, or anyone. And I never met her.*
*We dated for seven years, and I never met her.*
*Our friends, the parties we had every weekend in high school*
*were his escape, his chance to get away from his mom."*

—Margaret

*M*om isn't good at rehab.

She's been gone a couple of weeks when Dad and Uncle Mike wake me up. I'm ten.

*Come on, Johnny,* Dad says. Uncle Bobby is behind him throwing some of my clothes into a bag. *We have to go.*

I'm not sure who called, maybe it was Mom's brother, Uncle Charles, but the voice told Dad that Mom escaped from the Mayo Clinic. *You should probably pack up the kids and find someplace out of the way for them for a few days.*

*Why?* Dad asked.

*She's planning on breaking into the house and taking them.*

Groggy, Lisa, Joshua and I climb in the back of the car. Dad tells us to lie down, then covers us with a blanket.

*Why are you doing this?* Lisa asks.

Bobby calls from the front, *So no one sees you.*

Dad frowns at Bobby. *Don't worry about it.*

It's around midnight when Uncle Bobby pulls the car up to a friend's house. Dad thanks them for watching us, then goes home to confront Mom if she shows up.

The next day we go to school, but Dad's secretary Ginny Wiggins picks us up and takes us back to the friend's house. Later in the evening, Dad's maroon Toronado pulls up.

*It's okay to come home now,* he tells me.

*Where's Mom?*

*She's in a hospital in Baltimore.*

All I hear, or remember, is that Mom got sent away. That's all right with me.

I find out a judge committed her to a long-term treatment center. She lives there for a few months then after discharge she rents a fashionable apartment in Baltimore rather than live in a court-mandated halfway house. She may be a mentally unstable drunk, but she's still a Cella.

Her influence in our lives is no more than infrequent phone calls and rare supervised visits.

Life shifts to become something like normal. The adults continue to drink and smoke hard, as if it's their God-given right. Christmas is less of a zoo, but Uncle Bobby continues with his perverse rendition of The Little Drummer Boy and tipping the Christmas tree over. Some traditions die hard.

Friends, summer at the club, Lizzy, and school dominate life. One day folds into the next and memories fade and disappear into the foggier corners of the mind, though some stand out.

On a hot, humid summer day, I balance a pail of water on top of the kitchen door and hide behind some bushes with my buddy Gary Bender. Lizzy sticks her head out to spit tobacco juice and the water crashes down on her. She looks up and sees me laughing. Gary already ran off.

Lizzy stands to her full height, head sopping, *Boy! Today I am not Christ the redeemer. I am Christ the judge and I am going to make you look like the north side of a southbound mule!*

She whacks me with her broom before I get ten steps.

It's spring break of sixth grade and we are in Florida with Dad, where his latest girlfriend lives. He met her on one of his many shoe-related trips. I call her Aunt Cactus and have a monumental, teen-boy crush on her daughter. Her house isn't big enough for us all, so we're staying at our southern second home, the Sheraton Sand Castle, with Dad and Lizzy.

In the middle of the night I wake up to Dad shaking me. *Wake up, Johnny.*

*Why?*

*Your mother.*

*Again?*

*Sorry.*

Behind him Lizzy throws clothes into a suitcase, mumbling, *She ain't worth the salt in her bread, no sir, she's been beating the goat so hard the liquor does all the thinkin', damn . . .*

Sometime after midnight we arrive at Aunt Cactus' house. Dad goes back to the hotel to confront Mom if she shows up.

The next morning a cab pulls up and Dad gets out. *All's well,* he says, smiling.

*What happened?* I ask.

Dad's eyes glance away from me. *Nothing.*

That's the end of it as far as I'm concerned.

Already wound too tight, Lizzy is all but terrified Mom will come take us some night when Dad's out. True to form, Dad goes out a lot, but leaves the number to wherever he'll be and the time he'll be there.

*Hold on Mr. Lipscomb,* Lizzy says before Dad can leave. Then she dials each number to be sure it works. *All's well, Mr. Lipscomb; The lines 're clear.*

Dad smiles, *I can go now?*

*Yes sir.*

The second Dad steps out of the house I look up at Lizzy. *I want ice cream for dinner.*

Joshua looks at me, then Lizzy, *Me too!*

*So do I!* Lisa adds.

Lizzy rubs her hands, balls them into fists and puts each on a hip, *I'll tell y' all what; wish in one hand and pee in the other and see which one fills up first. You all havin' pork chops, fried, with extra greens.* As she walks to the kitchen, *These children, God love 'em, but livin' in high cotton too long, that's right . . .*

It's spring of 1970 and Dad takes a call from Uncle Charles. Despite the chaos Mom created, Dad and Uncle Charles remain close. After the call, Dad finds me and tells me Luju has lung cancer. I'm twelve years old and still possess a plentiful supply of youthful optimism, but all too soon she passes away.

Half, if not more, of St. Louis is at her memorial service and no one mourns the loss of Luju more than Aunt Mae. A bit of Mae's outsized personality is buried with Luju.

The same year Luju dies I begin eighth grade at Codasco. Like most things in Ladue, Codasco is a next step for the male members of my tribe: Bill McCandless, David Gardner, Rob Pierce, Allen Whittemore, and Gary.

All of us come from the kind of families and old money that calcifies our cliques, making it hard for anyone new to be accepted. The older your money, the more likely it is you were born in the same hospital as me, attended the same club, lived walking distance from my house, graduated from grade school at Rossman, and stepped into Codasco in fifth grade knowing everyone in your class.

Because our wealth is passed from one generation to the next, it's entrenched. People tend not to come and go.

So as I take my seat in homeroom I'm surprised to see a scrawny, pale, ginger-haired kid sitting behind me, wearing penny loafers with pennies in them and clothes straight out of Brooks Brothers. *Who the hell are you?*

He looks up from his desk. *George, George Love.*

*Hi, GeorgeGeorge.* I look up at Bill; according to last year's alphabetized seating he should be behind me, *Hey, McCandless, I guess we'll have to put up with this guy.*

The other mark of my tribe of boys is being athletic. Playing soccer, lacrosse, baseball, and football is important and marks you as one of us. George is hopeless at them all. Skinny to the point of being frail, he spends most of his time getting knocked around the field, or on the bench.

He's also a gangling, goofy kind of kid, never sure of himself and awkward, which in eighth grade means you get bullied without mercy. If you fight back, you get beat up. George gets the full Monty: picked on, beat up, and left out.

I won't hit him, but I'm mean. The least of it is bossing him around and calling him *Ginger.* The worst of it leaves him sunken, depleted.

George puts up with it and comes to school each day, but it wears on him. It's like watching a human body withdraw into itself. His shoulders stoop, his eyes never leave the ground, and he looks like all he wants to do is disappear.

One Wednesday, the week after Thanksgiving, George walks out of homeroom at the bell and stops at his locker. When he opens it everything is sopping wet. The pages in his textbooks and notebooks look like accordion bellows. The water, or whatever it was—maybe not water—ruined his notes and work as well as anything else in his locker.

A few boys snicker, *What's wrong, Ginger?* then walk to class.

Bill walks past me, *Come on Johnny Lippo,* and pats me on the back. Allen and Gary follow, but I pause by the doorway of our homeroom class. George is doing all he can to hide that he's crying, but his shoulders heave, his head droops, and even from behind he looks fragile to the point of breaking.

*George,* I say, standing just behind him, *I didn't do it, but I'm sorry. They went too far.*

He stands silent in front of his ruined work and belongings.

*Are you okay?* I ask.

*Do I look okay?*

*No.*

*Why do you guys hate me so much?*

*I don't know.*

George turns and looks at me. *Just leave me alone.*

*Okay. I'm done, no more.*

George wipes his nose with the back of his hand. *Thanks.*

From then on I ride the fence with George. We don't become friends, but I leave him alone. I also tell the tribe and anyone else to do the same, but I don't fight for George. Things get easier for him, but never easy.

The next fall the tribe returns to Codasco, but George doesn't. Rather than see his son so unhappy, George's dad sends him to Choate, a boarding school in Connecticut.

The year George goes to Choate, I turn fourteen. Every so often Dad takes me with him on business trips to Sedalia, Missouri, the heart and soul of Town & Country's manufacturing. We fly on a private, dual-prop plane owned by the company and piloted by a guy named Dick Carr. He's a good guy and lets me sit in the copilot's seat.

*Why don't you grab the controls,* he says one time.

I grab the yoke with both hands and feel the engine vibrate up into my arms, like I'm connected to the plane itself. I'm sure Dick has the autopilot on, but the thrill of feeling like I'm in control of the plane is unforgettable.

In Sedalia, Dad takes me around the factory where he's greeted as *Lippo* by some and *Mr. Lipscomb* by everyone else. While I'm with him, the place is all smiles, not a hint of trouble.

In the early spring Dad says, *Hey, Johnny-Jump-Up.*

I cringe a little. *Yes Dad.*

*Before you hear it from someone else, Celeste and I are getting married.*

*Married? Are you kidding?* Since Mom left, Dad is a dating tour-de-force. He won't tell me how many women he's been out with, but it is well over thirty. I think Aunt Cactus was somewhere around number five or ten.

*Yes, sir,* he says smiling. *A little surprised?*

Dad met Celeste the year before while on a business trip to Houston. I had met her twice, but given Dad's penchant for dating it never occurred to me he'd ask her to marry him.

She's nice enough, but I don't know her well. She's the daughter of a wealthy and well-connected Texas oil baron, which, like Mom, is a role she was born to play. She's tall, thin, good looking, has a honeyed southern drawl, and is confident to a fault. She reminds me of an older version of Cybill Shepherd's character in *The Last Picture Show,* the prettiest and wealthiest girl in town. Except Celeste's town is Houston, not atrophied and wasted Anarene.

The other piece that stuck out when I met her: she didn't drink. Wealth and a healthy sense of entitlement will go a long way in Ladue, I thought, but people consider alcohol and cigarettes to come from God.

*Well, yeah Dad, a little surprised.*

*Don't be so shocked, Johnny, it's a good thing.*

*When?* I asked.

Dad stands tall, hands on his hips like Superman. *May, a short while before school ends and you kids head off to camp.*

In late May, Joshua, Lisa, Dad and I board the private plane bound for Houston, with Dick Carr at the controls. From the airport we drive out of the city and into lush prairie in spring bloom. Dad drives the rental car, a large Cadillac, fast over slight rises and butterfly dips that you feel in the pit of your stomach. On either side of the road is a wide ribbon of wild flowers, blue bonnet and Indian paint brush, that runs off into the horizon, disappearing over the next rise.

The wedding is at the immense home and ranch of Wesley West, a close friend of Celeste's dad and a big ol' Texas oil guy, too. Both men have deep connections to Dallas and Houston, which include close friendships with President Lyndon Johnson. In fact, Wesley had a runway and bomb shelter built on the ranch so Johnson could visit for extended stays while president.

The wedding is a happy and fun time. My new stepbrother Cress—sixteen, tall, lean, good looking, hippie-esque—smokes a lot of pot. I drink some champagne, not much, meet my stepsister Chandler (the twelve-year-old version of Cybill Shepherd's character), flirt with a girl and even get a kiss. Joshua drinks Coke after Coke and goes a little wild. A few of Dad's buddies get drunk, crash their car and end up in the hospital; for them a regular weekend and part of the traveling show.

As I wind my way through the 300 to 400 guests under a huge reception tent, I hear Celeste chat with a couple of friends. *Well, there seemed to be a failure to get off the launch pad, you know, so I said 'John, make an honest woman of me or hit the road.'*

The clutch of women giggles. One leans forward, her wide hips challenging the seams of her tight, velvet off-the-shoulder-dress, *You're going to be step-mama to, what, three?*

*I certainly am. John's a saint, but his former wife gets so deep in her cups—* her eyes widen—*her own mother sent her away. So those children need a mother.*

*I don't need a mother,* I think to myself, *One's enough.*

On Sunday, we say goodbye and meet back up with Dick to fly home. In mid-June Celeste will move with us into a new house a few streets away from the old one, but closer to the country club. In a couple of weeks, Lisa, Joshua and I will leave for camp for July and August. Chandler and Cress will spend the summer with their dad, then move up in August.

Our new and expanded family, dysfunction and all, is only shifting to a new address.

When we pull into our driveway I'm exhausted, but I help Dad bring the bags inside. Lizzy is there at the front door and helps me carry Joshua's and Lisa's little suitcases to their rooms.

As we walk up the back kitchen steps, she places a hand on the back of my head. *John David, I already miss your blond hair bouncin' out the woods comin' back to me.*

*You're coming to the new house with us, right?*

*Nah, I've earned my retirement, pension and all.*

In my heart I can't imagine my life without her. Get rid of mom? Please. But Lizzy? Who'll take care of me?

*I don't want you to go, Lizzy.*

*It's all right, John David, things are changin'; it's the right time.* She pats the back of my head.

*Too much change.*

*Happens, John David, whether we like it or not; it happens.*

*I love you.*

*I love you as much as a kitten loves cream, John David, but don't let the devil get into you. You do that, everything'll be all right, ya hear?*

*Yes, ma'am.*

She turns, pauses for a moment then turns back to me, waving her hand in front of her face. *Lohd have mercy, John David. You went and lost yo manners again.*

She smiles and leaves me to tend to Lisa and Joshua.

What can I say? Camp is awesome. Lots of kids, archery (cliché, I know), shooting, sports, more sports, camping, canoeing, cabins and bunks, a mess hall, and crafts. I lie in my bunk each night, falling asleep to the snickering of kids, peepers by the lake, and crickets in the field. My muscles and body are sore and tired, but alive and filled with an energy that comes only from the soul of youth.

It's almost enough to take my thoughts away from the new house. I can't shake the image of Dad, his ginger hair fluffing out at his temples, oversized ears jutting at odd angles, saying, *Johnny, I'll need your help blending the families,* as movers wrap the piano in blankets and cardboard.

What the heck does that mean? He never explained it other than to say, *Be good, be helpful and be polite.*

*What're they doing with the piano?* I ask.

*No room for it at the new house, Johnny, so it's going to storage.*

*How's Uncle Bobby gonna play the drummer boy at Christmas?*

Dad smiles; hands on his hips, he stretches to his full height. *Hopefully, he'll give it a rest.*

A day later, Celeste arrives at the new house with two tractor trailers. The movers open the back of one, which is crammed with furniture, beds, and all their belongings. Then movers open the back of the second truck and it's like a jungle in there. She must have brought 500 zillion potted plants: ficus trees, pony tail palms, rubber trees, angel's trumpet, calla lilies, orchids, red torch ginger, tail flower, and on and on.

As movers pull out one lush, green plant that looks like a cactus with long, segmented tendrils from the back of the truck, Celeste calls out for Dad: *Ooh, ooh, John.*

*What is it?*

*It's a night-blooming cereus. It only blooms once a year, these gorgeous white flowers that look like a starburst, and only during the summer, at night.*

*Well, I'll be . . .*

Celeste lowers her eyes and leans in to Dad. *You and I can sit up and watch it bloom, together.*

I could just puke.

With all of this stuff, there are two cats, a French poodle named Garçon, and a double yellow-headed parrot named Mack.

Camp was a more than welcome relief from home.

Most of the kids at camp come from families like mine. They love each other, but send the kids away, each to their own. Kids indulge in the excesses of upper class camp life while Mom and Dad indulge in the excesses of upper class life. There aren't a lot of letters sent back and forth. Not much, *Hello Muddah, Hello Fadduh, here I am at Camp Granada . . .*

The same is true of Dad. He and Celeste are home alone and setting up house. They also find time to travel and do the sorts of things a newly married couple would do. This is why I'm surprised when a letter arrives from Dad.

It begins with the usual *Hope you are doing well,* but shifts to, *Before you hear it from someone else, your mother is coming back into your life. She bought a house and will move into it in August. As you can imagine, there has been a lot of discussion as to you, Joshua and Lisa. Your mother wants custody of you all and so do I. A judge will decide what's best. In fact, a judge has already ordered that the three of you live with your mother and spend every other weekend with Celeste and me.*

*Johnny, I can't tell you how sorry I am for this. It's a gut punch, to be sure, but I am optimistic the judge will see the light, so to speak, and make the correct decision for you three and for our family.*

*Be well and have fun Johnny.*

I shove the letter back in its envelope and go find Joshua.

Joshua is eight years old and the most excited he's been about anything to be at camp for the first time. When I find him with his tribe of young first-timers, his smile—a jumble of oversized adult teeth and crooked, too-small, child's teeth—looks as if it's etched it into his face by overuse.

*She's what?* His eyes dim and smile fades.

*Coming back to Ladue and thinks we're going to live with her.*

*You mean Dad, us, Celeste?*

*No, dummy; you, Lisa and me.*

*I don't wanna.*

*Neither do I.*

Joshua and I write back to Dad, telling him, *There is no way we will live with Mom. We don't want to do that and we refuse.* But it is not in our power to determine whom we live with. This becomes clear the day Dad picks us up at camp.

*Your mom's hired a couple of high-priced sharks for lawyers,* he says, edging the car along the rutted dirt camp road, *and there just isn't anything I can do about it right now. I wish to God there was, but there isn't. I'm going to fight for you, but this is how it has to be for the time being.*

We pick Lisa up at camp and Dad repeats what he's told us to her. She sits in the backseat next to Joshua, arms folded, a worn look on her face. Joshua stares out the window, eyes dull. Dad lights one cigarette after another and drives with his window wide open, elbow dangling out, thumb tapping the end of the cigarette.

We get off Interstate 64 at Clayton Road and wind up past St. Louis Country Club to a development of large, new houses not far from Codasco and Mary Institute. Near the corner of Warson and Pebble Creek roads Dad wheels the car into a short driveway that leads to a modest, two-story, brick colonial with an attached garage and sun porch to one side.

This isn't the first time we've seen Mom since she left. There was a brief trip to Baltimore, where she took us out to dinner. Afterward, we rejoined Dad and continued down to Florida for a vacation. There have been phone calls where we exchange a few words, then I pass her off to Lisa or Joshua, but no real conversations.

Stepping out of the car I hear, *There they are Dale, they're here.*

Mom scurries out the door and down a few steps and moves toward us with that same heavy, efficient heel-toe, heel-toe walk. She's let her hair grow out to shoulder length and she's a bit chubbier than I remember, though still pretty. She's wearing black heels and a red paisley dress that drapes down to below her knees.

Following her is a stout, solid-looking man with hair combed over the top of his head to hide his bald spot. He's wearing black leather shoes with gold buckles, polyester slacks and a white short-sleeved shirt with blue vertical stripes. His arms are thick and muscular with anchor tattoos on both forearms.

Both he and Mom wear glasses with large lenses—his metal and hers plastic frames—that darken as they near us.

Mom acknowledges Dad with a glance, then grabs Joshua in a bear hug. *Who's this?* I ask.

*Why, it's Dale,* Mom says, reaching behind and putting her arm around his shoulders, *my fiancé! Can you believe it? I'm getting married!*

*No,* Lisa says.

Mom hugs me and the scent of her is no different than the day she left: cigarettes and an acidic, boozy aroma from her breath and skin.

*Ohhh, Johnny-Jump-Up, you are sooo handsome.*

I cringe. *Hello mother.*

Dad leaves and we walk inside with our bags filled with dirty laundry and the detritus from camp. The foyer, living room and other rooms of the house are nicely decorated, but it feels staged, like a mockup of a real home. Lisa has her own room while Joshua and I share a room. There are a few of our belongings from Dad's house in each.

Mom follows Joshua and me into our room. *Do with it what you like,* she says with her hands pressed together. *Make it your ultimate boy room.* She wanders to Lisa's room and says much the same thing. Joshua and I overhear her say, *I'm sorry the house isn't more together, but I've been so busy with wedding plans, you know.*

There's nothing to say. The shock of it all is too much.

In the blink of an eye, Joshua, Lisa and I are at a church just up the street from Uncle Charles' house in Ladue. Aunt Mae is there, as well as Uncle

Charles and Aunt Susan. Mom and Dale stand before the altar as a minister reads a pro forma invocation. They exchange vows and they are husband and wife.

The reception is at Uncle Charles and Aunt Susan's house and involves hors d'oeuvres, champagne and cocktails. Mom chit chats as if she's the center of the royal wedding while Dale tells stories from his time as commander of a submarine. By early evening Mom and Dale are drunk and we're all out the door with Dale behind the wheel driving us to Mom's house. Fortunately, it's a short drive.

Clayton Road cuts Ladue in half, with the north section bisected by Ladue Road, which becomes the literal dividing line between the two warring parties of Mom and Dad. Their phone conversations devolve into arguments, with threats going both ways to sue the other for some breach. On Dad's side, he knows Mom's drinking is well beyond dangerous. On Mom's side, she is being grandiose and belligerent, doing whatever she can to deflect from her drinking and present herself as *the* responsible adult.

In the background, Dad's lawyer is doing all he can to win custody, or at least a fair custody agreement for Dad. Unfortunately, he's outmatched by a team of lawyers who've represented high profile clients, including alleged mob bosses. It isn't that Dad's lawyer is in over his head as much as Mom's inherited wealth is a bottomless well that her lawyers feel free to dip into. Dad has no such pool of wealth.

Not long after my fifteenth birthday in December, Mom and Dad go to court. One highlight is Aunt Mae taking the stand on Mom's behalf and telling the judge, *I haven't seen Eloise drink at all.*

I've never felt more betrayed than when I'm told Aunt Mae did this to Dad.

The other highlight is the judge calling each of us kids into his chambers. I'm in suit and tie, as is Joshua. Lisa wears her best dress. A court clerk leads me into the room with four lawyers—one is Dad's, three are Mom's—the judge, court reporter, and court clerk. Mom's lawyers—all large men, gold rings, loud—pepper me with questions.

*Have you ever seen your mother drinking, you know, more than is normal?* one of them asks.

I don't know what normal drinking is. *I think so.* I'm sweating and my stomach feels tight. I worry that I'll throw up.

*How would you know?*

*What do you mean?*

*How would you know she's drinking more than a normal person would?*

*I don't know.*

*Do you spend time around intoxicated people at your dad's house?*

*Well, yeah, I think so.*

*Would you say your dad drinks more than a normal person would?*

*No, I don't think so.*

Dad's lawyer tries to object to a question or ask his own, but Mom's three lawyers' protestations to the judge overwhelm him.

This lasts for about twenty to thirty minutes before the clerk leads me out into the hall. My face is burning red and I feel cut to pieces. Joshua looks up at me and the clerk asks him to go into the chambers next.

*Ay, ay, ay pee pot!* he yells, which is his signal that he needs to pee.

Despite months of fighting and arguing, the big court battle lasts a day. A week later, on a Friday that's Dad's weekend, Dad's lawyer calls.

Dad's new house on Brookside Lane in Ladue is smaller than the one on Oakleigh Lane. Cress and Chandler each have a room, as does Lisa, on our weekends there. Joshua and I share a room. There's a living room and a family room with a TV. When dad asks us to meet him in the living room, the piano feels conspicuously absent.

In a replay of the divorce announcement, the three of us sit on the couch. Dad has followed us in and stands with his hands in his pockets.

*Before you hear this from anyone else, the court thing didn't go well for us.* All three of our bodies stiffen. *Lisa, Joshua, you're going to have to live with your mother and Dale.*

I look at them both. Tears force their way from Lisa's eyes. Joshua's body deflates. I look back at Dad.

*Johnny,* he says, *since you're older, the judge says you can choose where you want to live. You'll have every other weekend with the other parent.*

Without even thinking, I say, *With you, Dad, I want to live with you.*

Joshua and Lisa look at me, mouths open, then Joshua says, *No way. You've got to be kidding.*

Lisa sobs, *No, Daddy, please.*

Dad takes a deep breath and stiffens his body. *I won't stop trying to get you back, but this is how it is for now.* Tears run down Joshua and Lisa's cheeks. Dad wipes his nose with a handkerchief, kneels down, and wraps his arms around them. *I promise I won't stop,* he says.

Relief that I can live with Dad balances any guilt I feel.

My report cards are pretty good up until Mom came home. Then they slide. For the remainder of my tenth grade year, they plummet. The bright spot is the tribe, which has grown to include a few girls, among them a girl named Margaret. She's intelligent and serious with autumn bronze hair, blue-mandala eyes and the lithe body of a ballet dancer.

As when we were younger, our lives remain mostly free of parents. At Dad's house Celeste wants to be a parent to me, but I don't need it or want it, which drives tension between us. To avoid it, I do anything and everything I can to be with my friends.

At Mom's house, she and Dale are constantly drunk. For the first few months Mom kept up appearances by drinking later in the day. Now it's a fulltime occupation for her. By three or four in the afternoon, still in her nightgown, she's passed out on a couch. Cigarette burns dot the rug that was spotless when she and Dale moved in. Her nightgown and the couch are equally spotted.

When she's not drunk on the couch, she's irrational and unpredictable. The click-click-click of her walk still reverberates up the spine. Joshua is nine and stands up to her, but Dale terrifies him. Lisa is twelve and scared to death of both Mom and Dale. With my friends, I call Dale and Mom the goons and spend as little time with them as possible. I also keep my friends away, as if the plague riddles the house.

I come back to Mom's one Friday night after being with the tribe to find Lisa and Joshua alone in the kitchen heating TV dinners for themselves.

*Where's Mom?* I ask.

*In the living room,* Joshua says.

*What about Dale?*

Lisa looks up from the kitchen table, where she'd been reading while waiting for the food to heat. *A bar, I think.*

I walk into the living room. Mom's passed out on the couch, her drink spilled on the carpet. It looks like Joshua or Lisa put her cigarette out for her. In the corner by the couch is a small bar set with an ice bucket, a few rocks glasses, and a bottle of vodka. In the cabinet below is more liquor.

I want to take the whole damn thing and throw it out the door and pour the liquor down the sink. *What's the point?* I think, *She'll just get more vodka delivered, and Dale might beat the hell out of me.*

I walk back into the kitchen and sit with Joshua and Lisa.

A couple of weeks later, the tribe is at the house of one of our friend's. Her parents are out; it's Saturday, so most of our parents are at some function or cocktail party. Until now, Margaret has been a desire, a gleam, a hope, but not much more. We talk and are friends, but her feelings toward me are opaque, hard for me to read.

*Hey Johnny,* someone says, *have a beer.*

He tosses the can at me and I open it. It's not my first beer or my first drink. I've had small glasses of wine at dinner parties with Dad and on holidays, as well as some champagne, but this is my first beer with friends, beyond the eyes of adults.

*Where's this from?* I ask.

*Beer fridge.*

I drink that beer and then another. Most of the guys have two or three, the girls one or two. We're worried our friend's parents will notice, but the beer fridge is so full, we barely make a dent in it.

I don't know if I feel drunk, but I feel light. There is a warmth to my body and a mood that is hard to describe, but it animates me and does the same to the tribe. The energy is different, more emphatic, easier and looser. There is also the sense of getting away with something, of privilege, that a culture of *having a few drinks* is something we are taking for our own and emerging into our own sense of what it means to mature. It's not about being an adult, but we are leaving our kidhood behind.

Walking home with Gary, we talk about girls and sports, but in the back of my mind is an intense realization that a few drinks does something for me that works, it really works. It's the lightness and all the rest of it, but it's also an escape. I haven't thought about Mom or Dad or Celeste or Dale, or anything other than being present with my tribe, my adopted family of friends.

Gary peels off toward his house and I head to Mom's, where I'm supposed to be this weekend. Neither Mom nor Dale knows I left. Through his silence, Joshua helped me sneak out while Mom was passed out in the living room and Dale was off at a bar he's found, where other former military guys like to hang out.

I walk down Warson Road toward Dale and Mom's house on the corner of Pebble Creek Road. In the distance there are flashing lights. As I get closer to the house I see a police car, an ambulance and fire truck out front. Two firemen are wheeling Mom out in a stretcher. An EMT is holding what looks like a folded white towel to her forehead. The towel is stained by blood that looks oddly luminous in the flashing lights.

*What happened?* I ask an EMT.

*Who are you?*

*Her son.*

*She fell and hit her head and has a fairly serious laceration across her scalp.*

*Is she going to be okay?*

*Yeah, I guess,* the EMT says, looking toward the ambulance. The firemen slide the gurney in and the EMT holding the bloody towel hops up behind her. *She's pretty incoherent and we can't really tell what part of it may be a brain injury or the fact that she's drunk. Her breath is God awful.*

I go inside and Dale is nowhere to be seen. In the living room Lisa and Joshua are crying. Joshua sees me and says, *I heard something downstairs and I thought it was you coming home, so I came down and I found her.*

I look over near the small bar set and there's a large, oblong blood stain in the carpet.

*Johnny,* Joshua says, *her scalp peeled off her head.*

*What?*

*When I found her, her scalp was peeled back, Johnny. I did my best to push it back on.*

I take a longer look at Joshua and see that his hands are smeared with Mom's blood and there's blood on his PJs. *Let's get you washed up and changed,* I tell him, and lead him by the hand toward the stairs. Lisa is silent as she follows.

Dale comes rushing through the front door, sees us and says, *What the hell?* Then to me, *That lil' sailor okay?* He leans on the door handle; his large rounded belly seems to sway and pull his body from side to side.

*It's Mom's blood,* I tell him.

*Oh, okay. I'll hitch a ride to the hospital with the cop. Hold the fort, will ya?*

*Yeah, no problem,* I say, then take Lisa and Joshua, both red-faced and weeping, upstairs. At the top of the stairs I look out a window down onto the street. The neighbor's lights are on and they're standing in their yard watching the ambulance pull away, lights flashing, and Dale, drunk, negotiating with the policeman for a ride.

Embarrassment stings and burns across my skin.

The tribe is my family, but Margaret is something else. The weekend beer drinking becomes the norm. The tribe becomes louder, more intense. Stealing beer from a friend's parents' fridge isn't workable so we figure out the stores in Ladue where entitlement grants us certain leeway. There are also stores on the outskirts of St. Louis where they are less determined not to sell alcohol to minors.

I am well in the mix of these parties and become known as the debater yelling out, *Oh, ptahhh!* if I disagree with someone. It is all in fun and we are completely loyal to one another.

As the night wears on everyone and everything becomes louder, like a slow engine throttling up. In the midst of it all, I always cut out a space for Margaret. Unbelievably, we become closer over the course of a few weeks. To me it feels like an eternity, but one night we are alone in a bedroom, kissing, when Laura walks in on us.

*When the heck did this happen?* Laura says, laughing.

*Last couple of weeks,* I say.

*Well, news to me.* She leaves and closes the door.

Later that night as I walk home my body feels light and my mind races with the excited insight that, yes, this really is working for me.

*Margaret and I*

George Love spent eighth grade at Codasco, but other than the day I decided to leave him alone, I don't think I spoke to him more than about five times. Over the course of that year, his dad and my dad became friends, but other than seeing Mr. Love in passing, I never got to know anything about him. Mr. Love was just another of Dad's many friends and George disappeared into the world of boarding school. If I thought of him at all, it was as a character in *A Separate Peace.*

So I'm a little surprised when late that spring Dad calls me into his office.

*Johnny,* he says, leaning back in his desk chair, *time you did some work. Listen, you know my good friend Lonnie Wallace owns a cattle farm in western Missouri, and he's agreed to take you and George Love on for the summer.*

Immediately, I think of Margaret. *The whole summer?*

*Yes, Johnny.*

*Can I come home on weekends?*

*I suppose.*

*Just me and George?*

*George and me,* he corrects, *and the other guys working at the ranch.*

The only image I have of George is a scrawny, ginger-haired kid wearing Brooks Brothers and penny loafers. When he and his dad arrive at our house to pick me up and I see this guy at the door, same ginger hair, but tall, filled out and rugged looking, it's hard to believe it's him.

*George?* I ask.

*Yeah, you ready?*

*What happened to you?*

*What ya mean?*

*You're not a pale, scrawny kid any more.*

*Yeah, I discovered rowing crew. Let's go.*

⁂

The ranch is a little patch of heaven. No parents, up at six then down to the ranch manager's house by seven to get our list of chores. Then we saddle up our horses—yes, we each have a horse—and round up cattle, tag cattle, give them shots, wrestle with calves to tattoo their ears to mark them, move and set irrigation pipe, and anything else that needs doing. At noon we eat a huge lunch of steak or pork chops, potatoes, corn bread, beans, the works. Then back to work in the long, hot Missouri afternoon until evening.

Each day lasts ten or twelve hours, but George and I couldn't be happier. At night, he and I sit by a fire talking and learning how to be friends.

On our third night, the ranch manager tells us to grab a few beers from the kitchen. He doesn't have to tell me twice so I grab six and George and I go to our little fire pit near where we bunk.

*I've never drank beer before, believe it or not,* George says as the fire grows.

*Well, now's as good a time as any.*

He takes a sip and his mouth puckers. *It's kind of gross.*

*Don't worry, you'll get used to it.*

Then George stands up and says, *I've got somethin' for you to try.* He walks into the bunk house and comes out with a joint. Smoking pot is another thing George discovered in a big way at Choate.

As we sit by the fire drinking and smoking, George talks a little bit about Choate.

*Why do you like it there so much?* I ask.

*Gets me away from my old man and the old lady.*

*Yeah?*

*Yeah. I don't really talk about it much, but I come from sort of the all-American corporate family. My grandfather ran Consolidated Coal and then Chrysler after the war, and basically saved the company.*

*Wow. I had no idea.*

*Yeah, he was the whole titan-of-the-corporate-world thing. And that's what my dad is, too, with a whole bunch of philanthropy thrown in. I never see the guy.*

I poke at the fire and hear my story in what George is saying. *My family on Mom's side is the Cellas—*

*The people who built nearly everything in St. Louis?*

*Yeah, The American, Millionaire's Row, all of that—*

*So you know what I'm saying, right?*

*I guess so.*

*My parents want me to just step into those huge shoes, but I'm not Mr. Corporate America. My parents are constantly like, 'God damn it, come hell or high water, your grandfather and your father and you are going to run a big corporation in the United States.'*

For the first time the reality of the legacy I'm being left by the Cellas and Lipscombs begins to form inside me. I'd felt the expectations from both sides, but I'd never internalized the reality of it, what it truly meant. I knock back a big slug of beer.

*I suppose my dad wants the same for me.* I don't even consider telling him about Mom. She's too toxic, too embarrassing.

*What's he do?*

*Runs Town & Country Shoes.*

*So, yeah, you've got it coming at ya from both sides of the family.* He tilts his head back with a can of beer to his lips and drinks deeply.

*Yeah.*

*I don't know if I'm cut out for the corporate world, much less be some sort of leader of it. So my parents are constantly like, 'We're disappointed in you, this isn't why we sent you to prep school your whole life, when are you going to get your act together, stop being such a loser,' but I'm not gonna do it.* George looks up into the sky. Without any city lights, the sky is dense with stars. *I can't, I just can't do it.*

*Neither can I.* I drain my beer. *Another?*

*Yeah. You're right. It isn't so bad once you get used to it.*

The rest of the summer is hard, hot work that we love, evenings drinking and smoking, and weekends partying with the tribe in Ladue, of which I've made sure George is firmly a member.

One night, late at a Ladue tribe party, George looks at me, sober in his earnestness, *Johnny Lipscomb, you are THE big, humble coxswain of Ladue.*

*What do you mean, George?*

*You tell 'em which way to row and how fast and they listen and follow.*

I'd never thought of myself in that way before, but it feels good. I like it.

I don't want to say goodbye to George at the end of summer. He'll be back for occasional weekends and holidays, but there's a kinetic spark between the two of us that's both fun and reassuring. We like partying together, and people like partying with us, but we also share something even more important. We're both lost in our lives.

Where Margaret knows what she wants and is driven to achieve it, George and I share not having any clue who either of us is or what our lives are meant to be. I feel a lot less lonely with him in the world. He is a brother.

When I come back to Codasco, my skin is bronzed and my muscles defined and strong. My hair's grown out so that stringy wisps of it sweep past and away from my face. Dad and Celeste call it *The Nest.* Just as George left the penny loafers and Brooks Brothers behind (for the most part), I now look less like I emerged from the Ladue preppy handbook and more like a son of Haight-Ashbury, although the transformation is incomplete. George and I both straddle the line between private school prepster and prep school hipster.

With George at Choate, my attention goes to Margaret and life falls into an easy routine. Weekdays are school followed by sports and spending as much time with Margaret as I can.

Her mother—I call her Mrs. Tice—lives across the street from Dad. Like my mom, Mrs. Tice has a petite build, but blond hair that she wears in a shoulder length bob. She believes I'm one of the good kids of Ladue with a fine pedigree but a troubled mother. She's kind, a good listener—which is rare to find in an adult in Ladue—and I feel a sense of belonging with her. I eat meals with Mrs. Tice and Margaret as much as I can and she is always happy to have me in the house. She also sets boundaries that I grouse about to friends, but in reality there's an attentive affection behind them that I've never experienced with my own mother.

On Fridays and Saturdays the tribe parties by night, and during the day I do my best to stay away from either home. At Dad's, I get the hairy eyeball from Celeste: *Where have you been? What have you been doing? Are you hung over? Your grades are horrible, you're overindulged, heading down the wrong path, and letting your dad down.* Dad isn't quite as loud or strident with me, but he's started calling me Unconscious, like: *Where you going, Unconscious. Hey, Unconscious, can you give me a hand? What the hell happened to your grades, Unconscious?*

At Mom's, it's her sitting in the living room by the bar like it's a life raft, getting passed-out drunk. Every so often, a couple of times a day, there's the clack-clack-clack of her heading toward whoever she's got a problem with. Dad tries to help, but any time he gets involved Mom's team of lawyers pounces. She sues him for anything and everything, such as letting me ride a mini-bike without a helmet.

Dale is almost always AWOL at some bar.

*Johnny,* Mom says one November day, *we're going out for Aunt Mae's birthday. Bring that girlfriend of yours.*

*I don't know.*

*Honey, do it. I need to meet this girl.*

Mom is like dark matter to Margaret. She knows Mom exists, but there's no evidence. She's never met Mom and I don't talk about her.

*Really?* Margaret says squinching up her eyes when I tell her. *What do I wear?*

*It'll be with my Uncle Charles and Aunt Susan, so something really nice.*

When I pick Margaret up at her house, her mother hovers around Margaret, making sure her hair is perfect. *Wow, Charles Cella, quite the occasion, I'm sure.*

Margaret smiles at me, but what I want is for her mom to offer me a beer.

We get in Dad's car, which I've borrowed for the night, and drive to Mom's before going to the restaurant for Aunt Mae's party. It's dark and in the distance there are flashing lights. I pull up to Mom's house and park in the street near a police cruiser and fire truck.

*She fell again,* Joshua says when he sees me. *Where's Margaret?*

*In the car. Where'd she fall?*

*In the driveway and cracked her head on the pavement.*

I look over toward the ambulance and the EMTs are loading her in. Dale is weaving a little as he talks to a policeman and Margaret is waiting in the car.

*Is she okay?* Margaret asks.

*Yeah, this isn't the first time and it won't be the last.*

*I'm sorry, Johnny.*

I like Margaret caring for me, but I don't like her feeling sorry for me.

*Let's get out of here.*

I'll never bring Margaret or anyone else I know to Mom's house again.

A few weeks after her fall, I come home late to Mom's and someone's locked the doors so I can't get in. I've been drinking beer with the tribe and think nothing of yelling up at the house. A light goes on in Mom and Dale's room.

*It's past your curfew, buddy,* Dale yells. The light goes off and that's it. I walk around to a window in the room I share with Joshua and toss some pebbles up at it. I'm freezing and I feel like I'm in some dopey movie, but it works and Joshua comes down to let me in.

Joshua's ten years old and starting to grow like a weed. I seem to have inherited Mom's height, while Joshua is definitely molded in Dad's image. *Thanks, buddy,* I tell him.

He looks up at me eyes tired, but bright. *Wanna watch some TV or something'?*

*Yeah, sure.* I don't spend much time with him and find it hard to say no. We go into the living room where the TV is and there's Mom passed out in her nightgown and bathrobe. You can tell how far she roams from the couch by the collection of cigarette burns and spill marks.

I walk up to her to nudge her to see if she'll go up to bed, but before I do, I notice the couch is wet around her and so is her nightgown and bathrobe.

*Let's just go upstairs and hang out,* I tell Joshua.

*Okay.*

Monday night I tell Dad about Mom and he shakes his head. *Not much I can do.*

*I know, but you have to do something.*

Dad's weary. Not tired like a bad night's sleep, but an emotional weariness that I see in how he carries his body.

*I'll do what I can.*

Two weeks later I'm at Mom's again and Joshua helps me sneak out of the house. It's more play for him as he edges around hallways to make sure the coast is clear and I follow him to the door.

*Hold on a sec,* he says at the door. He runs into the living room, sneaks past Mom and comes back with a bottle of vodka. *Here, you and your friends may want this.*

I don't know what to say other than, *Thanks.*

*That's just sad,* Margaret says when I show her the bottle.

*He's just trying to be nice.*

*Maybe, but it's sad.*

She's right, but I don't like the implication.

Life spins like a top. Dad calls me Unconscious. Celeste's overarching message is I'm no good and overindulged. Mom is Mom and Dale is Dale. The three things that slow the spinning are Margaret, the tribe, and beer.

After Mom's latest ambulance ride and Margaret's comment about Joshua—in reality, she was talking about me—there's been a shift. My order of preference for slowing the spinning top leans toward beer and the tribe.

*Come on woman, we're leaving,* I say late one night, loud enough for the tribe to hear. My body language is primal and I grab her as if she's a possession.

*Whatever, Johnny,* she says, but comes with me.

Outside I pull the car keys from my pocket, but Margaret snatches them from my hand. *There's no way you're driving,* she says.

I still depend on her and she's still willing to take care of me, but she's a little less important. Drinking becomes more of a priority.

Margaret has always been intent on college, so that spring she begins visiting schools, preparing for entrance exams, deciding what she wants to study and where best to do that.

*You know, Johnny,* she says with some frequency, *if you really want to go to college you gotta start doing something about it now.*

*I know, I know,* is about the only reply I can manage. My grades are not a full blown disaster, but I'm far from being a merit scholar.

Dad is equally worried about my attitude toward making something of my life, and is far more direct than Margaret. *Hey, Unconscious, graduation's coming so you better figure out what the hell you're going to do. I'll pay for college, but you're out on your butt if you screw it up.*

With the choice of working or staying within the warm embrace of school and a dorm room, I start to pick away at thinking about college. Meanwhile, Margaret is so serious about her life and future that she bails out on some weekend parties.

One of these nights I get pulled over near Dad's by a policeman.

*You been drinking?* he asks.

I'm sure my eyes are bloodshot and I reek of beer. *Yes sir, I had a few beers.*

*Where ya goin'?*

*My dad's house.*

*Here in Ladue?*

*Yes sir.*

*Who's your dad?*

*John Lipscomb.*

*Lippo?*

*Yes sir, Lippo.*

*All right, follow me.*

He walks back to his cruiser and pulls ahead of me and flashes his lights for me to follow. At Dad's house I park and say thanks to the policeman.

*It's okay, just be more careful next time.*

I feel a little invincible.

In June, there are the first of what people in Ladue call *Debut* parties, which are for girls after their first year of college. Invitations are sent only to people on the social register and young men are invited over a three-year period while girls only attend once.

I find it hard to believe that there's actually a social register, but there is and I'm on it. I receive invitations to a few *Debuts* spread out over two weeks. One of them is to former St. Louis Cardinal Stan Musial's daughter's *Debut*. I don't know her, but Stan-the-Man is a hero to anyone and everyone from St. Louis. Of course, I go.

George is home from Choate and with his family connections is on the social register too, so we go together. A cheap *Debut* costs the girl's parents around twenty thousand dollars. An expensive one is up around seventy-five thousand. This one must have been toward the higher end.

After the party, George and I are lit and I'm driving us to his parents' house in my little red Vega. I over-steer while going too fast around a curve and lose control of the car. I hit the brakes and the car swerves and skids into a tree. It slows enough before hitting the tree that we aren't hurt, just shaken up.

Soon after, a police car pulls over, lights flashing. He gets out of his cruiser and shines his flashlight on us. George and I are wearing tuxedos with top hats, and I'm cradling a Plexiglas cane in my arms.

*Who was driving?* he asks.

*I was, sir,* I say, squinting into the light.

He crouches to get a better look at me. *That you, Johnny Lipscomb?*

*Yes sir.*

*And who are you?* he asks George.

*George Love, sir.*

*George Love, Jr.?*

*Yes sir.*

*All right.* He walks back to his cruiser and calls a wrecker to come fetch the Vega, then walks back to us. *In the car. I'll give you clowns a ride home.*

He lets us off at George's house. *Let's be more careful, okay guys?*

*Yes sir,* we say at the same time.

Not only do I feel invincible, but I realize that my life has no consequences. I am free to do whatever I want.

I have this feeling of invulnerability when a girl approaches me that summer. It's Saturday night and George and I are home after a week working at the ranch. I'm tan, my muscles feel worked and taut, my body hard and lean.

*Hey, Johnny, what-a-ya say?*

I look around. Margaret's off visiting a college, or something. *I say whatever you want.*

Margaret finds out I cheated almost the instant she gets home.

*I can't believe you, Johnny.*

*I'm sorry*—I truly am, and desperate for her to forgive me—*I screwed up. It'll never happen again. I swear it.*

*You're such a bastard.*

I beg and plead and Margaret takes me back, but things are not the same. There's no way they ever could be. Where there was little light between us, now there is a growing cleft. She is committed to her path and I am lost, or as Dad says, unconscious in my own life; floating and drifting with currents wherever they take me.

Perhaps, if my family were different, if I weren't so dependent upon the acceptance and attitudes of the tribe, I'd float on amenable currents. Instead, my family is what it is and I am, to some degree, a product of the circumstances of my birth. My impulses tend toward self-destruction, self-indulgence, and escape, though I know in my heart that I am culpable for and sole owner of the consequences of my choices. Instead of humility and self-awareness, what shines out is a boy who believes he is free of account-ability or liability for his decisions.

Alcohol makes it possible to tune out this conflict.

After I tear Margaret's heart out and turn my back on Lisa and Joshua, Joshua especially, a thunderclap sounds and loss and change come like hard rain on a tin roof.

My senior year at Codasco begins with Lisa finally escaping Mom's house. She's talked mom into letting her go to boarding school back east, and the day she leaves she is not so much happy as relieved. Joshua waves to her as Dad's car pulls out to take her to the airport, almost like an inmate who's happy for a friend released by the warden.

The bitter pill is that this leaves Joshua alone in the house with Mom and Dale. Like a reliable first mate, Dale has all but taken up residence at a bar filled with ex-military men, all of whom miss the predictable cadence of military life and medicate the anxiety and loss of status with alcohol.

Mom is complete in her dedication to her alcoholism. She rarely leaves the house or her bathrobe, which between washings reeks of cigarettes, stale vodka, and urine.

Dad is concerned about Joshua when I speak with him, but his response lacks his former resolve. Rather than stand hands on hips like a ginger-haired Clark Kent, he says, *What can I do,* and plows his head into work.

A few weeks after Lisa's left for school, the weather is warm for early October so I've opened my window, which faces out toward the back yard. It's late on a weekday and I have a small bedside lamp on so I can read. Below the window, the back door opens and shuts and I hear Dad's shoes walk out onto the patio.

I lift my head up to look out at him and a match flashes as he lights a cigarette. He takes a deep drag off it and lets the smoke drift out of his mouth.

I look back at my book. From outside there's an awful sound, like a raspy, deep throated groan. I look out the window and Dad has covered his face with one hand. His shoulders are shaking.

When I step out onto the patio Dad turns and sees me, then wipes his face with one hand while bringing his cigarette to his lips with the other.

*Dad, what's wrong? Who died?*

He's still for a moment. *I did something horrible today, Johnny.*

*What?*

*I had to lay off more than half our staff at the company today. Nearly everyone from the office, and then I don't know how many in design and production and manufacturing in Sedalia. Some of them are people I recommended to my dad that he hire, they've been with us that long.*

*What about the other plants?*

*Oh Johnny, they've been gone for a few years now.*

*Why?*

*People aren't buying our shoes any more. All they seem to want are cheap knockoffs.*

*Dad, I'm sorry.* It doesn't occur to me what this means for our wealth.

*There's one other thing I better tell you before you hear it from the family. I fired your Uncle Mike, too.*

*You mean laid off?*

*No, fired.*

*Whatever for?*

*Johnny, I love him, I truly do, but he's a drunk and I just can't have that in the company as I'm laying off people who've dedicated their working lives to us.*

Over the next few weeks the business seems to level off, but Dad's work hours are intense and he can't fall back into the rhythms he used to inhabit. To fill the void, Celeste starts her own antiques store in Ladue—as predicted, she has seamlessly inserted herself into Ladue society. Our house is now a jungle overrun by a growing collection of vintage clocks; porcelain bowls, vases, urns, and tea sets; ornate chifferobes, canopy bed frames, cylinder-topped desks, and dining room tables; as well as a menagerie of brass, china, copper, wood, and ivory baubles and tchotchkes, as many as she can get her hands on.

Somehow I manage to graduate from Codasco in June and am enrolled in Drake University in Des Moines, Iowa. I just float and this is where the wind takes me.

At the beginning of summer, George's dad arranges interviews for us at his company, National Steel, to work at a pellet plant in Hibbing, Minnesota. The jobs are a foregone conclusion so I think nothing of getting tanked the night before. I'm so hung over the next morning that I forget to bring my shoes.

*What the hell, where are your shoes,* George says, when he hears my bare feet slap on the linoleum hallway as we walk to the interview.

I pull my suit jacket up over my shoulders, *Forgot 'em, I guess.*

When George's father finds out I didn't have shoes, he tells George, *Lippo owns a shoe company, for Christ's sake. Jesus, it's Shoeless-Johnny-Lippo.*

Of course, we get the jobs anyway. The first three weeks at the plant in Hibbing we spend our time smoking pot during work and drinking at night. Then one night George's dad calls and says there's going to be a strike at the plant.

*These guys are pissed so if they go on strike and figure out your dad is chairman of the company, they'll string you up,* he says to George.

*How do you know they'll be able to figure out who we are?* George asks, while holding a two-foot long bong between his knees. A bit of smoke swirls up from the bowl of the pipe.

*Because you're probably still wearing your Polo shirt and penny loafers, you idiot,* he says, laughing.

We skedaddle out of Hibbing and next thing its fall and I'm in Des Moines, kinda-sorta going to college.

A guy bangs on my dorm room door. *Lipscomb, phone!*

*Yeah, Dad, what is it?*

*Johnny, before you hear it from somewhere else, your Uncle Mike has throat cancer.*

*Is he going to die?*

*He says they can do surgery, but I don't know. Sounds like they have to slice him ear to ear.*

In what feels like the blink of an eye, I'm called to the dorm phone again. *Yeah, Dad.*

*Uncle Mike died, Johnny. It was the cancer, I guess, but I don't know, seems quick.*

There's a memorial service in Ladue that I go home for. Joshua's happy to see me. He's twelve, tall and turning into a good looking kid with a sad smile.

*You gonna hang out at the house, Johnny?* he asks after the service.

*Nah, I'm getting together with some friends.*

Margaret's off at college, as are most of the people who were in my class at Codasco or Mary Institute, but a few younger kids are seniors now. It's depressing how familiar the party is. I feel like the college guy who's so much more mature than this high school scene.

Then a cute girl walks up. *Hi Johnny, what-a-ya say?*

Cancer is something of a theme. Maybe it's that my dad's generation and the generation before him has hit some magical age milestone where cancer is simply more prevalent. Perhaps it's payment for the bodily sin of smoking or drinking. I don't know, but every so often there is word of a new case within his friends or our family.

Each announcement—usually from Dad—passes through me in a mix of sadness and resignation, but the interruption is brief and I continue in my unconscious posture. Then Margaret's mom is diagnosed with lung cancer.

At first, Margaret is told to be optimistic, there's reason for hope. Mrs. Tice is determined in her battle with the disease and inspires me with her bravery. It's a bravery and resilience I've never seen in Mom. The closest Mom has ever come to courageous was emerging from her stupor to attend my Codasco graduation.

There isn't a surgical option for Mrs. Tice, but she endures round after round of chemo and then experimental therapies and drugs through a well-known cancer specialist.

In the end, the cancer is terminal. When Margaret is told she comes to me and collapses in my arms.

*I thought she would be okay.*

I hold her close as she weeps. *I'm so sorry.* The pain of this news spreads through my body like an intolerable ache. *I'm more sorry than you could know.*

Something deep within me is shaken; something I can't quite name or place, other than to say it is a deep pain of loss. She is going to die and be gone from our lives forever. This is a certainty and a literal loss. What I can't decipher is that losing Mrs. Tice touches on the ambiguous loss of Mom.

Mrs. Tice is the mother I've never had. Mom will never be the mother I need.

A few weeks later, I go home to Ladue and walk across the street to see Mrs. Tice.

I knock on the door. When she opens the door she gives me a hug before either of us can speak.

*Johnny Lipscomb, so good to see you, boy.*

I pull back and look at her. The toll of chemo and cancer are unmistakable.

*You look good,* I say.

She smiles. *It's kind of you to say that.*

Mrs. Tice holds my hand and guides me into her home. She wheezes slightly and is frail, but manages well enough. In the living room she lets go of my hand and sits in a large chair. There's an oxygen canister next to her and she wraps a thin, clear plastic tube around her ears and adjusts the nose piece so it fits snug to her nostrils.

On the table next to her are a few prescription bottles, water, and tissue.

*My goodness, Johnny, I forgot to offer you something to eat or drink.*

*No thank you.*

I ask her if she's in pain and she says not too much. My hands are clasped in my lap and I look down at them.

*Johnny,* she says, *I want to tell you something.*

*Yes, Mrs. Tice.*

*I'm worried about you, Johnny. I'm worried about what you're doing with your life.*

I wipe my eyes with the back of one hand.

*I'm okay. I'll be okay, I mean.*

She smiles. *I know you will. You're a good kid, Johnny Lipscomb. Not always a great boyfriend, but in your heart, you're a good kid; kind and gentle. Let that be who you are and you'll be all right.*

Four months later, Mrs. Tice passes away. I'm proud to be a pallbearer at her funeral.

*Lipscomb, phone!* Someone yells into my room a few weeks later.

I pick up the receiver and Margaret says hello.

*I miss you, ya know.*

*Yeah, I heard how much you miss me.*

Immediately, I know what she means.

*You heard?*

*I ran into Chandler on Saturday. Johnny, I'm not going to do this anymore.*

I can't fault Chandler. Mrs. Tice was only partly right when she said I'm not always a great boyfriend. The truth is, I'm a terrible boyfriend and I've begged for Margaret's forgiveness too many times.

*Margaret, I'm sorry.*

*It kind of doesn't matter Johnny.*

*What do you mean?*

*I went on a date with a really nice guy.*

*You what?!*

*I like him, Johnny.*

My body feels like it's falling.

*I don't want the drinking anymore. I want to be serious about my life and, well, I just want my life to be about something. I can't do that with you. I'm sorry.*

She moves forward with her life and I continue to do what I do best: float.

The Wednesday before Thanksgiving I go home to Dad's house.

The next morning I meet up with Mom and Dale as well as Lisa and Joshua. Mom's body is thin, but bloated. Her skin is an unhealthy looking dim goldenrod and the whites of her eyes are gray and reddened. She sways when she stands to say hello.

*Johnny, look at you, my college boy.*

*Yeah, hi Mom.* She's made her hair and face up and is wearing a floral print chiffon dress that flows down her body. There are hints of her former beauty, but she is a faded woman.

We drive to Uncle Charles', where there's the usual over-the-top spread of champagne, caviar, and on and on. Uncle Charles hugs Mom tightly then shakes Dale's hand, *Hey Dale.*

*Charles,* he responds and that's as much as either will say. Dale disappears to get a drink.

Aunt Mae arrives and then a few other friends of Uncle Charles. The highlight of the day is a sleigh ride with Uncle Charles driving, a bottle of

Crown Royal next to him. Mom stays behind. The rest of us ride in the sleigh sipping—in my case gulping—Dom Perignon.

Before we leave, Uncle Charles leans over to his butler. *Alonzo, watch Eloise and make sure she doesn't burn the house down.* There isn't a hint of humor in his voice. In a rare moment of unity, Dale and I look away from Uncle Charles, embarrassed.

We eat a huge, multicourse meal in the afternoon. Afterward, Uncle Charles nudges me, *Let's go do a little duck hunting, work the food off.*

Joshua comes along, too, and we sit in a duck blind that's more like a half-buried cabin with an opening to shoot from. It's cold and Joshua and I are both wearing slacks, coat and tie with waders and a wool coat. We each hold a borrowed shotgun. Uncle Charles is decked out in hunting regalia. There's plenty to drink and the three of us tuck into it and blast away every so often if a duck comes close. I couldn't be happier.

I go back to school, then Christmas comes with the usual shenanigans, with the remaining family members at Dad's. I pay a quick visit to Mom and Dale, but spend most of my time with Dad.

*How are the grades?* he asks, but seems distracted.

*You know me . . .*

*Yeah, Unconscious.*

*. . . but they're okay,* I lie.

Back to school, where I kinda-sorta go to classes.

Around noon on a Tuesday in February, *Lipscomb, phone!*

*Hey Dad, what's up?*

*Did I wake you up?*

*No Dad.*

*Johnny, before you hear it from anyone else, Town & Country's going into bankruptcy.*

*I'm sorry,* I say, but to tell the truth it's not a huge surprise.

As the next few weeks pass, a buyer for Town & Country is found and they agree to keep Dad on as president. Life for the most part will continue as before, albeit without private planes and the other perks.

As this all plays out, in the back of my mind there's some relief. I'm no longer expected to inherit the mantle of president of Town & Country. If I'm lucky, I should be able to float for an indefinite period of time.

It's a Wednesday evening in May. *Lipscomb, phone!*

I pick up the receiver expecting to hear Dad's low, cigarette-grooved growl with bad news about the family or business, but instead its Joshua's breaking voice. *Johnny, its Mom, you've got to come home.*

*What happened?*

*She fell and hit her head.*

*She does that all the time.*

*This time it's different.*

*Why?*

*Her head hit the side of the fireplace. I couldn't get her to wake up, Johnny.*

I walk into a hospital intensive care unit. Dale is sitting on a bench. Joshua sits in a chair across from them. Lisa is on her way home from boarding school.

I walk into her room and Dale follows. There's an intubation tube stuck down her throat that's attached to a ventilator, which makes a rhythmic whirring sound as it breathes for Mom. There's an IV tube and monitors for heart, blood pressure and oxygen level. Another tube emerges from the bottom of the bed and leads into a catheter bag.

Dale coughs to clear his cigarette-roughened lungs, *There isn't anything anyone can do.*

*What do you mean?*

*The doctors can't help her.*

Lisa arrives the next day. She, Joshua, Dale and I stand next to Mom's bed as a doctor removes the intubation tube and turns the ventilator off.

The four of us watch her chest move up and down. Her body struggles for each breath, not wanting to let go. Our faces don't betray any emotion as her chest slows, even as her body works harder for each breath. A nurse stands off to one side of the bed. A heart monitor beeps, its cadence easing. Mom's chest lifts, beep, then falls, beep, then lifts, beep, then falls. A doctor checks her pulse with his fingers on her wrist. The cadence eases, her chest eases, Mom's eyelids flutter, and life slips from her body.

Dale walks away. I have no idea where he's going, but I'm glad.

Uncle Charles is in Europe and unable to return for Mom's funeral. The sun is shining and I know this section of the cemetery well. Mom's father, Lampau, and many of the Cellas who built the family's wealth are buried in the crypt where Mom is going today.

Dale, Lisa, Joshua, Aunt Mae and I listen to a minister say a few words. I look up at Aunt Mae and she is completely lost. The last of the people she loved most on this earth is dead, and died as most of them, from some alcohol-related disease or accident. She will never be the same woman I grew up with. When Luju died she lost a lot of what made her who she was, but it's all gone now.

The minister finishes and we stand in silent prayer. In my mind I see the photo of Mom just after my birth, pixie haircut like Audrey Hepburn, tired and smiling, holding a drink up to the camera. Then I remember that after my birth there was a week of parties attended by God knows how many people, all of whom were powerful and important. I think of stories of Mom and Dad's wedding, of more parties with hundreds of guests. The trips to Florida, high-stakes races at Oaklawn Park, family houses on Millionaire's Row, the parties I listened to as Lizzy put me into bed for the night. Mom was *the* debutante and socialite of Ladue, with hundreds of guests at her *Debut* party.

The four of us look impassively at the casket. Gone, too, is the woman who tore so much of our lives apart.

*Thank God, Joshua and Lisa can finally come home,* Dad says in the car after picking us up at Mom and Dale's house.

*You hear that, buddy?* I say to Joshua.

*Yeah.*

I look up through the windshield as Dad turns onto Ladue Road. *It's going to be all right, ya know?*

Joshua looks up at me and smiles.

# Chapter Seven

## ADRIANNE:
## SOME WOUNDS CUT DEEP

......................................................

*You're a manipulative bitch, Adrianne.*
*Ya know that? That's all you are.*

—Elaine Schoenowitz

*I can only love myself as much as*
*I believe I am lovable.*

—AL-ANON

......................................................

*E*laine stands over me while I'm trying to do my homework. *Jeez,*
*Adrianne, you're kind of an idiot.*

As usual, I'm slow to understand the work and even slower to finish it.

Wiping her hands with a kitchen towel, Elaine says, *Christ, look at Bina. She's already done and her work's a lot harder than yours. What're ya doin' anyway?*

I push my month-old glasses up the bridge of my nose. *An essay for English.*

*What on?*

*'To Kill a Mockingbird.'*

*I hated that book.*

*Why?*

*Dunno, just did.*

It's October 1974, I'm twelve years old and in seventh grade. Bina is thirteen and in eighth grade.

A little more than two years ago, Elaine put me on an airplane bound for Miami. I was alone and it was the first time I'd ever flown. Bina was already at Herb's mom's house and the two of us lived with her in Miami Beach until late August when we returned to Brooklyn for school.

When I walked into PS 238 in Brooklyn for the first time it felt like entering an overcrowded prison teetering on the brink of anarchy. The school was a large brick building with a tall chain-link fence and hard-topped playgrounds on either hip. Most of the kids knew each other, were loud, and stared at me. Inside, gray ceramic tiles covered cinderblock walls. The classroom doors were steel, with square windows covered by paper.

Teachers loitered in front of their classrooms, yelling at some students and letting others in. I had a vague notion of where my fifth grade classroom was, but no idea how to get there. Bina had walked with me to school and pointed in the right direction, but left me when she saw her friends.

I wandered the hallways lost, overwhelmed, feeling small, and like I was the only fifth grader wearing glasses.

Not long after returning to Brooklyn, Herb rented a new apartment for us on Avenue P and East 10th Street, about two blocks from the one on Coney Island Avenue.

This place isn't above a storefront; like the rest of our new neighborhood, it's on a small block of homes converted into two- and three-family apartments. It's a little bigger, but it has the same dreary, run-down feel as Coney Island Avenue.

Bina and I still share a bedroom and there's a third bedroom, but it's filled with Herb and Elaine's junk. There's a living room with a mix of old furniture and a few items Herb inherited from his aunt. Next to the living room is a dining room with more inherited furniture and then a wide entryway to the kitchen. There's also a short hallway with the bathroom on one side and Herb and Elaine's room on the other. At the end of the hall is a door out to the stairs that lead to the street.

Despite it being larger, the rooms are cluttered and unclean with dog or cat poop lying in a corner sometimes for a day or more. The change of address also hasn't changed the routine. Elaine is unpredictable and Herb spends hours in their room or locked in the bathroom. Sometimes he's in the bathroom for so long that Bina and I have to use a bucket.

Things haven't changed much since that first day of school, either.

Elaine hovers behind me as I work at the dining room table. Her hands are on her hips and I can feel her glaring at me. *I don't know why school's so hard for you, Adrianne, I really don't. Maybe you're just stupid.*

I clench the pencil. My Mom would never tell me I'm stupid, which makes Elaine's words sting all the more. *I'm not stupid.*

*Then it was those damn Cahns that ruined you.*

My shoulders stiffen and I duck my head. *It wasn't Mom and Dad, it's you.*

I feel Elaine's eyes looking through the top of my head and lower it a little more. The back of Elaine's hand strikes me so hard my glasses topple from my face and land on my notebook. My eyes water from the pain of her knuckles hitting my skull.

*Don't talk to me like that again, hear me?* She leans down, her mouth next to my ear. *They're not your parents and they spoiled you rotten.*

Herb comes out of their bedroom and down the hall. *What the heck's going on in here?*

*Your daughter's mouthing off again,* Elaine says, grabbing her cigarettes.

Herb frowns. *That essay done yet? What's taking so long?*

*It's hard.* I don't look at him. I feel the sting of Elaine's knuckles on my head and a tear streaks down my cheek.

Herb walks over to look over my shoulder. *Jesus Adrianne, who can read that chicken scratch?*

*I'm doing my best.*

*Well, you may have to do it over again. Don't forget to bring it to me when you're done.* He walks back into the bedroom. Elaine lights a cigarette and walks into the kitchen, where she grabs a vodka bottle from the freezer and pours some in a glass with orange juice. Bina is in our room, listening to music with headphones on.

There's nowhere for me to be alone. I have to sit at the kitchen table with Elaine smoking and glaring at me every so often. I close my eyes and pray to my grandmother in heaven, *Please, help me go home.*

*About time,* Herb says, when I hand him the one-page essay. He has a red pen near the bed and begins reading. He doesn't get far before the red pen starts marking up my essay. In a few moments he hands me the page, which looks as if it is bleeding from a hundred different cuts. *Fix those mistakes and then you're done.*

I walk to the dining room table, pull a fresh sheet of paper from my notebook, and start again.

The next day of school is the same as ever. I walk from a crazy house to an overcrowded prison on the brink of utter chaos, where most of the kids look at me like I'm trash and not worth even saying hello to.

I push up my glasses and, head down, keep moving forward. With each step I remind myself what Mom says when I talk to her on the phone, *I love you very much, Ady. Stay strong and when you're eighteen you can come home.* Two years done, six to go.

At night I pray for someone to rescue me.

The only bright spot in all of this is Bina. At times she is an aloof older sister—especially around school friends her age—but at other times she understands my sadness. Like Harry, she takes it as her job to make me laugh and forget about all the bad things.

I call Mom and Dad once a week. I pull the phone as far away from Elaine as I can, but the cord is only so long and she can still hear, so I can't ever talk about anything other than to say I'm doing okay. If I say what I really think, Herb gets mad and Elaine gets meaner.

When he's not working, Herb is in the bedroom. If he wants something, like a cigarette or coffee—he smokes and drinks coffee a lot—he calls out to Elaine for it. Elaine looks at me: *Well, go see what the hell he wants.*

On weekend mornings, everyone except me gets up late. Herb spends hours in the bathroom. *Coffee!* he'll yell, *Cigarette!* If we have something planned, which is rare, we are hours late. The only time we are on time is for Bina's dance or gymnastics classes.

*Hey Adrianne,* Herb whispers into my ear as we watch Bina. *Why can't you do a handstand like that?*

*I don't know.* In my head I think it's because I'm uncoordinated and weak, while everyone else is normal and can do these things.

The only escape I have from the crazy house is walking the dogs or doing laundry with Bina, which we haul to the laundromat in a grocery cart. Every so often, Elaine trusts me with a small amount of money to pick something up at a grocery a few blocks away.

One day in mid-November, I come home from school and Elaine tells me she has good news. *I called my ma and sister and they said its okay for us to come visit, so you'll get to meet some more of your family.*

Each new family member I meet makes me feel as if I'm sinking deeper and deeper into the quicksand that is Herb and Elaine, and further from Mom and Dad. *What're they like?* I ask.

*My sister's okay, but Mom's a drunk.*

I sit at the dining room table to begin my homework. Herb isn't home from his job at the methadone clinic, and Bina is walking home with friends.

*They live in Hollywood, Florida, not THE Hollywood.* Elaine is sitting at the table with me and takes a long drag off a cigarette. *That's where I grew up, if ya didn't know.*

*I do.*

*Oh. I never liked my mother much, but my dad was something else. He owned a few nightclubs in Hollywood and hung out with guys in the mafia. He probably was in the mafia.*

Elaine is often a relentless fountain of disturbing information. She once told me she earned her GED in Attica prison and then prattled on about the ins and outs of prison life; she loved to talk about it. Another time, she told me how she got hooked on heroin.

Her favorite topic is her family. *Dad was a real character, ya know, and I loved him*—she takes a deep breath—*but he got cancer. He didn't want me to know about it or see him go through it. I was fifteen, so they sent me to boarding school up north.*

Elaine takes another long drag. *But I knew something had to be wrong. He wouldn't of sent me away. He loved me. So after a few months I snuck out of school and went home. We had a nice big house with a small front yard, Bermuda grass, coconut palms, a hedge of Spanish Stopper, that sort of thing. In the back were hibiscus, gardenia, key lime, and a grapefruit tree, a real nice place.*

*Anyway, I walked in and there's Dad with an oxygen tank and practically a pharmacy on the table next to him. He looked like crap. So he died. It seemed like a week or two later, after his funeral, I came home and found my mom screwin' some guy. She kept him around even after I told her he tried to get with me, too. She called me a liar.*

*Mom blamed me, of course, and we got in this huge fight so I packed my stuff up, I was sixteen, and left. Ended up in New York, started doin' smack, met your dad—*

I jut my lower jaw out. *He's not my dad.*

Elaine looks at me with her neck craned. *Whatever, you manipulative bitch. Anyway, you know the story. Life sucks then you die, right?* Elaine takes a drag off her cigarette and stamps it out in an overflowing ashtray. *The dogs need to go out. You're good at that, aren't ya?*

I put my pencil down and grab the dogs' leashes.

A few days later the phone rings in the afternoon and Elaine picks it up. *Hi Ma—*

After a bit, she says with one hand over the mouthpiece, *Say hello, Adrianne.*

I put the phone to my ear. *Hello?*

*Soooo, thith is my little granddaughter Adrianne,* she slurs. *I can't wait to see you*—the pitch of her voice rises as she speaks—*for our first ever Christmas tomorrow.*

*But Grandma, Christmas isn't for another month and we aren't coming for another two weeks.*

*What?*

Elaine grabs the phone from my hand. *Don't worry about it Ma,* she says, and frowns at me. *We can't wait.*

Two weeks later, early in the morning, Bina, Elaine and I take a taxi to the airport. Elaine pulls a wad of bills from her bra to pay the cabbie and off we go for my second plane ride.

When we get off the plane in Fort Lauderdale, Elaine's sister Joyce and her daughter Kim meet us at the gate. Joyce couldn't be more different than Elaine. She's two inches shorter, with a thin waist, rounded hips, modest bust, and red hair cut to shoulder length. She wears white Capri pants and a sleeveless powder-blue blouse. She has the odd habit of lifting her eyes when she speaks, as if she's trying to visualize the words in the air above her head.

Kim is her mother's daughter, though her outfit has a slight disco-esque flare to it.

We walk to the parking lot and I'm struck by how bright and warm the sun is and how green and exotic the plants are. It seems like magic that in a few hours we've gone from the cold gray winter of Brooklyn to a world of warmth, flowers and sun.

Elaine sits in the passenger seat of her sister's robin's-egg blue, wood-paneled station wagon. Bina and Kim sit in the back seat while—lucky me—I have the whole way-way-back foldout seat to myself. As she drives, Joyce points out projects her husband the engineer helped build. *Ooh, and he worked on that, and that.* She tilts her head back, *Bina, Adrianne; we can spend a day at the beach, too. It's sooo beautiful.*

Elaine bristles and pulls a cigarette from her purse.

*Please don't smoke, Lainey.*

I've never heard anyone call Elaine *Lainey,* so I turn to look.

*Jesus,* Elaine huffs.

Joyce's body stiffens. *Still keep your cash in your bra?*

Elaine shoots her a look, but doesn't say anything.

We pull into a small, U-shaped driveway in a neighborhood of identical large, single-story ranch houses. Joyce's is corn yellow with white trim on the outside. Inside, everything—the two couches and three easy chairs, television, tables, walls, everything—is bright white. I almost expect to hear the voice of HAL from "2001: A Space Odyssey" ask, *How was your trip?*

About an hour later, an orange Chevrolet Vega pulls up in front of the house. A tall woman, nearly six feet, with strong features and white hair, wearing black polyester pants and a sleeveless white blouse, steps out and wobbles toward the door in high-heeled sandals.

*You ready, Lainey?*

*As ready as I'll ever be.*

The two women go outside to meet their mother.

*Hi, Mother,* Elaine says.

*Why Lainey,* her mother says, holding both hands in the air so they flutter about her head like two birds, *you've put on weight. Where's that new granddaughter of mine?*

Bina, Kim and I watch from one of two windows framing the front door. Kim whispers, *There's Grandma in all her glory.*

The door opens and there she is, hands still flapping around her head. She pauses to look me over, *You look like one of us, so good for you. Come 'ere honey so I can give ya a smooch; you too, Bina.*

The women sit and chat on the back patio while Bina and Kim go for a walk. I sit and watch the ladies talk and drink gin and tonics. Every so often, small, thin lizards skitter by. I try to catch one, but Joyce says for me to leave them alone.

*They're stinky,* she says, wrinkling her nose.

Then Elaine's mom asks if she can take me to lunch tomorrow.

*What about Kim and Bina?* Elaine asks.

*Oh no, the two teenagers don't want to spend the day with an old bitty like me. Let them put their bikinis on and go to the beach to tease boys.*

*Whatever,* Elaine says.

I smile a little when Elaine says it's okay. The thought of getting away from Elaine for even a little while is nice. Who knows, maybe Elaine's mom will be fun.

The next morning, I keep walking past the windows on either side of the front door to look for the orange Vega. When it pulls up at eleven I'm more than ready to go.

*Hop in, honey,* she says. With a wave she lurches the car out into the street.

*Where are we going to eat?*

*Oh, a nice little place I know.*

Elaine's mom wears much the same outfit as the day before, with a white scarf to hold her hair in place. She is a bundle of energy that never stops talking about her four marriages, the failings of each man, how she fooled around on each of her husbands.

*Honey, a woman doesn't get any younger and there is soooo much out there; soooo much.* She looks over at me with a wink. Without any doubt, she is the source of the fountain of disturbing information that is Elaine.

We pull up at an old building with a stucco exterior that looks stolen from the Southwest. Above a green fabric awning are three big, red letters, *VFW*. Next to the letters is a red and gold cross with words in blue circling the center: *Veterans of Foreign Wars.* Three small windows face the street.

I follow Elaine's mom as she wobbles around to the side of the building, where there's a heavy glass door. She holds it open and says, *Come on in, honey.*

We walk into a large room with a handful of tables and chairs scattered around and a stage with a small rostrum up front. In the back of the room is a bar inhabited by four or five older men wearing military baseball caps and significant bellies. To one side of the bar is a swinging door that leads to a kitchen.

*Hey boys,* she yells, *this is my granddaughter Annie—*

Adrianne, I correct.

*Oh, Adrianne. Isn't she a beauty despite the glasses?* She leans down to my ear and waves her hand around my head. *Maybe we could do something about the hair.*

We walk up to the men at the bar and I say hello as Elaine's mom gives each a kiss and then nestles in among them. *Gin and tonic for me and do you think you could set the kid up with a sandwich or somethin'?* she says to the bartender.

*Yeah, of course,* the old guy behind the bar says.

She turns to me and leans down. *Adrianne, honey, go on into the kitchen and they'll fix you up somethin' while I chat with my buddies.*

As I'm eating my sandwich and chips in the kitchen I can hear her laughing out at the bar. After a couple of hours, she stumbles to the car and drives me back to Joyce's.

Back in Brooklyn, it's the Saturday before Christmas. I wake up early and pack a small bag, nothing too big or conspicuous, and sneak out of the apartment.

Because Herb and Elaine never take Bina and me anywhere, we've gotten good at finding our way around the city by ourselves. I take the subway to Penn Station and buy a ticket to Wantagh. As I board the train I feel a little bit like Huck Finn escaping down the Mississippi on a raft.

I look up at the conductor when he gets to my seat to see if he suspects anything, but he isn't looking at me. *You on your own,* the conductor says when he stamps my ticket.

*Yeah, I'm going home.*

*Where's home?*

*Wantagh.*

*Okay, I'll let you know when we get there.*

I hop off at Wantagh and wave back to the conductor. Everything is the same as I remember it. I can't believe I'm almost home. I'm so excited that I hurry as fast as I can and walk through the door at ten.

*Ady?*

*Dad, I'm home, I'm home.* I run into his arms. He holds me close and I can smell his aftershave and feel the warmth of his bear hug.

*Bea!* Dad yells, *Ady's home!*

Mom comes running into the kitchen. *Oh Ady, we've missed you so much.* She looks at Dad, then at me again. *How did you get here? Why are you here?*

*Aren't you proud I found my way all the way home from Brooklyn?*

*Yes, Ady,* Mom says. *But why? How?*

*I escaped, Mom. I got away from them and I don't ever want to go back.*

*Oh, jeeze Ady,* Dad says. His eyes water. *I'm so sorry honey, but I have to call them and tell them you're here.*

Head slung low, he calls Herb. *Yeah, she's here. So you did notice she's missing?*

While we wait for Herb I tell Mom and Dad what life is like. For the first time in a while I can speak to them directly. I look at Dad and tears never stop welling in his eyes. Mom keeps saying, *Oh, Ady,* and her eyes water too. I wish we could run away together, but we can't.

We are sitting in front of the only place I've ever known as home, but it isn't my home anymore. It's Mom and Dad's, Harry and Jeffrey's, but not mine. *I want this to be my home again,* I tell Mom and Dad.

Dad pulls me close. *This will never not be your home, Ady. I still believe, truly believe, we haven't reached the end yet.*

Hours after he said he would be there, Herb pulls up in his beat-up car, but this time I'm not waiting for him on the ledge.

Herb is furious. *You could've been killed.*

When we get to the apartment Elaine yells, *You manipulative bitch!* I can tell she wants to hit me, but won't because Herb is standing right there.

I go to my room and bury my face in a pillow. *If I can't escape, what can I do? Maybe if I'm just good it won't be so bad; she'll stop yelling or hitting me.*

I pick my face up off the pillow. I can feel its warmth from my tears and I look out the window into the street. Though we are two blocks from Coney Island Avenue, we live on a busy street. There are kids out playing while cars, buses and trucks rumble by. I watch as the kids play, laughing and looking happy. I want to be one of them.

Elaine comes into the room and slams the door shut. She stands, hands on hips, and looks at the closet I share with Bina. There are two rods with hangers, no door, and some clothes have fallen off the hangers.

*Where's Herb?* I ask.

*Out.*

*Out where?*

*I don't care.* She looks back to the closet. *Why are there clothes on the floor?*

*I don't know. They fell off the hangers.*

*Why didn't you pick them up? Why do you treat everything we get you like crap?*

*I don't.*

*Yes you do, you spoiled manipulative little bitch!* As she yells, spit flies from her mouth. She walks to the closet, grabs a wooden hanger and walks over to me. I cover my head and she starts to hit me with the hanger. *Whap! Whap! Whap!* Over and over. I feel the sting of the hanger on my side, my back, my stomach, any part of me that I can't cover with my hands.

*Stop, stop, please just stop, ow, please just stop, stop, ow, ow, ow—*

She points the hanger down at me.

*Don't push me!* She throws the hanger at me. *Pick these clothes up, you spoiled bitch!*

Each day I wake up in the crazy house. I walk to the prison. Then come home to the crazy house. I escape by walking the dogs, doing laundry, volunteering to run any errands, doing dishes, cleaning Bina's and my room, picking up around the apartment, anything to stay out of Elaine's way.

It doesn't work. She still hits me and calls me manipulative and spoiled, and complains that Mom and Dad ruined me. Herb still checks my homework and cuts it up to a bloody mess with his red pen and asks me why it's so hard for me to learn even simple things.

When I'm out I stop at a playground and press my face into the chain-link fence. The cold metal feels good against my skin. I spend as much time as I dare watching the other kids. I watch them play, talk, smile, laugh, run. I want to be one of them so much, it makes my heart ache.

When I'm home and not doing chores or homework, I stare out the window for hours, watching people on the street. I'm not lonely, precocious *Eloise,* a character from my favorite book, looking down on Central Park from the Plaza Hotel in Manhattan. I'm a lonely twelve-year-old girl in a world that is all too horribly real, looking out onto Avenue P and East 10th Street in Brooklyn of the mid-1970s. I'd do anything to be like the people I see walking by—free.

Spring comes, then summer. Life remains the same even as the seasons change and I turn thirteen. Then fall and another school year. Bina goes into ninth grade at Edward R. Murrow High School and I'm in eighth grade at PS 238. The red pen comes out from storage and Herb returns to being my schoolwork editor. Elaine is Elaine.

In November, I have a book report due the week before Thanksgiving that I must type. In Herb and Elaine's room there's an old, gray Remington-Rand typewriter. Elaine is out on a vague errand, something she has done frequently over the past few months, and won't be back for hours. Bina is in our room doing homework on her bed and Herb is working at the methadone clinic.

I walk into Elaine and Herb's bedroom, which reeks of cigarette smoke more than the rest of the apartment. Cigarette burns dot the bed. Elaine's stained and cigarette-burn-dotted nightgown lies across the bed. On a table in the corner is the typewriter.

I walk over to it and there's a sheet of paper in the spool. I pull the paper up so I can look at it:

*Dear Mr. Elroy Stark,*

*As you know I came to you some years ago seeking a respectable home for my son born in 1964. Perhaps you remember I was paid a sum of money for him by a family seeking a child. I'm not sure if this was some sort of black market arrangement or even if it was legal, but I would like to find my son so I can contact him. It seems to me that you would be interested in helping me with this so I don't have to go elsewhere for help.*

*Sincerely, Elaine Schoenowitz*

*Holy heck. Bina! Come 'ere!*
Bina wanders into the room. *What is it?*
*Look.*
She reads the letter. *Wow. I had no idea.*

*Neither did I. He's two years younger than me.*

*Yeah—*

*Do you think Herb knows?*

*I would imagine,* Bina says, rubbing her chin.

I pull the sheet out from the typewriter. *What are you doing?* Bina asks.

*I still need to type my essay.*

Bina picks the letter up, folds it and puts it in her pocket. *I'll take care of this.*

A couple of hours later, Herb walks through the door. He walks into the dining room and raises his eyebrows, which lifts his whole face in a tired, sad smile. Bina walks up to him and hands him the folded piece of paper. Herb looks at it as he walks into his bedroom and shuts the door.

I look at Bina and she looks at me. We both look at the door, but there's only silence.

Bina makes dinner and calls for Herb to come eat, but he says no. *Not hungry.*

Around nine, Elaine comes home. Her eyes sag and red veins map through the whites in jagged lines. She walks through the dining room and looks at Bina and me. We're on the couch watching TV. *Hi, girls.*

Neither of us says a word.

Elaine shrugs and walks into the bedroom and shuts the door.

Through the door we hear Herb: *Look at this.*

Silence.

*What about it?* Elaine bites back.

*We have a son out there somewhere? That you sold?*

Pause.

*I have a son that I got paid for when he was adopted.*

And it begins. Herb yells. Elaine yells. The two of them escalate.

*Where were you tonight? The other nights?*

*Out!*

*Out where?*

*Socializing!*

*With who?*

*Friends!*

*You don't have any friends.*

*Ta hell with you.*

*Who were you fucking tonight!*

*No one!*

Bina leaps from the couch and bursts into their room. *Stop it, just stop it!*

*Get out!* Elaine yells at her.

*Don't talk to her like that, Elaine.*

*I'll talk to her any damn way I want! Get out! Now!*

I hear Elaine move toward Bina and know she's going to hit her.

In a forceful, controlled voice, Bina says, *I hate you.* Then she strides hard out of their room to me and stops. Herb and Elaine are trying to yell over each other as Bina says, *You don't do anything when they fight.*

I don't know what to say because what I'm thinking feels so horrible. I'm not going to break it up because I'm praying that one will kill the other so I can go home.

The bedroom door flies open and Elaine tries to walk out, but Herb grabs her arm in the doorway and the two stumble into the hallway. Herb yanks Elaine's arm as his feet stutter one or two steps, then he hits Elaine in the jaw. The impact of his fist makes a sickening, dull thud as it meets her chin. His fingers come apart and his wrist goes soft with the impact.

Bina and I run to our room. From the corner of my eye I see Herb go to the kitchen and grab a knife. The punch slows Elaine for a moment, but she shakes it off and is yelling at Herb again. Bina and I close our door. There's a crash, like broken glass, and I hear Elaine run into their bedroom and slam the door shut.

Bina pounds on our door, screaming, *Stop it! Stop it! Stop it!*

Herb bangs on Elaine's and his bedroom door. *Let me in!*

Elaine screams, *Stay out, stay out!*

*Damn it, Elaine.* With almost the same speed that his anger escalated, it ebbs away. *Please Elaine, open the door so I can see if you're okay.*

I hear the door open. Bina waves at me to follow her then presses her finger across her lips, *Shhh.* We walk to Herb and Elaine's room, expecting to see Elaine lying dead. We look in and there's blood on the bed and floor. They're sitting on the bed and Herb is wrapping Elaine's arm with a towel.

*I need to take her to the hospital,* Herb tells us.

They stand together, with Herb holding her arm and the towel in place. Bina and I step out of their way as they pass.

Elaine looks at me and whispers, *I wonder who gave him that letter?*

Herb glances at Elaine and then me. He grabs his car keys and the two of them leave.

Maybe she'll die, I think. There's no way Elaine will tell the police because she knows if she did, I'd get to go home.

When Herb and Elaine come home, she has a few stitches and that's all. Herb is nervous; Elaine is angry.

The next afternoon Herb is at work and Elaine walks by me in the kitchen. Without a word she swings the back of her hand at my face, catching me right on my nose. A jolt of pain shoots up into my head, making my eyes water. I bring a hand to my nose and pull it away. There's blood on it.

Elaine hands me a paper towel. *Be more careful. And by the way, you don't go out of this apartment unless I say you can.*

I spend more time sitting by a window, watching people, people who are free, and I pray that someday it could be me. *Please, God, let me go home.*

Two days later, I've finished my homework, but Herb is still at work so I have to wait to show it to him. I'm sitting by a window in the living room watching people when Elaine hits me with the back of her hand, making my forehead slam into the window pane.

Bina stands up from the couch. *Don't do that again.*

*What?*

Bina takes a step back. *Don't hit her!*

Elaine steps toward Bina. *Don't tell me what to do,* she says, making a fist with her right hand.

Bina is tall and trim, fit and athletic, and quick. In an instant she leaps forward, hands up, and pushes Elaine with so much force that Elaine falls backward onto the floor near the couch. Elaine struggles to get up and holds the couch for support. Her cigarette-scorched lungs wheeze as she pulls her body up.

Before she can gather herself, we are in our room, door locked.

*Come out now.* Elaine pounds on the door. Bina leans her shoulder against the door so Elaine can't force it open. *I'm going to kill you two when I get my hands on you.*

I sit on my bed and watch Bina. I can't believe what she's done, what she's doing now, to fight Elaine and protect me. Why is Bina so brave when I am so scared? Why am I paralyzed with fear when Bina isn't? I envy her courage.

Elaine is beating on the door with all of her might. Like in a cartoon, the door bends open and looks like it will splinter any second. I don't know why, but Bina opens the door and Elaine walks in. Bina steps in front of her and Elaine trips her so that she falls to the floor.

Elaine's eyes are enraged slits, her fat body tensed with blind anger.

She turns to look at me. *You manipulative little bitch. Ever since you came into this house you've done nothing but screw our lives up. So you know what? That's what I'm gonna do to you. You're going to wish you were dead.*

*I already wish I were!* I yell at her. *All I want is to go home!*

Elaine takes a step forward and rears back her right fist.

*Elaine, what the hell are you doing?* Herb yells from behind her.

Bina rushes past Elaine and out the door to Herb. *Elaine hit Adrianne again!*

*Elaine, Jesus, stop. Do you hear? Stop.* Herb holds Bina around her shoulders. She's crying into his chest. Herb looks at me and then down at Bina. *I can't do this anymore, we gotta get out of here.*

*Then get the hell out,* Elaine yells.

I get up and walk past her, expecting that at any second she's going to backhand me in the head. I get to Herb and he leads us out the door to his car.

*Where are we going?* Bina asks.

*Friends,* is all he says.

The next morning Herb drops me off at school wearing the same clothes from the night before. He hands me a couple of dollars for lunch and says he'll pick me up after school. I didn't get much sleep, and I'm tired. Herb's friends are a couple whom he's worked with at the methadone clinic, but all they have to offer is a couch and floor.

What his plan is, I have no idea.

After school, we go back to Herb's friend's apartment and try to settle in. I have no idea if we'll be there long, but Herb tells me this will be our home for now. At evening, I hear the adults talking quietly while Bina and I do homework in the kitchen.

*Jesus, Herb, you have two teen girls,* the woman says.

*Yeah, what do you think you're going to do?* the man says.

*I don't know.* Herb's voice is soft and trails off.

*They don't even have clothes or anything,* the woman says.

*I know, I know,* Herb says. *I gotta get them their things, okay. I get it.*

He walks into the kitchen, his eyebrows lift his face in a half smile. *Let's go, girls, we've gotta grab a few things.*

*Where are we going now?* Bina asks as we climb into the car.

*You'll see.*

Herb pulls the car up into the driveway in front of the apartment.

He turns to us and gives each a large, black garbage bag. *Okay, we go in, grab clothes and whatever stuff we can and then get the hell out as fast as we can. Got it?*

*Yeah,* Bina and I both say.

The three of us walk up the steps to the door and Herb knocks.

*Is that you, you God damned coward?* Elaine yells from inside.

*Let us in!* he yells.

*Piss off.*

*I mean it, Elaine, let us in.*

*PISS OFF!*

*One last time, Elaine, let us in!*

*P-I-S-S O-F-F!*

*All right girls,* Herb says, waving one hand at us to move, *stand back a little bit.*

He takes a few steps back and kicks the door down like you see in the movies. The door splinters and the latch and deadbolt fly off. I can't believe this is my life.

*Don't you dare!* Elaine yells, but it's too late. Herb's rushing through the door and pushing her out of the way.

*Go girls!* he yells as he runs at Elaine.

Elaine rushes into the kitchen yelling, *I'm going to kill you, you son of a bitch,* and grabs a large knife.

Herb is right behind her and grabs the thing nearest him, a broom. He waves it at Elaine, yelling, *Go girls, go. Grab as much as you can!*

Elaine slashes at Herb with the knife as he jabs the bristles of the broom into her face to prod her back into a corner of the kitchen.

Bina and I run into our room and grab whatever clothes we can carry and anything else we might need. I start to run out the door, but remember and go back for my floral overnight case. Bina pushes me through the door and we run past Herb, who looks like a rodeo clown trying to avoid the horns of an enraged bull.

*I'll kill you!* Saliva spews from Elaine's mouth, and her face, normally a dull yellow, is florid.

Bina and I run out the door and Herb hops backward as he pokes Elaine in her face with the broom. He reaches the door and pulls it shut. *Run!*

The three of us fly down the steps and out the door with Elaine chasing us in her housecoat, screaming profanities. We jump into the car—Bina and me in the back—and Elaine slams into the passenger side. She grabs hold of the inside door handle through the open window. Herb guns the engine and we speed off dragging Elaine, until she can't hold on any longer and is left lying in the street, yelling at us.

A few blocks away Herb eases his foot off the gas. Sweat drenches his body and he wipes his face with his hand. He looks at Bina and me in the back.

*Well girls, that was something,* he says, and lets out a nervous laugh.

Bina smiles. *Yeah, I guess.*

I smile, but think, *Please God, let me go home now.*

God and Herb have different plans.

Herb is doing his best, but it's not enough and he knows it. Staying with his friends in their tight apartment will work for only a short while and Herb is desperate to find a long-term solution, a home for the three of us. We look at apartments, but there are few he can afford without Elaine's welfare check.

One night, I ask if I can call Mom and Dad and Herb reluctantly says okay. Even though Herb is listening in, I tell them we've escaped from Elaine.

*Oh Ady,* Mom says, *where are you staying?*

I look up at Herb. His eyes are wide. His eyebrows can no longer make his face rise up in a smile. Instead, his face sags.

*We're looking for an apartment now, but it's hard, Mom.*

Herb looks down into his lap.

*So where are you staying?* Mom says, her voice a bit more insistent.

Herb raises his eyes toward me.

*Friends of Herb's, for now.*

*Oh my, Ady.*

Dad breaks in on the other line. *What about Elaine? Is she trying to get you back?*

*I don't think she is,* I say. *I don't know what she's doing.*

Herb raises his head. *Time for dinner, Adrianne.*

*I have to go.*

*Ok, Ady,* Dad says. *I love you, little doll.*

*Love you too,* I say.

*Love you, Ady,* mom says.

*Love you too.*

I hang up the phone and Herb looks up at me. His eyes are soft. For the first time since he came into my life, I feel like there is truth behind his eyes.

*I'm doing my best, Adrianne,* he says.

*I know, but I want to go home. Please can I go home?*

*I'm your dad, Adrianne,* Herb says, *and your home is with me.*

Two weeks later, Herb rents a small, dingy furnished apartment. There's a tiny bathroom, kitchenette and tiny living room-type space, and one bedroom. Herb sleeps on a small, stained couch while Bina and I share the bedroom. Cockroaches run across the floor and scatter whenever a cupboard is opened. We can hear them and mice moving in the walls at night, but the apartment's close enough to our school that we can walk and the neighborhood isn't so bad.

Still, neither Bina nor I have any idea what his plan is.

The next morning I walk to school, but have to pass the old apartment. I cross the street so I don't walk past the front door. I'm scared Elaine may leap out and grab me. After school, I walk past the apartment again and Elaine is on the front stoop.

*Adrianne, wait!* she calls. *I have something to show you!*

People look at me and I wonder if they know about Elaine and the big fight or that I've escaped her with Herb and Bina. Elaine rushes up the stairs and then a moment later reappears on the stoop with the broom Herb used to fend her off.

*Look what I got for Herb!* She holds up the broom and there's a knife taped to the handle.

A few people look at Elaine and then me. I look away from them, scared, and walk as fast as I can back to the apartment.

When I get there, Bina isn't back from school and Herb is still at work, so I go to the lone window and look out onto the street. It's a different view, but my feelings are the same: I want to be free in my mind and body, and I want to be free from fear.

The weeks between Christmas and Thanksgiving used to be the longest of the year. There is an exquisite agony to waiting for Christmas when you're a kid, but not this year. Time moves quickly, too quickly and days feel like they're bunching up on us.

When Christmas break starts Bina and I are happy to be free of school, but feel no joy at spending the break in our apartment. Then on Christmas Eve, Herb gets the mail and there're progress reports from school. I'm not doing well and neither is Bina. She's failing a couple of classes and there's a note saying she's missed school on more than a few days. Herb is beside himself.

He calls his mother and asks if we can live with her. She says yes, but when he calls the local school district to ask what he needs to enroll us, a woman tells him our mother will have to sign a permission form.

When Herb asks Elaine, she says, *No God damn way.*

That night, Herb takes Bina and me out to a diner. A light snow falls. Most of the stores and apartments have Christmas lights in the windows. Every so often we pass a plastic Santa with a red cheery face, bag of presents slung over one shoulder and hand held up in a wave, standing in a tiny patch of yard. Lights are strung on some streetlight poles and an occasional tree. It's not what I remember in Wantagh, but it's pretty.

*I gotta tell you something,* Herb says when we sit down. *This isn't workin'. We can't go to Florida and this apartment's no good for us.*

Both Bina and I look at him. It's chilly, but he's sweating and his head bobs. He wipes his face with one hand and lets it remain on his forehead, eyes closed.

*I love you two so very much.* His voice breaks. *But I can't keep you, not like this.*

Bina looks at me. *What does that mean? Can I live with Grandma?*

The features on Herb's face, his forehead, eyebrows, eyes, cheeks, lips, and chin, all melt. *No sweetie, your mother says she won't allow it.*

Bina's body stiffens. *So where are we gonna live?*

His eyes open and drift down to the Formica tabletop. *You'll have to go back to your mother, but just for a little while, until I can sort things out for us.*

*What?* Bina says.

I feel my body stiffen and then release, as if I'm sinking into the diner's vinyl bench.

*It'll only be for a little while, until I sort things out.*

*How long?* Bina asks.

*I don't know. I'll do my best.*

*She won't let me live with Grandma?*

*No, Bina, she won't.*

*What about Adrianne?*

Herb looks at me and then at Bina. His eyes narrow. *No, Bina. I told you, we're a family and I'll get it all sorted out for us, okay?*

*How did that experiment work out for ya?* Elaine says as we walk back into the apartment. Her eyes are sunken and her skin is sallow.

Bina and I walk into our room, which is still dumped out from when we broke in. I drop my small, floral suitcase onto the bed and Bina flicks the light switch, but the light doesn't come on.

*The bulb in here burned out,* Bina calls to Elaine.

*It's not burned out,* Elaine says. *No electricity.*

Elaine is lost without Herb. Her life has no structure, nor does she have any income other than welfare and whatever money she manages to pick up. I don't ask her where her money comes from, but I assume Herb wasn't too far off the mark in his comment after finding the letter in the typewriter.

Herb comes by for New Year's Eve and there is a tense peace between the two of them. Afterward he visits when he can. Elaine disappears for hours at a time and sometimes is gone overnight or even for a few days. When she returns, there is something different about her. She's a bit more up and relaxed, but it fades until she disappears again.

When she's home, Elaine ignores Bina, but still goes after me verbally and physically. She's stuck on calling me a manipulative little bitch and I learn to stay in my room when she's home. Otherwise, I have no idea when she'll smack me across my head or face with the back of her hand. There's never any warning or reason for it.

I do my homework, but not with the same effort as when I knew Herb would check on it. I still do the laundry in a laundromat down the block by wheeling the clothes back and forth in a shopping cart. There is dog poop on the floor all the time so I clean it when I find it and walk the dogs as often as Elaine lets me. I also empty the kitty litter and do what I can to keep the apartment clean.

None of it buys any sympathy from Elaine. Nor does it ease my constant fear.

In late February Elaine walks into my room, where I'm looking out the window at the people in the street.

*What did I tell you about hanging your clothes on a hanger?* Elaine wobbles and her skin has a yellow hue. She takes a long pull from a cigarette.

I look at the closet and there are some dirty clothes piled at the bottom. Bina isn't home from school.

*What did I tell you about leaving clothes on the floor!*

*I'm sorry. I'll pick them up.*

*Damn right you will.* Elaine walks toward me.

*Please, no,* I cry.

Elaine winds up and hits me hard, and again, and again, and again until her arm's too tired to swing at me.

*You listen to me, ya hear!* Then she walks out into the living room, puts a coat on and leaves.

My arms, belly and legs are red and welted. Bruises begin to form. I take a shower, hoping it will help the pain, but purple bruises blotch my body. The skin is broken in a few places.

When Bina comes home I show her, but beg her not to say anything to Elaine. I don't want her angrier at me than she already is and I don't want to see another fight between her and Bina.

The next day at school I cover my body as best as I can, but after I take off my coat my homeroom teacher walks up to me.

*Adrianne, are you okay?*

I don't know what to say so I look away from her. She places a hand on my shoulder and gently turns me. Across my neck and down along my arm is a deep, black bruise.

*Adrianne, who did this to you?*

*Elaine.*

*You mean your mother?*

I nod.

Soon after, a woman comes into class and whispers with my teacher. She's young with red hair and a modest-size pregnant belly beneath a plaid wool dress and leggings. As she speaks, one hand rests on her belly.

The woman walks to me and leans over as if she's trying to bend her body around the baby in her womb.

*Adrianne,* she whispers, *I'm Mrs. Whorley. Can we talk?*

I nod and follow her out of the classroom, down the hall, and into a small office. There're two chairs on one side and her desk on the other. She sits in her desk chair, rubbing her belly, and I sit in the seat.

*You're pregnant, right?* I ask.

*Yes, I am.*

I can't move my eyes from the round, taut bump in her stomach. *When are you going to have it?*

*Not for another four months.* Mrs. Whorley smiles and looks at me, head tilted. *Adrianne, you have a pretty big bruise on your neck and shoulder.*

I nod.

*And your teacher tells me your mother did this to you?*

I nod.

*Your teacher also tells me things have been rough for you lately?*

I look up from her belly. *What do you mean?*

*Well, she noticed you've not been very happy and your school work isn't as good as it used to be.*

I nod and look back to her belly.

*And she says you've lost a lot of weight, you're very thin, and often very tired.*

It hadn't occurred to me that people could see these things, or that anyone was looking.

*I'd like to see if I can help you.* She leans down a little to look into my eyes. *You're such a pretty girl, Adrianne. Could you tell me how you got that horrible bruise?*

Mrs. Whorley's plaid, round bump draws my eyes again. I'd never been so close to a pregnant woman before and the whole thing is such a mystery to me. My mom never carried me in her belly, but she loves me so much.

I look up into Mrs. Whorley's eyes. They're expectant, hopeful; her hand rubs her belly. There's love in her gentle touch.

Her plaid dress stretches over the bump, which moves slowly, like a napping baby bundled beneath a blanket.

Mrs. Whorley smiles. *She's just started doing that.*

*You know it's a girl?*

*No, I just think it is, I guess.*

*Okay.*

*Okay, what?*

*I'll tell you about me.*

My story begins like a mist, but soon develops into droplets and becomes a torrent.

When I finish, Mrs. Whorley reaches out a hand—the other still rubs her belly—and places it on my wet cheek. *I'm going to do what I can to help you, Adrianne.*

What I don't know is that Bina is sitting in an office like Mrs. Whorley's telling a counselor like Mrs. Whorley our story. When Bina finishes, the woman makes the same promise and says she's going to call child services.

*Can I speak to my dad?* Bina asks.

The woman says yes and when Bina tells Herb what's happening he says, *Whatever you do, don't let child services take you.*

Mrs. Whorley and the other counselor talk and they do call child services, but we aren't taken away. Instead, they and child services confront Elaine and tell her they will remove us from her home, one way or another.

*Fine,* Elaine says. *They can go, but there is no way Adrianne can go to the Cahns or Bina to her grandmother's.*

*Mrs. Schoenowitz, you don't have much say in this. You realize that,*
*don't you?*

*Listen you, I know what say I have and I know I can get a lawyer and be*
*a major pain in your ass, or not.*

*Where would you like them to go?*

*I don't care.*

That night, Elaine tells us to just forget about living wherever we want.

*Why can't I go to Grandma's!* Bina yells.

In a quiet voice spoken at the same time as Bina, I tell Elaine, *I just want*
*to go home.* I'm tired of being afraid.

Elaine puts one hand on a hip and raises the middle finger of her other
hand at us, *Agency kids can't go wherever they want.*

It is beyond Herb to take care of us, but he is able to get friends of his
in upstate New York, the Breens, to take us. Elaine doesn't care. Her victory
in all of this is keeping Bina and me from living with people we love.

A few days after speaking with Mrs. Whorley, I'm sitting in the front
seat of Herb's car with Bina in the back, going to the Breens. I'm excited to
be away from Brooklyn and Elaine, but nervous to be with a whole new
family, again.

*Don't worry,* Herb says. *They're nice, not like city people. They do a lot of*
*sports and activities like that.*

Great, another home where I'm no good at what everyone else wants
to do.

After about an hour, we pull off the New York Thruway and drive for
another thirty minutes or so before turning into a tightly packed neighborhood of modest houses. We climb out of the car and Mr. and Mrs. Breen

come out. I hold my floral suitcase in front of me when we say hello.

Herb spends some time chatting, but before too long he says he has to leave.

He walks outside with Bina and me and gives each of us a hug and kiss. *Be good.*

*We will,* Bina says.

Herb starts to walk to his car, but turns. *You know, your mother's either going to be dead or in jail within six months.*

Neither Bina nor I say anything.

*See you girls soon.* And he leaves.

Four months after leaving us with the Breens, Herb calls.

*Your mother's dying.*

*What of?* I ask.

*Liver failure, of all things. I always thought she'd overdose.*

I feel nothing when he tells me this, other than the same, deep longing to go home. Life with the Breens is far, far better than with Herb and Elaine, but I don't fit. This isn't home and they aren't Mom and Dad or Jeffrey and Harry.

Two days later, Herb calls. *She's dead.*

I grip the phone. *Please, now can I go home?*

Before Herb can answer, Mrs. Breen, a large, direct and self-confident woman says, *Let me speak to him, honey.*

I sit on a chair and listen to her tell Herb, *I love you, but it's time to do the right thing. You've got to let go of this girl.*

*Let me sleep on it.*

*No Herb. I know you, you'll avoid it. Do the right thing for Adrianne, Herb. Let her go home.*

*Are you saying you don't want her anymore?*

Mrs. Breen looks at me. *No, of course not. Herb, Elaine's dead, there's no way you can take care of her. Let her go home.*

I hear Herb's voice break. *All right, all right, yes, okay. She can go to the Cahns if they'll have her.*

Two days after that, Herb and I pull up in front of my home.

*I did my best, Adrianne.*

*I know.*

His eyes tear and his body shakes as he reaches out with both arms and hugs me. *I love you so much.*

I look to the front door, which opens. Dad is the first through it, followed by Mom and Harry and Jeffrey. Herb follows my eyes; his mouth slackens. Mom and Dad, the four of them, stop near the ledge I spent so much time sitting on, waiting for Herb and Elaine.

Herb looks back at me and wipes his eyes. *I really do love you so much, Adrianne.*

I look up into his eyes. There is truth behind them. *I know, but this is my home.*

*Okay.* Herb reaches across me to open the door.

I step out to grab my floral suitcase from the back seat and look at Herb. He turns to look at me. Then I pull the suitcase out, slam the door and run to my family.

Mom reaches her arms out to me. I drop the suitcase and fly into her arms as they pull me in.

*Oh Ady, my baby is home, my baby is finally home!*

Wrapped in her arms, I hear the rattle of the engine start and Herb pull away.

৩৵৩

That night we're in the car coming home from Kwong Ming, where Dad's had them sing Happy Birthday to me. My birthday still isn't for a couple of months.

*Hey Dad,* Jeffrey calls from the backseat, where I'm snuggled between him and Harry. *So who's your favorite?*

*Favorite what?* Dad calls back.

*Favorite kid.*

*Ady, of course.*

*Welcome home party*

*College graduation with my parents*

# JOHNNY:
# HITTING BOTTOM

*A person falls into a hole. A priest says three Hail Marys.*
*A doctor sends down a prescription.*
*A friend goes down into the hole.*

—Overheard by Johnny at an AA meeting

cidic bile rises up into the back of my throat, which is dry and jagged from smoking. My head pulses with pain. An ache suffuses the marrow of my bones.

Sleep eases from me, but I wake up into an alcohol-fueled torment twenty-five years in the making. My fingers are pudgy, inflamed little stumps. The gout—my God, I can't believe I have gout—feels as if some cruel imp is jabbing knitting needles into the joint of the big toe on my left foot. It is freezing cold outside, one of the coldest stretches ever in the Midwest. My house is chilly but my face feels florid and hot.

I rub my eyes with the heels of my palms, hoping that if I grind them hard enough the pressure will force the poison from them and my head might at least clear up. Lights flash inside my eyes. Bile rises with more force.

I turn my body on the couch so I can reach a small rubbish bin. On the coffee table, kicked at an angle to the couch, there's one lone unopened can of beer. It stands among fifteen or twenty empty red-and-white cans scattered around the coffee table and floor. From my angle on the couch, the tableau looks like a perverse shrine.

My stomach roils and twists as I reach a shaking hand toward the can of beer. I open it and, in one long draft, kill it. I swing my legs around as my stomach reacts to the first waking assault of alcohol and the blackness of its contents spills out into the rubbish bin.

It's the morning of January 4th, 1999. My mother died eighteen years ago at age forty-seven, an appalling drunk to the end. I'm forty and two weeks ago I ate what I believe will be my last meal—lamb, potatoes, and broccoli.

I see no reason to do anything other than drink.

The day I took my first drink is the day my life started spiraling out of control. It was slow at first, barely noticeable, but alcoholism is a progressive disease. It's like a storm gaining strength, spinning faster and faster, its center tightening and accelerating, pulling me deeper into it, away from life.

I've been powerless in its grip for years, but since shortly before Christmas, I exist within a surreal world of physical pain and emotional torment. I am completely under the influence of this disease.

Though it's been long in coming, I'm not sure what sparked this final fall.

Is it memories of long-past Christmases that overwhelm me each year?

Or maybe the spark was Dad and Celeste walking into my home on my birthday—December 17th—to plead with me to stop drinking?

*Go to hell,* I said.

Dad hadn't taken his coat off. *Okay, Johnny. I'm here if you need me.*

Perhaps it was my last call to Margaret, a few nights before Christmas?

*Hello,* she said. Her voice was tired and faint.

*It's Johnny, Margaret.* My tongue was inept, unable to manage words and sentences without elongating and contorting them.

*Oh, Johnny.* I heard bed sheets riffle as she sat up. *Do you know what time it is?*

*I don't know, midnight?*

*Yeah, Johnny, it's after midnight.*

*I just wanted to hear your voice.* I felt my face flush and my eyes were wet and itchy. I ground my fist hard into my knee.

*Johnny, I'm married and it's time for you to grow up.*

*I just wanted to talk.*

*I can't do this. You have a problem and need help.*

*Come on, Margaret. Don't be like this.*

*Johnny, please, please don't be this guy.*

*What guy?*

*The guy who calls old girlfriends late at night, drunk. You have to stop.*

I imagined putting a gun to my head, pulling the trigger, and the sensation of instantaneous blackness.

*Okay. I love you,* I said, and hung up.

The next morning I woke up on the tile floor in the kitchen. A vague outline of the call to Margaret formed in my head and I began to cry.

I pulled myself up and opened the refrigerator door. Week-old left-over lamb sat uncovered on a plate. It was bluish gray. Next to the plate were two cans of beer. I grabbed one, drained it, then raced to the toilet to throw up.

I grabbed the last beer from the fridge and was sitting in the living room, trying to pull myself together enough to buy more beer at the package store down the street, when the phone rang.

*Johnny, it's Lisa.*

*Merry Christmas.*

*Merry Christmas, Johnny. Look—*

*Your house full yet?*

*Not yet. Johnny, I gotta say something.*

I drained half the beer. *What?*

*I don't want you to come tonight.*

*You're not having your party?*

*We're having the party, but I don't want you to come.*

*Did Margaret call you?*

*What? No. Why would she call me?*

*I don't know.*

*Johnny, I don't want you to come because you're going to get drunk and cause a scene and I just don't want it in my house. Not anymore. Between you and Mom, I've had enough.*

Tears welled in my eyes. My hands and body shook as I brought the beer can to my lips.

*I'm sorry, Johnny.* There was a break in her voice, a slight catch.

*You know what? I'll eat at the club.*

My house—a small brick colonial in Kirkwood, a few miles from Ladue—is in foreclosure and the bank repossessed my car a few weeks ago.

I'm months behind on child support and haven't paid taxes in three years. Yet, I still have my five-hundred-dollars-per-month membership to the club.

*I love you, but I can't do it anymore. Goodbye.*

*Lisa?*

After Lisa's call, I dedicate myself to the slow suicide of addiction. I drink. I cry. I sleep. I drink. I cry. I sleep. Pain throughout my body, night sweats, unceasing shakes, and vomiting punctuate the routine. It is an out-of-body experience where there is no hope, as I surrender to the disease and fade into it.

Johnny Lipscomb no longer exists. Alcohol has subsumed my identity, my life, everything. There are no sober moments. I have fallen into a deep, dark hole. My mind and body rise from unconsciousness into painful, formless, floating delirium, crying because I hate who I've become, but I'm powerless to stop, to keep my head above the waters.

I am emotionally, spiritually and physically dead.

For twenty years or more I have flailed at the water as I drowned. I wanted to live, but refused to learn how to swim. I've pushed away anyone who's tried to save me, who wanted to reach in and pull me to safety. And I ignored those who so long ago offered their love.

There is the faint murmur of Lizzy: *I love you as much as a kitten loves cream, John David, but don't let the devil get into you. You keep the devil away, everything'll be all right.*

And Mrs. Tice: *In your heart, you're a good kid; kind and gentle. Let that be who you are and you'll be all right.*

I haven't kept the devil from me, nor have I let the good kid determine the man I've become. I sit on my couch drinking and sobbing because I've failed those who love me most. My loudest wails and greatest despair is for the young son and daughter who've escaped me for all the same reasons I wanted to escape mother.

Coiling in and around my bottomless self-pity like a snake, is anger. I am angry at mother for thinking alcohol was more important than me. I am angry to have been born into a family of willful drowning victims; people who accepted slow death rather than reach for life. I am angry at every person who failed me (in my confusion, the list is long). I am angry at those who are no longer alive and available for me to berate.

As I sit on my couch, stewing, I am most angry at Mary. An ardent and committed alcoholic, she is the woman with whom I had the affair that ended my marriage and led to the loss of my children; the woman whose capacity for physical abuse is written in the scars on my body, and the last woman to abandon me.

It's the evening of January 4th.

My hand shakes uncontrollably from delirium tremens as I reach for the phone. The answering machine blinks an angry red number that I can't quite make out. Holding the phone as steady as I can, I'm careful as I press each number.

*Hello?* The voice on the other end of the line is soft, reassuring, maternal.

Deep in my memory a faint signal reaches through the noise . . . *In your heart, you're kind and gentle . . .*

*Hello, Mrs. Godfrey. It's me, Johnny.*

All I have is Mary's parents' number.

*Johnny, are you okay?*

*Is Mary there?*

*No, Johnny, she's not.*

*I need to speak with her.*

*You don't sound so good, Johnny. I'm worried about you.*

Like vibrations along a taut string disappearing into the mist, these words connect me to my better self.

*You've always been good to me,* I tell her.

*Mary's father and I love you, Johnny.*

I wipe tears from my eyes with the back of my hand. I feel the beer can I'm holding brush against my hair.

*I love you, too.*

My trembling hand brings the can of beer to my lips.

*Johnny, are you drinking?*

*Yes, Mrs. Godfrey, I am.*

*Are you okay?*

*No, ma'am, I'm not.*

*Johnny, Dr. Godfrey and I haven't been able to help Mary, but maybe we can help you.*

*I'm beyond help.*

*If I make an appointment for an interview at a place that helps people like you, will you go?*

I lay my hand with the phone on my lap and push the fingers of my other hand into my forehead. The beer can presses against the side of my face. I'm sweating and squeezing my eyes so hard that luminescent waves pass before them.

*Johnny?*

I bring the phone to my ear.

*Yes, Mrs. Godfrey.*

*Yes, what?*

*Yes, I'll go.*

The morning of January 5ᵗʰ starts much the same as the days before. I wake up on my couch. A nest of empty beer cans surrounds me. The ashtray is full to overflowing. It's cold inside the house. Just to get my mind and shivering, shaking body moving toward some sense of equilibrium I drink a beer, wretch, then drink two more.

I don't know why I said I would go to this damn appointment.

I respect her. So I suppose that's enough to get up off the couch, pull on my coat and drag myself out into air that is so cold, it hurts my face. I toss three beers into my dented and rust-spotted red truck. In the bed are tools for installing the DogWatch hidden dog fences I sell.

Two beers are for the ride there and one for the ride back with a stop for a couple more cases and maybe some wine, or better yet, vodka, in honor of Mom.

The engine is slow to turn over. In the foot-well of the passenger seat is a pile of beer cans, half crushed, and tossed aside. The ashtray is over-flowing. I wind the window down and dump it out on the side of my street as I pull away.

I open a beer and take a long sip, then set it between my thighs. The heat starts to blow through the vents, but my body can't stop shaking. I take another pull from the beer.

Edgewood, the rehabilitation center where Mrs. Godfrey set up the appointment, isn't far. Twenty minutes on a normal day, but in the cold and fearful of speeding, I take an extra five minutes to get there.

The tools in the bed rattle as I pull into the parking area. I step out of the truck and kill the last of the second beer, crumple the can, and toss it into the truck. It lands next to the last full beer.

Heat blows from a vent as I walk through the automatic doors into the building. Then there is noise. I look into a large room near the entrance and some twenty to thirty people are laughing, hugging, smiling, and talking loudly to be heard above the din.

I have no idea what the hell this is.

There's a bathroom a few feet away. I duck into it and splash warm water over my face. Looking into the mirror, I don't recognize the man with black eyes looking back at me. He's bloated, shaking, sweaty, and his skin and the whites of his eyes are sallow, jaundiced. My breath is stale and smells of beer and cigarettes.

I shake my hands off in the sink. *This is horrible,* I say to myself. *I want out.* My body already needs more alcohol. The pain of that need is sharp, and aches into my chest and bones.

I walk down the hall to where a large sign says INTAKE. There is a window and a woman opens the glass.

*I'm Johnny Lipscomb. I have an appointment.*

*Take a seat.*

In a moment a middle-aged doctor with salt-and-pepper hair and wearing a white coat, greets me and guides me into an exam room.

*Why are you here?* He leans back in his seat. His eyes narrow. He looks me up and down.

*A friend is worried about me so I said I would come and get checked out.*

*What is she worried about?*

*My drinking?*

*Are you worried about your drinking?*

*I suppose.*

*Have you been drinking today already?*

*No,* I lie.

He looks at me for a moment. Then he asks me to roll my sleeve up to take my blood pressure.

*Your blood pressure's sky high. Did you know that?*

*No.*

He checks my pulse.

*Your pulse is racing. If you don't do something about this, you're going to have a stroke or heart attack soon.*

The pain of no alcohol becomes panic as I realize my beer, my last beer, will freeze in the truck if I stay much longer.

*How soon? Today?*

*Soon.*

He hands me a three-page form and asks me to fill it out. There are twenty-one questions and I answer yes to all twenty-one.

The doctor looks at the form for a moment, then to me. *I'm probably not telling you anything you don't already know, but you have a serious drinking problem. If you don't do something about it, you won't live much longer.*

There isn't any emotion behind his words. His tone is flat. His attitude and bearing is of an expert stating an obvious fact.

My brain and body are screaming for me to run away. Get to that beer before it's too late and go to the store and drink this away. I feel sicker than when I walked in and my shaking intensifies to near convulsing as my body warms with anxiety, embarrassment and fear.

*Okay.* I squeeze my hands so tight that my fingers are white.

*We need to check you in.*

*When? Tomorrow? A week?*

*Right now, Mr. Lipscomb. I can't compel you to enter our program, you have to agree to it, but if you walk out that door I'm afraid I'll never see you again.*

*Can you do something to stop the shaking?*

*We can help.*

*Okay, but please, I'm begging you; I'll do anything if you could just stop the shaking.*

An hour later, I'm in a hospital room in the basement, detoxing. The pain is unreal. The shaking won't stop, even though the doctor gave me Librium. The drug makes me feel like I'm in even more of a haze. I'm tired, but can't sleep. Every muscle in my body twitches, I'm damp from sweating so much, and my stomach is cramping.

*If this doesn't get better soon, I'm out of here,* I say to myself.

I lie in bed almost twitching, the shaking is so bad. All I want to do is leave, but I'm too afraid to get up and walk out. I clench the under-sheet with my hands and literally hold on for dear life. I look at the clock and it says 1:32. Then I clench the sheet harder. I squeeze my eyes shut and it feels as if my entire body is pulsing. Every muscle can't stop trembling, and yet I am so damn tired.

*For God's sake, why can't I sleep?*

I look back to the clock and it says 1:34.

Adding to the stress is my roommate. His name is JR and he's going through drug detox. He's in his mid-thirties, tall and lean, with a wisp of straight black hair that hangs across his eyes. He pushes it back like a tic as he paces back and forth, muttering to himself. He's like Lizzy, only he's white, male, and an addict.

*What are you here for?* I ask.

He turns and looks at me, but keeps pacing and muttering. I ask again and he still doesn't respond. I try once more.

*I work, I should say I worked, because there's no way that guy's ever going to have me back, so I worked for a veterinarian, I love animals and that's something that isn't germane to why I'm here, but is very germane to who I am, but I'm here because I found out that the doggie downers we had at the clinic are really great to shoot up, but now, apparently, they are absolute hell to come down off of, so if I stop walking or have to answer another question too soon I'm not going to do it because the only thing that helps with this absolutely miserable pain is to keep moving because, God damn it, if I could sleep I would, but every muscle in my body is twitching like it's connected to some sort of electrode.*

*Me too,* I say.

I keep my body pressed flat into the bed and hold onto the sheet for dear life. JR looks down at me, eyes wide, his face burning and fevered.

*You too, what?*

*My muscles twitch too.*

*Doggie downers?*

*No, alcohol.*

*Got it. Can't stop, can't talk.*

He goes back to pacing. I shut my eyes tight.

Every hour a nurse comes in to take my vitals. I see worry in their eyes and wonder if they'll just send me to a hospital ICU unit.

Every so often a doctor or counselor comes into the room. He asks how I'm doing and then asks me why I'm here.

*Mrs. Godfrey asked me to do it.*

*Why did she ask you to come here?*

My body is bloated, sweaty, yellow and the DTs cause me to rattle. *Dunno. I drink too much.*

*Would you say you're an alcoholic?*

*Yes.*

*Okay, then you're in the right place.*

After he leaves I lie flat in bed, shaking and sweating, swearing that if it doesn't get better I'm going to walk out of here and buy a bottle and a case of beer.

I'm exhausted, but don't sleep. The Librium makes consciousness distant, like looking down a tube through a cloud. My body aches and my muscles twitch. I can't find a position where I am not in pain. I can't stop shaking. I hold on to the bed for dear life.

Late at night, consciousness fades and I lapse into a state that is neither awake nor asleep, but is restful.

*Mr. Lipscomb, time for me to take your vitals.*

The soft voice is unwelcome.

*How are you?* She wraps a blood pressure cuff around my arm and starts pumping it up.

*Not great. If things don't get better, I'm outta here.*

*There's an AA meeting this morning you could go to.*

*Alcoholics Anonymous?*

*Uh huh.* She unwraps the cuff. *Your blood pressure is still very high.* She grabs my wrist to take my pulse.

*I feel horrible.*

*Well, we aren't allowed to give you any stimulants—that includes coffee— but if you go to the meeting they have coffee and maybe a donut or muffin, something like that.*

*I think I'll try it.*

An hour later I walk upstairs in a bathrobe and hospital socks and go into the room I'd passed the day before. There are the same twenty or thirty people and they are laughing and hugging each other.

I walk toward the table with coffee and donuts. As I pass small groups of two or three people, they smile and say welcome.

A guy says, *One day at a time,* and pats me on the back.

I overhear a woman say, *The definition of an alcoholic is an egomaniac with an inferiority complex.* The two men beside her smile and look down at their shoes. They've heard that one a lot.

Another man says, *I'm glad to see you made it today.*

My hands shake so much I have difficulty holding a Styrofoam cup steady and pumping the coffee dispenser. An older woman, in her mid-fifties, says, *Let me do that.*

I look at her. She has untamed, gray-streaked hair and smiling little brown eyes.

*You're a Lipscomb, aren't you?*

*How did you know that?*

*I waited on your daddy at the club for many years.*

She hands me coffee. I turn and look around the room. Almost everyone is smiling. There are a couple of people who, like me, seem lost and confused.

*Are you Johnny Lipscomb?*

I turn and there's a tall, lean man in his forties with close-cropped hair.

*I'm sorry. I recognize you, but I can't place where or why.*

*That's okay, it's been a while. I'm Dave and you used to buy flowers from me, both you and your dad. Your dad still does.*

*You're a florist. Right, I'm sorry.*

*It's okay. I'm glad you made it here. It gets better, I promise.*

We all sit in folding chairs and the meeting begins with, *God grant me the serenity to accept the things I cannot change, the courage to change the things I can, and the wisdom to know the difference.*

After a few announcements the leader—a middle-aged woman—asks if there are any newcomers. I raise my hand with three or four others. People turn to us and say welcome.

Then a woman stands to speak. She looks tired but confident, comfortable.

*Hello, my name's Alice and I'm an alcoholic.*

Everyone responds, *Hi Alice.*

*When Nancy asked me to speak I wasn't sure what to say. Like most of you, the day my life started falling apart was the day I took my first drink. It took some time for me to recognize it, but I think when I was in my mid-twenties I knew I was alcoholic. For some reason, it wasn't until I was forty-five that I finally got sober—*a number of people in the room smile in recognition—*For twenty years I knew I was killing myself with alcohol. Why did it take so long for me to stop?*

Around the room, heads nod.

*It's as if half of me knew I had to stop, but the other half that wanted to keep drinking held more power over me. It wasn't until I knew, I mean, I really knew that death was coming.*

I see myself in her story.

She finishes and everyone says, *Thanks Alice.*

A few more people share their stories and then the group stands in a circle holding hands. I stay in my seat, but no one seems to notice. Together they pray:

*Our Father in heaven, God is almighty hallowed be your name Your kingdom come, your will be done, on earth, as it is in heaven. Give us this day our daily bread, and forgive us our debts, as we also have forgiven our debtors. And lead us not into temptation, but deliver us from evil.*

Then it's over.

A few people introduce themselves and say they're glad I came. One man says, *Easy does it.* Another, *One day at a time.*

They put their coats on and go out into the world sober, working to become better people. I walk back downstairs to my room. JR is relentless in his pacing and muttering. My body is in pain and shuddering so hard I feel like I will shatter.

*If this doesn't get better soon, I'm leaving,* I murmur to myself. But, I've seen a way forward. I've seen what it looks like to reach the other side.

That day is discussions with a counselor, a group meeting of inpatients with JR pacing behind and around us, and lots of time lying in bed holding on for dear life. The twitching in my muscles, the stomach cramps, and the Librium haze create a sense of confusion. I feel overwhelmed by the misery of it all.

*Can I make a call?* I ask a nurse.

*Who to?*

*My dad. Please, I need to speak to my dad.*

She frowns a little but says yes.

*Dad,* I say, *I can't do this. I gotta get out of here.*

*Johnny, please. I love you so much. Please don't.*

*Dad, I'm walking out of here. You have to listen to me. I can't take it anymore.*

*You're stronger than you think.*

*No, I'm not.*

*You are, Johnny. Your mother wasn't, but I swear to you, you are.*

I decide to stay, but repeat to myself, *If it doesn't get better, I'm getting a drink.*

It's Friday, January 8th. I've been in rehab for four days.

*Johnny,* one of the counselors says, *your insurance won't cover your stay here past tomorrow. I can't over-emphasize how important it is for you to be here for thirty days. Can you afford to stay here?*

I don't have to consider this question too long. Town & Country Shoes filed for bankruptcy twenty years ago. Mom had incredible wealth, but she was a tragic, helpless drunk. Dale and others preyed on her and left little for Joshua, Lisa or me. What they didn't take was used for college and for providing us a modest start in life.

I grew up with a nanny, private planes, grandparents with homes on Millionaire's Row, private schools, and all the rest, but now I'm broke with a flagging hidden dog fence business.

*No, I can't afford it.*

*I'm sorry, but we have to let you go home tomorrow. Is there anyone you can call?*

*No.*

*Okay. Listen, you aren't fully cooked yet.*

*Fully cooked?*

*You won't make it out there on your own. You'll start drinking again, only this time you may not find your way back here.*

*Okay.*

*You need an outpatient program.*

I think for the hundredth time, if the shaking, pain and craving don't get better, I'm going to drink.

*Where should I go? I ask.*

*We recommend a program called Exodus. They're your best bet. Can you do it?*

*I think so.*

In the early evening the next day, I walk out the front door for the first time in five days. This is the longest I've gone without a drink. I'm shaking, on Librium, in pain, clueless, scared, and alone.

The temperature is near zero. The door to my truck squeaks as it opens. Inside there are nine or ten beer cans scattered on the seat and floor. The lone unopened beer rests against the seat back where I left it, looking as if it's been waiting for me. Without thinking I pick it up and pull the pull-tab, but the beer is frozen solid. I throw it as hard and far as I can across the parking lot.

The engine is sluggish to turn over, but it does and within half an hour I'm home.

I walk through the front door and the house is like a time capsule of my final days. Other than my body lying on the kitchen floor, the tableau I walk into is what the person finding my corpse would have seen.

The angry red light on the answering machine blinks. There are beer cans all over the kitchen and living room. Ashtrays are full to overflowing. The plate from my final meal four weeks ago and a few other dishes sit in the sink with food remnants crusted on them. The trash reeks.

I move through the house looking at it all, almost like Scrooge in *A Christmas Carol* witnessing the wake of his death. I am overwhelmed and fall to my knees, sobbing. I bury my face in my hands.

Six days ago, I would have drunk myself into oblivion, but my best friend, alcohol, is gone. Among the papers the counselor gave me is a list of Alcoholics Anonymous meetings. I find one that starts in an hour. I wash my face, brush my teeth and do what I can to pull myself together.

I climb into the truck and head down the road. In about twenty minutes I pull up in front of a Methodist church. It's quiet and there are no lights. I go to the large wooden doors leading to the nave, but they are locked. I walk around the side to a small door, but it's locked, too. I walk back to my truck and wait, but it's obvious someone canceled this meeting.

I look through the list and there's a meeting in the morning at a Congregational church not far from my house. If I can make it, I'll go.

I don't sleep well, but I haul myself out of bed. Trembling, pain, and the deep, persistent compulsion to drink have not left.

It's Sunday, so I put on a *Brooks Brothers* wool suit, nice shoes and tie.

I look at my yellow, bloated body and florid face in a mirror. Tears flow without restraint. *I'll give this another day or two, but if it doesn't get better, I don't care. I'm going back to what works.*

I walk into a basement meeting room of the church. About twenty or thirty people are there; some I recognize from the Edgewood meeting. There's a table with coffee and donuts so I walk to it.

*Johnny, glad to see you here.*

An older man, gray hair, ruddy Irish face, smiles and holds his hand toward me. *I haven't seen you in years, Johnny. I'm a friend of your dad's. We sold shoes together.*

*How are you?*

*Good. Say hello to your father for me.* He pats me on the back and walks away.

I pour coffee into a Styrofoam cup.

*You know what?* There's a guy standing next to me who looks to be about my age. His neck is thick and muscular, hair black and cut short. He's dressed in jeans and a brown sweatshirt with *NCAA Wrestling* written across it. He stands and walks like a wrestler.

*What?*

*I took one look at your sad, bright red face and one-size-too-small Brooks Brothers suit and thought, "There's a guy I can help." You look like hell.*

*I feel like hell.*

*I'm Pete.*

*I'm Johnny.*

*Look Johnny, we're about to start, but here's my number. Call me. I'm nothing special, just another guy white-knuckling it through each day and holding on for dear life.*

I go home after the meeting and try to pick the house up, but the shaking and Librium make doing anything impossible. The obsession to drink is strong and unceasing.

*Please God, just make this shaking end or I'm going to drink.* Tears continue to come easily.

Without thinking, I pick up the phone and dial Pete's number.

*That didn't take long,* he says.

*I'd do anything to stop shaking.*

*Me too. There's a coffee shop down the street from where the meeting was this morning that has great donuts, lousy coffee, and bubble hockey.*

*Bubble hockey?*

*Yeah, it has a Plexiglas dome over it and levers to work the players. Meet me there right now.*

I try to work the lever to make the little plastic hockey player hit the small black puck, but my muscles twitch too much and won't cooperate. Pete is strong and fit, but the craving for cocaine and alcohol are too much for him. We hold onto the levers to steady ourselves as much as to play the game.

Pete spins the lever and the machine shudders from the force.

*Damn it!* he yells as the puck rolls away from his player. *The obsession of needing a drink or drugs is twenty-four/seven and it's like the devil working on me. I can't take it.*

I manage to hit the rolling puck with one of my players and it goes in Pete's goal.

*Damn it to hell! Damn it twice! Damn, damn, damn.*

He shakes the levers and I laugh, laugh hard.

*Brooks Brothers one, Wrestling champ zero,* I say.

Pete laughs. *If I don't take myself too damn seriously who else will?*

*Isn't that one of the steps?*

Pete laughs again. *Yeah, I'm the most important living thing in the known universe. Play again?*

*Yes, please.*

*Where ya from, Johnny?*

*Ladue.*

*Born with a silver spoon in your mouth?*

*More like a silver martini glass.*

I tell Pete about Mom, her drinking, and her death. I tell him about Lizzy, he laughs, and I tell him about Dad and the family of drunks I grew up with. He nods and says, *Been there, done that.*

I tell him about marrying a woman I didn't love because it seemed like the right thing to do. I told him about losing my wife and how she accused me of abusing one of the kids.

*Did you?*

*No, well, I was a drunk, so I guess that's a form of abuse, but I sure as hell didn't do what my ex accused me of.*

Pete's quiet as he concentrates on the puck, but he can't get the little hockey player to do what he wants.

*Damn! You know, Johnny, when I first saw you, I figured you for a Ladue guy.*

*Oh yeah?*

*Yeah, I thought, here's a guy who looks like hell, but probably has every-thing. Money, family, good job or trust fund, the whole deal.*

*No, no trust fund, at least not anymore. What about you?*

Pete spins the handle to slap the puck forward.

*What about me, what?*

*Your story, what's your story?*

*I grew up on Long Island with six brothers and sisters, so I always felt like none of us ever got much attention from our parents. They were just trying to keep everything together. And, you know, life happens and drinking leads to more drinking and then drugs and next thing I know I'm an addict and an alcoholic.*

*I've tried to get sober more times than I can count. I'd do it for a little while, Addicts Anonymous, Alcoholics Anonymous, rehab, all of it, but I didn't want to do what anybody told me to do. It was always Pete's Anonymous.*

The machine shudders as he spins the handle, hard.

*My mind was always racing and I had no filter,* he says. *I remember a guy at a meeting came up to me—I call guys like this drones—he came up to me after a meeting and tried to tell me what he thought I should do. I got so belligerent the whole room went silent.*

*Anyway, I put too many conditions on my own sobriety. I put conditions on saving my own life, ya know what I mean? I was saying, I'll stop slowly dying from drugs and alcohol, only my way, and the rest of you can screw off. The result? I never got sober and kept dying.*

*Then one night, in a blackout, I robbed a McDonald's and got arrested. I realized if I can rob a McDonald's, what's next? I could kill someone or get killed, so I realized I needed to do something different.*

*I got probation for the robbery and the judge told me to go get help. That was about six weeks ago and I've been going to two or three meetings a day.*

Pete speaks so loudly that people glance at him, not sure what he may say or do next.

*I'm sorry you had to go through that,* I tell him.

*Ya know what? Whenever I tell anybody else that story, they tell me what they think I should do, that I'll be okay and don't worry, or they walk away. Thanks for not doing that.*

Pete spins his player near the puck. The little black disc flies across the white, fake ice and slides into the goal.

*Again?* he asks.

*Yes, please.*

We spend the rest of the evening playing bubble hockey, drinking coffee, eating donuts, talking, and hanging on for dear life.

Monday, January 11, 1999, I walk into Exodus. They're expecting me. A tall man, dark hair, wearing khakis and a dress shirt, meets me at the desk.

*I recognize you,* he says.

*You do?*

*Yeah, you came in a few weeks ago, but I'm not surprised you don't remember.*

*Why?*

*You were speaking Chinese.*

He leads me down a hallway into a room that looks like a combination of an exam room and therapist's office.

*You'll be working with Barbara; she's a counselor, and she should be here in a moment. Good luck, Johnny.*

He closes the door and a few minutes later a tiny, middle-aged woman walks in. She has black hair, crinkled eyes, and is composed of spit and confidence.

She asks me to tell her my story, which I do. She asks me many more questions and I do my best to be truthful.

*I think we can help you.*

*I hope so.*

She says, *We run a twelve week program, two nights per week. The rest of the time we want you to go to as many AA meetings as you can; ninety meetings in ninety days is what I recommend. Think of them as your lifeboat until we can get to the root of your drinking. Okay?*

I think that many meetings is ridiculous, but I say, *Okay.*

*During the evenings we do a lot of work in group, but you'll also spend time with me one-on-one. One of the nights, Thursday, there's time for family to come in. Usually, that would be a wife, kids maybe, but given your situation, could you find someone?*

*Yes.*

When we finish I go home and call Dad.

*Johnny, I told you, I'm here when you need me. I love you. Of course I'll do it.*

Of the twelve sessions, Dad will make it to eleven.

The first few weeks are okay. I go to an AA meeting each day and Exodus two nights per week. I listen and share when I feel like I can, but am not leaping out of my seat to share with the group.

Barbara knows everything there is to know about the disease of addiction and has something new for me to try every session. The problem is, I don't engage with any of it or internalize it.

After about five weeks, Barbara's fed up with offering guidance that I don't listen to. And yet, I come to her each session and tell her I'm still barely holding on.

Pete and I spend a lot of time together, but that's a temporary salve. My mind and body burn for a drink. Ten or twenty times a day I tell myself if it doesn't get better, I'll drink. There are a few times I drive to a package store, slow the truck, but find the strength to pass it by. One more day, I tell myself.

One day Dad calls. *Johnny, I wanted to tell you before you hear it from someone else, but your Uncle Bobby died.*

*How?* Uncle Bobby, Dad's best friend, player of *The Drummer Boy*—images of him flashed through my mind.

*This may not be the right time to tell you, but he just holed up in his house and drank himself to death.*

A week or two later a friend from Codasco shoots himself to death. Another friend tells me he wrestled with alcoholism.

Within about this same time, a kid from my old neighborhood makes the conscious decision to drink himself to death. We used to play pickup football games together and run around the woods and creek.

I can't help but think of George and wonder how he's doing. Last I saw him—was it two years ago?—we both drank into blackout.

*Barbara, I'm miserable. If something doesn't change soon, I'm not going to keep hanging on.*

Barbara runs her fingers through her hair, then puts both hands in her lap.

*Johnny, this is a simple program for complicated people. If everyone who wanted to get sober would just show up, shut up, listen, help others and do what people who know what they're doing suggest, there would be more sober alcoholics. The program isn't failing you, you're failing the program.*

*What do you mean? I've been doing everything—*

*No, you haven't. You've been putting conditions on what you will or won't do to save your own life, to stay sober. You're unwilling to do this or that, many of the things you need to do. What you're trying to do is personalize your program so it's Johnny's Anonymous.*

*Do you know Pete?*

*Who?*

*Nothing.*

*Johnny, this is a family disease. Think of your mother. Think of the effect her drinking had on you, your sister and brother, your father, everyone around her. Think of how she never engaged with the cure, only the problem. And think of the effect your drinking has had on you, your family, your ex-wife, the decision to marry her, but most importantly, how has your drinking affected your children?*

*They won't see me.*

*Your own children don't want to have a relationship with you, Johnny. I think you even said that they escaped you the way you wished you could have escaped your mother.*

Tears well and then stream down my hot cheeks.

*I've become my mother.*

*No, not yet. You're still trying to get better.*

I put my face in my hands.

*Johnny, you need to forgive your mother and let go of what she's done to you.*

*She's dead,* I say through my fingers.

*I want you to write a letter to her.*

*Why the hell would I do that? I hated her and she was a complete wreck and probably why I'm here right now.*

*Shut up and go do it.*

I drive home and sit down with a pad of paper. I stare at it for an hour. I throw it. I pick it up and sit down again. I stare at it. Then I remember a bit of writing advice a friend once shared: *Start with just one true sentence.*

I write: *As of this date you have been gone from my life for eighteen years.*

Then: *In reality I feel like I have never had a mother and honestly remember very little of you.*

Followed by: *I am filled with so many what ifs? Maybe I should start at the beginning.*

One sentence follows the next and for two hours I hover over that pad of paper sobbing. I speak with Mom in a way I never have or could. I feel each resentment like a cancer, its black tendrils penetrating deep into the tissue of my heart and psyche. As my words touch each of these lesions, they burn and throb. They awaken a child's yearning for a mother's embrace, a mother's love, to understand why she didn't love me enough. Was I unlovable?

My body shivers, not just from the raw sweat of withdrawal, but from rage, anguish and loss.

The next evening I bring the letter to Barbara.

She is quiet as she reads. *This is good, Johnny. It reads true.*

*Thank you.*

*Now, I want you to read it to the group.*

*Tonight?*

*Yes.*

*No way.*

*Johnny, I am small, but I am tough. Let go and stop placing conditions on how you stop killing yourself. Read this letter, tonight.*

And so, an hour later I stand before about twenty people. Tears fall down my cheeks even before I start. I struggle to keep my body still and my voice steady, but it's no good. I melt.

*Mom, up to age nine I have very few memories of you. I have fond memories of Lizzy and, in all honesty, I consider her my mother. I remember our walks down the lane, spending most of my time with her and feeling safe in her presence. She would have laid down her life for me and I know she loved me. "As much as a kitten loves cream," she used to say. I remember, too, when I was a boy, she would say, "John David, I knew you were coming to me because I could see your soft, blond hair bouncing from the woods and up the yard."*

*I have no memory of you saying such things.*

*What I remember is after Dad and you told us the two of you were divorcing, you took us to Florida and the hotel staff carried you up to our room because you were so drunk. And I remember Dad tying you up in the pantry. He told me to untie you once he left.*

*Then you were sent away.*

*Then you came back and we went through the custody fight. How could you put us through that terrifying ordeal and then separate us? On top of that, you married Dale, who was verbally abusive to all of us, and physically abusive to Joshua.*

*Most of my memories of you are from age fifteen on, and they are not pretty. Didn't you ever wonder why I didn't bring friends around? Not one friend, including Margaret. Would you even know who she is and what she meant to me?*

*My memory of you is lying passed out on the couch in your urine-soaked nightgown day after day, night after night, with cigarette burns in the carpet below you.*

*I remember thinking I am never going to be like you. The many ambulances in the driveway, the trips to the hospital because you fell. Being rushed out the restaurant on a stretcher, and the only time I remember you driving, you got pulled over for your drunken driving.*

*At age twenty-two, I received a call you were in a coma. Looking at all the tubes coming out of you, yellow skinned, bloated. That is the memory I am left with. None of us shed a tear at that moment or at your funeral, where there were only five people in attendance.*

*I am mad, Mom, angry and full of resentment. How could you? I have grown close to most of my girlfriends' mothers over the years. I guess it is my way of having a mom. I have never understood the closeness my friends feel for their mothers.*

*As I stated in the beginning, I did not want to relive these memories or write this letter. I told my counselor, "Why do I want to write a letter to my dead mother?" She said, "Just do it."*

*In my six weeks in the program I have learned one thing, which amazes me. I have learned that you did the best you could and I have to accept that fact. I have the same disease as you and my life hasn't turned out very well up to this point.*

*I do want to thank you for my life. Obviously, without you it wouldn't be possible. I hope God is looking over your soul.*

*Love, Johnny*

I stand sobbing before the group.

*Thank you, Johnny,* a man says.

Another says thank you, and then another.

I am drenched in sweat. Every muscle in my body eases from absolute tautness to a tranquil calm. My mind is still. I am hollowed of the burning compulsion to drink. It is impermanent; I am not done with my work, but it is real and I feel that I can now, finally, let go.

It's the twelfth week and I'm sitting with Barbara in her office. Sobriety is still work, but the intense need for alcohol has dissipated to a slight yearning.

I feel comfortable, relaxed as we talk. Why do you think I've been able to get sober—

*You're doing well, but there's more to do,* she reminds me.

*True, but I've done more than my mom ever did. Why?*

*Johnny, I don't know, other than to say that we aren't here for those who need it. We're here for those who want it.*

The next day I take the letter to the crypt where Mom's body rests and read it to her. I fold it and put it in my pocket. Margaret's mom is only a few feet away.

Standing before Mrs. Tice's stone, tears well.

*You were right. I was a terrible boyfriend, horrible. I'm sorry, truly sorry. But you were right, too, when you said that in my heart I'm a good kid. I'm sorry it took so long to figure that out. I love you.*

Today is Monday, May 30, 2005. Memorial Day. It's seven in the morning and I step out of my red pickup truck, which is still dented and beat up, with tools rattling around in the back as I drive from one client to the next—I'm pretty busy—but there are no more beer cans cluttering the seat.

I walk into the same morning meeting where I met Pete six years ago. He sees me and we hug.

I tell Pete that I'm worried about one of our friends, Martin. He hasn't shown in quite a while, which usually means the person is back drinking.

Since my own sobriety began, I've committed myself to helping anyone who wants help in any way I can. Unfortunately, both Pete and I have learned that within this group, sobriety is hard won and hard to keep. We've had one friend start drinking again after fifteen years sober, and die of a heart attack a month or two later. Suicide is another common form of death, though we are all aware that addiction itself is slow suicide.

We've also seen people come into the program, succeed for a number of years, leave for a year or more and return. There are quite a few who become fixtures in our lives then walk out the door and we never see them again.

Sobriety is a tough road. I heard one estimate that ten percent of the population is alcoholic in one form or another. Ten percent of those people seek help and then ten percent of *them* manage to maintain sobriety for a year or more.

Those with five or more years sobriety is an even smaller fraction of the people committing slow suicide.

I've learned to love everyone I meet in this group, and leave the sobriety out of it. We share alcoholism, but connect as people. I want them to find lasting sobriety because I believe it's the path to lasting happiness, but I know we are all doing our best. That has to be enough.

*Did you call him?* Pete asks.

*I did, but he told me to piss off. I told him I love him and we're here for him when he's ready.*

*You know, maybe we should go see him. I hate to sound like a drone, but our friend's in a hole. I don't want to be the priest or the doctor; let's go in after him.*

Pete's body stiffens and eases as he speaks. There's an intensity to him that contrasts with his innate gentleness.

*Yeah, okay.*

I pat Pete's arm, tell him I need a coffee, and walk to a table where there are donuts and strong, bitter coffee.

A woman stirs her coffee. Her eyes are soft and preoccupied. She taps the wooden swizzle stick on the side of the cup and tosses it into the trash.

*Are you new here?* I ask.

*Yeah, you could say that.*

*Well, you're in the right place.*

*I hope so.*

*I'm Johnny. What's your name?*

Her lips press together. Her eyes drift over the room.

*I'm Adrianne.*

# Chapter Nine

## ADRIANNE: IT'S NEVER OVER

*Often when you think you're at the end of something, you're at the beginning of something else.*

—Fred Rogers (Mr. Rogers)

When I was a girl Dad said, *It'll be okay in the end; we just haven't got to the end yet.*

I thought when I came home to Mom and Dad I'd reached the end, a fairy tale happy ending, but the story wasn't over. Thirty years later, it still isn't.

*What happened to happily ever after?*

I'm sitting in my black Suburban on a cold December afternoon, waiting in the car pickup line at my daughters' Catholic, all-girls school. Frankie is ten years old and the youngest. Sam is twelve and Alex fourteen.

I look out at the other moms in their expensive cars. They are beautiful and smart-looking. They appear confident and free from fear as they talk into cell phones, sip coffee, or look expectantly at the school doors.

In their bearing I see devoted husbands, beautiful homes, and lives filled with loving friends and family.

Compared to them I feel as if I'm nothing, as if my life is an ever-shrinking circle condensing all my fears and insecurities into the hole I am falling through.

I look in my purse and hear the reassuring rattle of my pills in their small, decorative pillbox. I pull my cell phone out. No calls, texts or messages. My husband seems to have vanished.

I call his number, but it rings once and goes to voicemail.

A few months ago, he would be apoplectic if he couldn't reach me or didn't receive check-ins from me at regular intervals. Now he's quiet, no longer needy; from one extreme to the other.

I look at the other moms and imagine them preparing for Christmas with warm, frenetic anticipation.

I dread my sister-in-law's annual Christmas party tonight. She and the rest of my husband's family—disciples of upper class, suburban St. Louis—make me feel so small.

As we planned our wedding his mother said to him, *I am sorry, but I'm not excited that you're marrying that girl.* Shortly before our big day, his mother announced that my bridesmaids were not invited to the rehearsal dinner. There were only two. My soon-to-be sister-in-law—at the time a post-season debutante studying in Florence and a graduate of the Mary

Institute in Ladue—wrote: *If I see chiffon and feathered hair, I will throw myself down the aisle.*

I've tried to be the devoted daughter-in-law and sister-in-law, but they want nothing of it.

For fifteen years I've suffered through the symptoms of lupus, a painful and unpredictable autoimmune disease that flares up and falls into remission on its own schedule. Flare-ups cause fevers and my fingers and joints swell and ache to the point where simple tasks are difficult to impossible.

At first, doctors only treated the symptoms and said they would have to watch me before they could provide a definitive diagnosis. Then last spring it was so bad I was finally referred to a rheumatologist who formally diagnosed me with lupus.

Braided in with lupus attacks are herniated discs in my back and neck that so far have led to three surgical procedures, none of which relieved the primary symptom: intense pain that radiates through my body.

I'm in continual pain and bouncing from one doctor to the next, either from spinal issues or lupus or both. And then there are health issues that pop up every so often due to the pain, lupus or medications.

My husband's family has never shown much sympathy. They react to my health challenges in a way that makes me feel that they view illness and needing medical intervention as a sign of weakness.

Just before Thanksgiving, the lupus flared up and my rheumatologist prescribed a new medication. After starting it, I became violently ill in the parking lot of a strip mall, which required a trip to the emergency room and a brief hospitalization.

My mother-in-law's reaction to my Thanksgiving health setback was, *How in the world did Adrianne land herself in the hospital, again?*

I've given up on them. I don't believe they'll ever embrace me as worthy of their love or friendship. I can't imagine them seeing me as anything other than their social inferior, the calamity and striver who married their heart surgeon son.

Just the thought of the party tonight sends me into my purse for another Percocet with a Xanax chaser.

I swallow the pills with a sip of water. My eyes wander to the other moms. A shiver of embarrassment runs through me as I realize I've just exposed my secret to them.

They all seem so placid, so normal, as they wait. I want what they have, but I have no idea how to get it.

The doors to the school open and a rush of girls in plaid, pleated skirts and white polo shirts bursts through them. I smile as each of these Catholic, tartan-clad penguins tumbles into the correct car.

My girls come out at their own pace and rhythm. They smile, laugh, wave and find their way to me through the waddle of other penguins. They are so normal and happy, though Frankie seems a bit off. A quiet has settled over her, but only recently. As with her older sisters, she's resilient and will find her way through.

They climb into the Suburban and I wend the large vehicle through a clutch of BMWs, Audis, Volvos, and Cadillacs, all the mothers trying to get to the next activity on time.

The girls ask what we are doing. I tell them I need a nap before the party and they scrunch down into their seats. They ask what I did all day. I say it was another busy day. I don't tell them that I went to the pain clinic—I'm too ashamed of the pills to even hint at my need for them—or that I slept and failed to go to the gym, again. I neglect to mention I've not walked our golden retriever and Saint Bernard in days, preferring to open the door for them and let the hidden fence keep them in the yard.

I ask them how the last day of school before vacation went and stories spill out all at once. Each wants me to hear them, to feel loved, and I do.

When we get home the girls make snacks and argue over what to watch on TV. I tell them to behave and go to their bedrooms. I'm so tired.

My head feels fuzzy when I wake and my vision's a bit blurry. My body is sore, legs restless and my neck and back are in pain. I reach for the pillbox and take a couple of Percocet, sit up and remember the party, which sends me fumbling for a Xanax.

I hear my husband talking on the phone. It's late so I get dressed and prepare to be with the in-laws. I look at myself in a full-length mirror. My eyes are weary and I realize I never became the tall, lean woman I'd always hoped I'd be, though I'm not unattractive.

The girls get themselves dressed and I pull a bottle of *veuve-clicquot* champagne from the wine rack in the kitchen and place it on the counter so I don't forget to bring it to the party. I wander the house, compulsively picking up glasses and plates left by the girls and my husband, and rinse them in the sink before placing them in the dishwasher.

The house is spotless and I am so obsessive about laundry the girls often joke that I'm a load ahead. Cleaning and organizing are peace-making activities I'm too afraid to let slip, lest I bear the brunt of my husband's anger or allow myself to completely sink into addiction. A clean, well-kept house and all's well.

I look out the bay window in the living room. Across the street, our neighbor's house is lit for Christmas. I turn on our lights as a beacon to show that all is well in our home.

My husband is loud when he calls for the girls to hurry. Dressed in a blue blazer, he turns and looks at me like a drill sergeant reviewing a plebe. His behavior is volatile. I never know when he will tear into me and I live in fear I've done something to upset him. Is the house not clean enough? Did I come home too late? Sleep too long? Buy too much of the wrong food? Spend too much time with a friend? Can't account for my whereabouts for every minute of the day? Gain weight? Or simply fail to be the arm jewelry and trophy wife he desires?

When he drinks, his moods become even more erratic and explosive. One minute he's uninterested, the next a lout, and the next rage reddens his face and he's screaming at me, then he's back to uninterested.

Ours was a whirlwind romance. We first saw each other while working at the same hospital—I was interning in *Recreation Therapy*—but we didn't actually meet until we bumped into each other while on vacation. Six months later were engaged. Rushing to get engaged was a mistake, but so too was ignoring the warning signs even a short while after we met. I thought they were minor faults or momentary lapses. I wanted his love, I wanted the security of marrying a doctor, and I wanted him to need me. His constant, urgent demand that I account to him for my whereabouts felt like need, not control.

Over the years his drinking increased, and with it the intensity and instability of his moods. I sought refuge in Al-Anon and even had a sponsor and worked the program, but now it feels too hard to manage and I've let it fall by the wayside.

We have also spent what seems the entirety of our marriage in counseling. Each session is a draining experience that never achieves reconciliation or resolution to the many spats, disputes, and sins we hold against each other. Often, we return from a session angry and hurt. My husband either stews silently or gives me the full force of his wrath.

Now he turns from me and calls up the stairs for the girls, which means I'm found to be adequate.

I place my pills in a clutch, put a coat on, grab the champagne and off we go.

His sister answers the door by swinging it wide and saying, *The famous heart surgeon is here,* which brings his mother and father to the foyer. They hug and talk in staccato bursts between smiles and subdued laughter. The girls receive their due of hugs and kisses and, *Can you believe it's Christmas and Santa will be here soon?* They dote on the girls and tell them how pretty they are—they truly are beautiful—and they float in the embrace of this home.

I stand in the foyer, coat on, holding the champagne with both hands across my chest. My sister-in-law sees me and reminds me that they have plenty of wine and champagne, but thank you, anyway.

My husband's sister and mother treat him as the hero of the family and the other guests—the house is filled with the cream of the social register—see him as an old-friend-done-well.

I find my way into the kitchen, open the champagne and pour some into a fluted champagne glass. With clutch and champagne in hand I wander through the house saying casual hellos to people, but am unable to break into any conversation. The girls are happy with their cousins and friends. My husband, a tumbler of scotch in one hand, talks with his male Ladue friends. They speak in loud, confident masculine tones. Sister-in-law is chatting with her friends in loud, confident feminine tones.

Watching them, I am back sitting in the windowsill of Herb and Elaine's apartment.

I drain the glass and go to the kitchen for another. When I place my clutch on the counter I hear the reassuring rattle of my pills and sneak off to the bathroom, glass in hand, to take a Percocet.

I pause in the mirror to fix my hair, but my hands fall to my sides. My eyes look so tired.

Dinner is served and I sit next to a man I've known for quite some time, but have little in common with. He talks to friends across the table. The woman to my left is amiable in her conversation, but the rhythm of it feels off, stunted, difficult to maintain.

My neck hurts, as does my lower back. I notice a slight headache and wonder if my fingers are swelling. I hope it's not the lupus flaring up. Sliding out of my seat, I return to the kitchen and pour another glass of champagne—my third, or is it my fourth?

There is the consoling rattle of the pills.

In the bathroom, I sip another Percocet down with champagne. Tilting my head back causes me to wince. Who is the woman looking at me in the mirror? She looks tired, unhappy, afraid, and sad. It's Christmas. Why am I here, with these people? Why am I so afraid? Where's Ady Maidy's smile? Why am I so far from Dad?

Tears roll down my cheeks. Dad's the kindest man I've ever known and he loves me unquestionably, but I worry so much about him. Mom died of breast cancer a little more than ten years ago, while I was pregnant with Frankie. She and Dad had something of a cobra/mongoose-like relationship, but losing her is a pain that is too much for him to bear.

He's not good at being on his own, nor is he well. Diabetes and heart disease have taken so much from him, but he remains resolute in his optimism. He is frustratingly, unreasonably positive and optimistic, to the point that he doesn't take good care of himself.

*Yeah, I'm watching my diet,* he tells me, but he rides his scooter—he has trouble walking—from the assisted living facility he lives in to a Denny's near him. Harry visited him recently and told me when the waitress at Denny's got to their table she asked Dad, *You want the usual, hon?* Then she brought out a plate of eggs, pancakes, butter, syrup, bacon . . . the works.

*Don't worry, doll,* he tells me, *I'm all right. In fact, I'm great!*

But this isn't true. He often requires care in the emergency room for both his diabetes and his heart disease. The last time I saw him—for two weeks around Thanksgiving—I hired an in-home nurse to help look after him.

I don't talk about my troubles with him because I don't want him to worry, but when he returned to his home in southern California after a visit here, he said, *Doll, I could've cut the tension in that house with a knife.*

I don't know how to fix what's broken in my life, but the pills make it easier.

I didn't seek these pills out. They found me after my third spinal surgery a year ago. The pain dulled, but never left. I went to a pain clinic for relief and told the doctor my biological parents were heroin addicts. She listened, then prescribed what I thought was a large amount of Percocet.

With my lupus diagnosis, the rheumatologist prescribed Percocet to treat severe joint pain that radiates through my body during flare-ups. She also prescribed Xanax to help with anxiety and insomnia.

Two doctors prescribing Percocet and Xanax and I'm flooded with little blue pills that lighten the pain, and have the coincidental effect of creating an emotional *pied-à-terre* to escape into.

For a few months, I was able to balance life with the escape offered by the pills. I maintained friendships, managed parenting, and remained engaged with the world.

But last May my husband and I returned home from a difficult counseling session, once again. The entire car ride, he yelled. We got home and he kept yelling. I tried to get away, but he followed and wouldn't stop screaming at me. My head pounded and my body felt swollen and as if it was on fire. My neck and back burned with pain. A wet film of tears covered my cheeks and I pleaded with him to stop.

For more than an hour he berated me and when the storm passed I lay on the bed, my knees curled to my chest, shaking from frustration, emotional exhaustion, pain and fear. I wanted it all to go away, to have some respite where time stopped, a safe place I could crawl into. I reached for the pillbox and a Percocet, knowing what I was doing, and tapped two pills into my hand. I wanted to get high, to escape.

*Screw it*, I thought. *What do I have to lose?*

Now, six months later, I need the pills.

When I don't have them, I don't feel normal. Within a few hours my emotions are raw and withdrawal washes painfully through me: stomach cramps, diarrhea, shakes, nausea . . . the works.

Pill planning is a necessary compulsion. Do I have enough? Are they with me? Should I put some in the car so they're never too far away? Am I running low? Which doctor will give me more? How long will I be away from the house? Do I have a backup supply? What do I do if I my special little box disappears?

Managing the pills is all-consuming and I build an entire set of obsessive behaviors around ensuring I am never without pills. I all but strap them to me when I travel and hide the bottles in a pocket in my closet so no one will find them and realize I'm taking more than I should. On a few occasions, I've panicked as I've torn through the clothes in my closet because I've forgotten the new hiding place.

Life falls away in bits and pieces. I sleep during the day. I no longer go to the gym or see many of my friends. Life grinds into a tight routine of pills, pain, obsessive cleaning, and watching the world as an envious outsider.

As I look deeper into my tired eyes in the mirror, my throat thickens and my face reddens. I mouth the words, *I hate you,* then wipe tears from my cheeks. With my fingertips, I tease my hair so that it falls across my eyes, and take a sip of champagne.

Back out in the party I pour another glass of champagne and watch the others as they celebrate. I'm drunk and high, going through the motions of a Christmas party. I'm a movie extra in the background, trying to look natural behind the main characters. People talk loudly, a woman's high-pitched laugh rises above the muddle of voices. Nothing makes sense. I'm the trembling woman in the corner. I'm the scared little girl watching out for the back of Elaine's hand as life passes like a party I was never invited to.

Christmas comes and goes. New Year's is a blur. The girls return to school and January melts into February. My days are waking the girls, making lunches, dropping them off at school, sleeping, withdrawing further into myself, feigning alertness in the car line with the other moms, and enduring the buoyant energy of teen girls in the afternoon. Frankie is still off; something isn't right with her.

And, of course, the pills. They are the solution to sadness. They are the cause of shame. Stopping is impossible.

Other than the girls, the deepest connection I have is to Dina. She's the coolest woman I've ever met. She's pretty and funny, but never makes me feel left out or other-than. I sense strength emanating from her in much the same way I admired and envied Bina's courage. I feel protected and safe with her, and her words and grace toward me allow me to believe I belong in the world of strong women, that I can be admirable and beautiful in my own right. Everyone should have a Dina in their lives.

We've planned to have coffee, but I wake from deep sleep to see I'm already late. I splash cool water on my face and take a pill from the pillbox in the medicine cabinet, then rush out the door.

Sliding out of the Suburban, I hitch my leather bag up my shoulder and hunch my shoulders against the cold wind. The large glass windows at the Starbucks are opaque with condensation from the cold outside and the heat inside.

Dina is sitting at a corner table, pecking at her phone with one finger. Her other hand sweeps a lock of reddish-brown hair from her face. She sees me at the door and her eyes widen.

Though she's sitting, her five-foot-four inch, taut, lean body bounces as she turns back to finish with her phone. She taps one last message and deposits her phone in the handbag slung over her chair. Watching her, all I can think is, *Why can't I be more like her?*

*How's my favorite mama?* Dina asks, smiling.

I set my coffee on the table and turn to sling my bag on the back of the chair, but bump the table. Coffee spills out of both our cups and I grab mine before it falls. As I do this, my bag slides off the chair and lands on the floor with a thump.

There is no reassuring rattle.

I take my coat off, sit, pick my bag up and look through it. Tissue, wallet, keys, day calendar, phone, mints, lipstick . . . everything except my pills. I bite my lower lip as I search through the bag one more time. No pills.

Dina tilts her head over the table into my bag. Her tone feels sharp to me. *Did you lose something?*

I run a hand through my hair. I can stop at home before picking the girls up at school.

*It's okay,* I say.

I reach into my bag one more time and set my phone on the table next to my coffee.

Dina looks at me, lips pressed together.

*You don't have to be at his beck and call,* she says.

*If he texts or calls and I don't answer, there'll be hell to pay.*

She leans toward me. *You don't have to be this way. You didn't do anything wrong.*

I turn my eyes from hers. *I know, I know. I don't like it.*

*If you don't like it, get out.*

*And be a single mother? Or lose the girls? Or be broke?*

I don't mention our deep debt. The guilt of lying to everyone, Mom and Dad, his family, friends, eats at me.

*It wouldn't go that way.* Dina sips her coffee then crosses her arms.

*I don't know,* I say.

There's an echo of Dad saying *It'll all be all right Ady, don't worry.*

*Well, he's stopped calling so much lately,* I add.

Dina's eyes narrow. *He's having an affair.*

I can't tell if this is a statement or question.

*I don't know. Maybe. I suppose.*

*You're a beautiful, smart, wonderful woman, Adrianne. You don't have to put up with it.*

I don't believe her, but I smile. A little love is a welcome balm for my sick soul.

Dina leans back and takes another sip of coffee. *So, how are those young beauties of yours?*

*They're good.*

For the next fifteen or twenty minutes we talk and laugh. I forget the pills, my husband, everything. If I could put Dina in pill form, I'd do it in a heartbeat. Her friendship, her love, nourishes and nurtures. It's the closest I get to feeling normal, to feeling like the women at school. For these minutes I'm one of them, having coffee with a friend.

When my phone vibrates on the table, I tense. Dina studies my reaction. I can read her mind: *You don't have to be this way.* But I do.

*Hello?*

*This is Terrie Faulk, the nurse at school.*

I intuitively know its Frankie.

*Frankie is with me and she's in a lot of pain, in her abdomen.*

Frankie is the kind of kid who would shake off a broken limb. For her to say she's in pain means she's scared.

*We haven't called an ambulance, but you need to pick her up right away and take her to the emergency room.*

*I'll be there in a minute.* I look up at Dina. *I have to go. Something's wrong with Frankie.*

*Anything I can do?*

*I don't think so.* I stand and grab my bag and phone. *I'll be in touch.*

The air is cold and I rush to the Suburban as my mind runs through the fastest routes to the school. I slide into the seat and toss my bag into the passenger seat. There are no pills to clatter in my bag. I pull open the glove compartment, then search the other spaces where I might have stashed some pills. Nothing. I can't worry about that now.

At the school, Frankie is curled up holding her stomach, crying from pain and fear. The nurse and another woman help me get her into the car and I pull out of the parking lot, the quickest routes to the hospital still running through my mind.

Then I remember the pills. And I remember that without them there will be nausea, cloudy thinking, shakes, more pain, stomach cramps . . .

I could take the highway directly to the hospital, but . . . *We have to make one quick stop at home.*

Frankie's my little stoic, never complains, nothing is ever too much, but she's lying across the back seat sobbing.

I wipe tears from my eyes. My hands tremble. I'm ashamed of myself and what I'm doing.

*I just have to . . .* and I trail off as my mind concentrates on the quickest route to my pills.

I race inside, grab the pillbox, take one, pocket the box, then dash back to the Suburban and Frankie.

At the emergency room I call my husband, but there's no answer. He must be in surgery. Dina picked Sam and Alex up at school and is taking care of them, so I know they're okay.

At the hospital they give Frankie meds to stabilize her pain and doctors ask questions before blood is drawn and an abdominal ultrasound ordered. The doctor believes her appendix may be the cause of her pain and warns me that if that's the case, she will need surgery.

I sit on a hard plastic chair in a small cubicle. Frankie lies in the bed. We talk and she's at ease, though medicated. I'm scared for her at the thought of surgery, but there is nothing to do other than wait.

After about an hour, Dina calls to ask how Frankie is.

*I don't know,* I tell her. *I'm alone.*

*I'm sorry.*

*It's okay.* It isn't. I'm a horrible mother.

My phone beeps. It's my husband calling.

*I have to go,* I say, then answer his call.

*What's happening?*

I tell him and he asks questions, none of which I have answers to. I assume he'll just call in to the ER to speak directly to the doctor.

*It's good her pain is stable.*

*Yeah, it is. Maybe it's nothing.*

*Maybe.* He pauses for a beat. *Where are Sam and Alex?*

*They're at a friend's, getting ready for the father/daughter dance tonight.*

*That's right. I promised I'd take them.*

*I know. You still want to take them?*

*I do.*

I don't want to be alone, but I know this is important to Sam and Alex so I tell him it'll be all right and that I'll have Dina drop them off at the house.

An hour or so later a nurse comes into the cubicle and says it's time for Frankie's ultrasound. With her pain manageable, she's back to being my little stoic. She's concerned, but calm.

I follow them down the hall to the imaging department, and watch as Frankie is wheeled into a small room with an ultrasound machine and a sonographer. The door closes and I sit to wait.

About twenty minutes later a doctor walks into the ultrasound room and closes the door.

Ten minutes later the doctor emerges and calls me into the room. His lips form a straight line and he looks concerned.

He shows me an image of Frankie's abdomen.

*Here, you can see an inflamed lymph node, and more over here.*

*What does that mean?*

He guides me to a corner of the room, away from Frankie, and tilts his head closer to my ear. *It means there's something wrong. It could be lymphoma.*

With the word *lymphoma* my breath leaves me. *Lymphoma?*

*We don't know that she has lymphoma.*

My hand shakes as I push my fingers through my hair. I touch my mouth and feel warm breath on the tips of my fingers.

*Mrs. Lugo, there's a pediatric oncologist at St. John's Hospital, Dr. Bergamini. Frankie should see him, tonight.*

*What will he do?*

*I'm not sure, but the usual protocol is a CT scan. Depending on the results of the scan, there may be a biopsy.*

The word *biopsy* shudders through my body. I'm as afraid of that word as I am of *cancer.*

I reach into my bag and fish through it. The pills slide in my pillbox and I wonder if the doctor's heard their telltale sound. I pull out my phone and call my husband.

He's shocked, but there's an aloofness in his voice. We agree that we shouldn't tell Alex or Sam yet. He says he'll put on his happy face and take them to the dance while I see the oncologist with Frankie.

The doctor leaves the room to call the oncologist and set things up. I reach in my bag for a Xanax.

Almost as a reflex, I call Dina.

*Oh my God. Are you all right?*

*I don't know what to say,* I tell her. *I just want it to stop, to go back to normal and have everything okay.*

*I know.*

*But it won't. Nothing's okay.*

Tears fall from my eyes and I wipe them with one hand. There's a smear of makeup on my hand and I wonder what I must look like.

*There's still room for it to be something else.*

*What do you mean?*

*No one's said the words 'She has cancer'?*

*No.*

*I don't know, but there's reason for hope.* Dina pauses and I hear her soft breath on the other end of the phone. *I love you.*

*I love you, too, but I have to go.*

When we reach St. John's, Frankie's eyes are wide with fear. I've told her in vague terms that she might be sick, but that the doctors need to be sure.

I hold her hand and she stares up at me as an orderly pushes her wheelchair through a series of hallways. She searches my face for a clue as to what's happening to her. She wants to gauge how afraid she should be by how afraid I look. I'm terrified.

I hitch my bag up on my shoulder and hear the subtle rattle of pills. A deep shame underscores my fear.

Dr. Bergamini meets us at the imaging department. He's a large, friendly looking man with glasses, salt-and-pepper hair, and a brightly colored sweater with wavy, vertical stripes. He says hello and explains what will happen in the CT room. Frankie is wheeled away and Dr. Bergamini sits with me. He explains what they are looking for and tells me not to worry. *We'll track it down.*

I'm not sure how much time's passed, but I'm in Dr. Bergamini's office waiting for him. Frankie's in another room reading a magazine. I wonder how many people have sat in these chairs and heard a doctor say their child's cancer journey has begun.

There's a knock on the door and the doctor bounds into the room.

*It's not cancer,* he says quickly.

Before relief sinks in he asks me a number of questions. I answer as best I can, but nothing connects until I tell him she gets mouth sores similar to when my lupus flares up. This seems to spark a thought and he asks us to come back to his office Monday morning.

*Thank you, Dr. Bergamini.*

*Oh, everyone calls me Dr. Bob, you can too.* He smiles and looks a little funny in his sweater.

Monday morning, Alex and Sam go to school and my husband to work. It's just Frankie and me walking into Dr. Bob's office at the pediatric cancer center at St. John's. I do a short accounting in my head and realize that my husband has missed nearly every one of these major life events, whether it's for me or the kids. The thought makes me a little angry.

In the sitting room, a handful of patients wait for their turn. Many of them are bald with dark circles under their eyes and I realize that by the grace of God, this is not the path we are on.

We are called into an exam room. There's a knock and Dr. Bob comes through wearing another bright, colorful sweater. This one almost looks as if he tie-dyed it.

He asks Frankie how she is and she says fine. Then he asks me a couple of questions about Frankie's health history. Then he says he suspects an immune deficiency and orders a blood test to confirm the diagnosis.

The results point to *common variable immunodeficiency*.

Our next appointment is with an immunologist at St. Louis University Hospital. My husband isn't at this appointment either. I wonder why he isn't here. *Is this normal? Is he having an affair?*

The immunologist begins by telling me that Frankie could die from an infection. My mind races and my stomach cramps and feels hollow. He keeps talking, using words such as *hypogammaglobulinemia* and *intravenous immunoglobin*. The long and short of it is that Frankie's body isn't able to produce enough antibodies to fight off infection. She's not at the level of the boy-in-the-bubble, but she needs antibody infusions every three weeks for the rest of her life.

My head drops and my mouth is dry, my throat sore. I listen, but all I hear is the immunologist laying out a life of medical dependence for my daughter.

The pills in my bag call to me and guilt burns across my skin. I've let so much of my life slip and fall away, but I never thought I'd fail my children. Frankie needs a mother, not an addict.

I can't imagine hating myself more than I do right now.

The story of Herb and Elaine is part of who I am, but their story doesn't have to be mine. At least, that's what I say to myself as I wait to see my therapist, Nadia.

Nadia invites me into the archetype of a therapist's office. It's a small room with couches and chairs, a couple of bookshelves. Large pillows are piled in one corner. Her credentials and a few photos adorn the walls, each frame hung with a strong sense of precision and proportion. Everything is neat and organized.

Nadia is without any doubt the woman who inhabits this office. She wears little, if any, makeup. Her light brown hair is neat and pinned back, but obviously not obsessed over. She is wearing fitted black twill pants, a white blouse and a thin black cardigan.

For two years I've worked with her so that I could learn to live with my past. To say the least, her process is unique, but helpful. When we started, and in every session since, we each sat on a large pillow facing one another. I started talking about Elaine and Herb, telling her my story. Every so often she stopped me to ask how I felt about something. With each question she dug a little deeper, getting closer to the heart of what living with Elaine and Herb did to me.

The sessions were difficult and painful. It was hard to go back to a time when I was so vulnerable, when so much was being done to me beyond my control. I remember coming home after those early sessions and falling apart sobbing in bed.

After a few sessions, Nadia felt I was ready to include group sessions in my therapy. She does what's called psycho drama, where individuals bring up a particularly painful or difficult event. They tell their story and the rest of the group asks questions, then we role play.

There is also a bat in the office. As the emotional intensity builds, the person at the center of the drama beats a pillow with the bat. When I leave for these sessions I tell the girls, *I'm off to beat the pillow.*

Many of the people I meet in group are there for addiction issues. Nadia is more than familiar with addiction treatments and often receives referrals to her practice because her techniques are so good. When I joined her practice, she asked me to sign a contract that said while I was receiving therapy from her I wouldn't drink or take drugs.

This is also where I met Dina, there for her own troubled past. Watching her in group, I was so impressed with her honesty and compassion. And, of course, I thought, *She is soooo cool.*

There's a directness to Nadia, in her look and in the way she carries herself, that contrasts with Dina's looser, lighter mien. They are both strong, confident women, traits I aspire to, but each in her own idiosyncratic way.

A few days after Frankie's diagnosis, I sit on the pillow across from Nadia and put my purse next to me. Gone is the rattle of the pillbox; I'm trying to wean myself off the pills. I feel and look horrible.

Nadia smiles. *Adrianne, what brings you here today?*

By omission or outright, I've been lying to her for a long time.

I twist the strap of my bag between my fingers. *I'm an addict.*

Nadia crosses her legs. *Alcoholic?*

*I don't know. Drugs, but probably alcohol, too.*

*What's your drug of choice?*

*Percocet.*

That I'm not saying heroin allows me to believe my addiction has a more refined grace than Elaine's.

*How long?*

*A while,* I say, *maybe a year or a little longer.*

She adjusts her weight on the pillow.

My eyes wander from hers. *Remember a few weeks ago when I called after a big fight with my husband?* Compared to many therapists, Nadia is open and accessible. She knows her people will need her at any time, day or night, and allows us to call her as that need arises.

*Yes.*

*I was so high I think I was probably incoherent.*

*I remember.*

*Did you know?*

*I don't know. I think I've been worried about you for some time, but I knew, and know, you have the tools and the wherewithal to reach out for help.*

I think about Elaine. My story makes me feel broken, like I'm someone to feel sorry for.

*I hate myself for coming here with all of these people working on their sobriety and their issues, and here I am leaving them and popping pills. I've been so dishonest. I'm so sorry.* I wipe tears from my eyes.

*So, tell me about your drug use.*

I tell her about the marriage counseling session and how I just wanted the yelling to stop, how I wanted to escape my fear, everything that's hard in my life, which feels overwhelming. *I thought, what do I have to lose? Screw it; I'm gonna take a pill to get high.*

Her almond-shaped eyes remain focused and rarely blink. They aren't soft or sympathetic, but neither are they hard and unsympathetic. She is purely observing.

*You mean to escape?*

Nadia knows about Elaine and Herb. She knows that I live in constant pain, and she knows that I struggle with my husband's anger, but she doesn't know the extent of our troubles.

*Yeah, to escape, but it's more than just pain or dealing with his anger. We're in a lot of debt, to the point where we owe years of back taxes and have overspent and over-borrowed. And we've been lying about it to his family, my family, everyone.*

*That's a lot. It must be difficult.*

*I sit in my car at school waiting for the girls and I look at the rest of those women and think, why can't I have what they have?*

*And what's that?*

*A happy, normal life.*

*The pills help with that?*

I rub the back of my neck, which feels sore and stiff, and rest my other arm across my belly. The lack of Percocet makes me nauseous and causes my stomach to cramp.

*Nothing helps. I don't know how to get what I want and I'm so overwhelmed I don't even know how to take the first step.*

*So what do the pills do?*

*They make me less sad, less afraid. They make everything stop so I can just be. So I can empty my head and think about one single thing at a time and not worry so much.*

*They don't make you feel overwhelmed, too?*

*I don't know. Yes, of course.*

*What happened to get you to ask for help?*

I wipe tears away with the back of my hand.

*I let my daughter writhe in pain in the back seat of my car because I had to get my pills rather than take her to the hospital.*

I wipe more tears from my eyes and Nadia hands me a tissue.

*For all I knew she was dying, but I had to stop for my pills.*

*How does that make you feel?*

*Shame. I hate the woman I've become.*

I wipe my eyes with the tissue and look up at Nadia. *I don't want to end up like Elaine.*

She leans forward, arms resting on her knees, and looks into my eyes. *You already did.*

I bury my face in my hands, crying. I can't believe I've become the woman I've spent my life hating.

*There's an important difference: you're seeking help.*

I raise my head from my hands. *And, I love my daughters.* My love for them is a thread connecting me to the person I want to be, the person I believe I am at heart.

*And, you love your daughters.*

Nadia sits back and crosses her hands in her lap. *So, there's a lot we can work on here, but you need help staying sober every day. Do you think you can do ninety meetings in ninety days?*

*You mean AA?*

*Well, I think alcohol is part of your story, but you also seem to have some comfort with AA through your experience with Al-Anon, don't you think?*

*I do, but there's no way I could do that right now.*

*Why not?*

*I can't do the detox on my own, I just can't. I already feel like hell.*

*Okay. There's a facility here that's a satellite for a rehabilitation center called Sober Living. I want you to go there after you leave here, for an evaluation.*

*Rehab?*

*I think you need it, don't you?*

I'm humiliated, but there is no choice.

My voice wavers as I say, *I do.*

We stand and Nadia goes to her desk and writes down the name and address of where I'm supposed to go. She hands me the paper and wraps her arms around me in a warm hug.

*You are loved. Take care,* she whispers in my ear.

When I walk through the door of Sober Living I'm met by a man and a woman. They look to be my age and are polite and well dressed. I'm led to a room where I undergo a brief physical—blood pressure, pulse, that sort of thing—and answer a series of questions. I fill out a questionnaire and then answer a few more questions.

My life is changed forever and I've fallen into if not the same hole as Elaine, one too close to hers, but there's a banality to it all. Another pro forma evaluation of an addict.

The result of their assessment is a foregone conclusion, but my stomach knots when they say I'm clearly an addict and will need inpatient treatment to detox and begin the work of sobriety. They want to send me to their primary facility in Newport Beach, California, for a ninety-day detox and rehabilitation program.

I nod. Over the next few hours they call my husband and ask him to come in. When he arrives he gives me a cool look, but it otherwise calm, impassive. A social worker irons out the financial details with the two of us and I am surprised and unsettled by my husband's calm.

When it's done, my husband goes back to work and I go home.

I call Dina and ask her to come over and help me. Withdrawal, grief and shame render me unable to function. Dina comes over and books my flight, cleans up around the house, keeps tabs on the girls, talks to Nadia to let her know where I'm going, and helps me pack while I lie on the bed.

I'm so detached from the reality of the moment, probably the first whispers of withdrawal, that I tell Dina that I want to go out and buy some cute clothes for rehab. She's folding a pair of yoga pants to put in my suitcase and looks at me with a wry smile.

*Cute clothes for rehab?*

*I want to look good, right?*

Dina laughs so hard she nearly folds in half. *Honey, you're not going to a deb party up in Ladue.*

*What's so funny?* I ask, a little hurt.

*It's not like here where people wear heels, designer purses, and ball gowns to drop their kids off for the first day of elementary school.*

I still don't get it. I feel as if I'm living a painful dream. I'm humiliated, embarrassed and afraid to tell the girls their mother's addicted to pills. My head is pounding, I have double vision, my stomach feels as if it's twisted in a knot, and I'm not thinking clearly. As time passes I become so nauseous I can't imagine putting food in my mouth.

Once my suitcase is packed, Dina calls the girls up. *We have something to tell you,* she says.

They walk into the room and each notices the suitcase sitting by the bed. They are quiet. They know something's wrong.

Dina is on the bed next to me, one leg curled under the other and her back resting against the pillows. The girls sit around us on the bed.

I pause for a moment and look at them. I can't believe what I've done to myself and how I'm hurting them. I look to Dina, then say, *I've become addicted to my pain medication and need to go away for a little while to a place that will help me.*

Alex, the oldest, smiles a little. *Really?*

*Yeah, really.*

She looks at Dina and then to me.

*I thought you were going to tell us you and Dina are lesbian lovers.*

*What?*

*Well, you spend so much time together, I just thought . . .*

*No,* I smile, *we're not lesbian lovers.*

We talk a bit longer and I tell them I'm going to a place in California and that their dad will take care of them and Dina will help out. I tell them I love them and they say the same. I hold my arms out and they come into me and I wrap as much of me as I can around them.

I may have Elaine's addiction, but I'll never be her. I have the love of my children.

My husband doesn't return home until very late in the night. I don't have the energy to ask him where he's been; clearly not work.

The next morning Dina arrives at our house to offer help and support. This, as I know from our group therapy sessions together, is a trip she's familiar with. She and I load the car and call the girls out. My husband slides into the driver's seat with no more emotion than a trip to the grocery store, the girls climb in the back and Dina squeezes in with them. I ride in the front. We are all going to the airport and we are all silent.

*How you doing?* Dina asks as he drives.

*I'm afraid.*

*Anything in particular?*

*Missing the girls, where I'm going . . . just afraid.*

At the airport, just before I pass through security I say goodbye to the girls and Dina with weepy hugs while my husband stands like a stoic with a cup of coffee in his hands. The last image I have of them is waving goodbye as I walk from the controlled chaos that is airport security.

What can I say? Rehab is rehab. It's a nice place near the ocean, but it isn't a vacation.

I feel like I'm too close to being Elaine, to walking in her shoes and seeing the world through her eyes.

I hate being away from the girls. It's like a constant ache, not being with them.

Over the first week, the withdrawal gets worse. I've never felt this bad, not even after the surgeries. Then it starts to fade, but it takes more than a month to feel anywhere near normal.

I'm afraid and anxious. I worry about the girls, what's happening at home, what my life will be like, how I'm going to manage my back pain and lupus, my marriage, debt; everything. Sobriety isn't an end. It's the beginning of life without my coping mechanism.

There's a lot of group and one-on-one therapy. At first it's hard for me to open up; my body is too sick and many of the patients are young women, girls really, who aren't serious about sobriety. They all smoke and act as if this is just a rest area, a break from partying. They drive me nuts.

I do my best to ignore them. As the withdrawal wears away, I start to open up about my life and why pills were an answer to it. My counselor tells me that only a handful of people manage to remain sober. Looking at the party girls, I can see why, but I tell her I'm going to make it. Whatever I have to do, I'm not going to end up like Elaine.

After a couple of weeks, Dad and Jeffrey come to visit. I still feel like hell and look pale, withdrawn. Jeffrey is fascinated by the place and can't stop looking around.

When Dad sees me he says, *Doll, you look great!*

I tell them about how all of this started and how things are going.

*I'm afraid I'm too much Elaine's daughter.*

Dad stiffens. *You'll never be anything like that woman.*

Jeffrey leans in. *This isn't your first detox, you know?*

*I know. Born addicted to heroin, right?*

*Yeah, Elaine gave you a head start, but you're strong, you'll be okay.*

*Okay?* Dad says clapping his hands together. *Okay? You're going to get through this and you'll be great. I know it, Ady, I just know it.*

Their love sustains me more than either will ever know.

Over time, the party girls filter out and a new set of young women filters in. Some of them are the rest-stop types, but more of them want to be sober. Like me, they've reached their end with drugs and want off that path before they die. At age forty I'm older, like a rehab mother to them, and they call me *Sexy mama,* which I like.

I talk with my daughters as often as I can, and with Dina, but it never feels like enough.

During spring break, in late April, my husband brings them out to visit. I'm delirious with joy to see the girls and I'm allowed to go out for dinner with them. I love being in their presence and doing something that feels so normal, a family meal, but my husband drinks three martinis during dinner. I wonder if he needs them or is just being obtuse to the fact that I'm in rehab. Maybe this is just him being passive aggressive.

When his credit card is declined, it sets him off and he's irate at the waitress. Then he starts yelling at Alex. I start to cry and beg him to stop, to not ruin this dinner, this first chance to be with my girls in more than two months. He yells back and we are in a shouting match in the restaurant. The girls are beside themselves.

I feel horrible. I wanted to show the girls that I'm okay, that treatment is working and things can be different, but it's more of the same. I need a better way to manage his anger and my emotions, but there is no doubt that he's still the same man I left behind: tense, nice, angry, distracted, and then I'm on the receiving end of his temper.

I tell my counselor about the fight. She knows our story from our weeks of sessions. Without any change in her expression or emotion, she says, *He's having an affair.*

I know it's true, but the same fears about money, losing the girls, making a life as a single mother are too much, too painful. I put this in a little box and pack it away.

When my husband and the girls come to say goodbye, he is silent. I have nothing to say to him, either. The girls are quiet, sad.

*We spent more time in the car than seeing you,* Frankie says.

I hold her and tell them I'll be home soon and that I love them.

When I call home over the next couple weeks, I don't speak to my husband, just the girls. One evening I call to speak to the girls and he answers. I don't know what sparks it, but the call becomes a hard fight. When I hang up, I realize I've had it with rehab. I'm done. I can't stay here any longer. I have to go home, back to my girls, back to life and whatever that holds.

I go to the main desk and ask for my credit card—I had to hand over a number of personal items during intake—and use it to buy a plane ticket home. When I tell my counselor, she's worried, but says I've come a long way.

*Get to a meeting as soon as you can,* she says. *Do that, and I think you'll be okay. You were in Al-Anon, you've done a lot of work, you get it.*

On Friday, May 28, 2005, Memorial Day weekend, I walk out the front door of Sober Living and climb into a cab that takes me to the airport. By that evening I'm home having dinner with the girls.

They are excited to have me home and I'm in love being with them. I promise never to leave them for this long again; never to go back to the pills. I can do this.

They're also excited for a swim meet at the club the next day. There's no question I'll go, but this is a big club event. The in-laws will be there, as will most of the members, and it'll be an afternoon-long cocktail hour as the kids swim and summer season begins.

My husband is working and doesn't come home until late. He's distracted and doesn't seem interested in me. I ask him when we'll leave for the club. He says he has to work, but he'll head to the club when he's done. I beg him not to be late and he asks why. I tell him I'm not sure I'm ready for so many people or for being at a cocktail party and that this is something we talked about in treatment; that I have to ease back into life sober.

*Don't worry, I'll be on time.*

The girls and I leave for the club the next day. People are friendly and welcoming, but I've never felt I belong here and that is truer now.

*The Club* is by definition a clique within a community of people who define themselves by the social circles they travel in. I'm *the dalliance, that woman who can't get her life right* and now, *the pill popper, the addict.*

Standing alone in the middle of all these people, I close my eyes and breathe deep. I look down at my bag and begin leafing through it until I realize this is nothing more than the reflexive act of an addict. I ask the bartender for a bottle of water so I have something to hold, but then I feel self-conscious that it's only water. I walk to get a better view of the pool, but the girls aren't swimming and I feel self-conscious for ignoring the people around me to watch the pool. Everything I do to feel normal, to look normal, only makes me more aware of the fact that I'm not.

I'm an addict days out of rehab at a cocktail party, trying to look natural and trying not to drink.

Where is my husband? He's late and he promised he'd be on time. I pull my phone out of my bag and call him, but it goes to voicemail. Damn him.

I dial Dina's number, thinking that all I want is to be a mother. I'm so done with all the rest of this crap.

*Hello?*

*Dina, hello.*

*How are you? Where are you? Are you at the meet?*

*I am.*

*Is it okay?*

*No.*

My voice breaks, but I catch it.

*I'm the addict at the party and I hate it.*

Dina and I talk. Her voice is calm, reassuring, loving and she reminds me that swim meets are part of being a mom. I know this, but I'm so overwhelmed. She says it'll be okay, I'm strong, my husband will be there, and the girls won't hate me for leaving.

I back away from the metaphorical ledge and look up to see my husband.

*I have to go,* I tell Dina.

I walk up to my husband and tell him I need to leave. It's too difficult being among so many people so soon after coming home. I'm angry and afraid he may cause a scene or that we'll cause a scene. It's obvious he's angry, too, but there isn't an argument.

We need a better way to manage how we treat each other, but I don't know what that way is.

⟨⟩

Sunday is a day of tense détente with my husband and I spend the day with the girls, getting caught up and introducing myself back into their lives. I also know that I need to continue the work of being a sober person. There's Nadia, but daily AA meetings are an important piece of my recovery plan.

I look online and there's a daily 7 a.m. meeting at the church next door to our home.

The next morning I walk into a basement meeting room of the church, where about twenty or thirty people are talking in small groups. Most of them hold a coffee cup in one hand and look comfortable chatting as they wait for the meeting to start.

To one side of the room is a table with coffee and donuts. I'm feeling anxious and awkward, like I'm an outsider intruding on their morning ritual and friendships. I walk to the table, but am so conscious of the effort to look as if I belong that my face reddens.

As I stir cream and sugar into my coffee a man walks up to the table and picks up a cup. He's wearing a white polo shirt with a green DogWatch logo, worn jeans, and LL Bean duck boots. He's smiling and there's something familiar about his eyes, his face.

*Are you new here?* he asks.

*Yeah, you could say that.*

*Well, you're in the right place.*

*I hope so.*

*I'm Johnny. What's your name?*

I press my lips together and let my eyes drift over the room. I'm not used to being noticed like this.

*I'm Adrianne.*

# Chapter Ten

## JOHNNY: LOVING ADRIANNE

- - - - - - - - - - - - - - - - - - - - - - - - - - - - - - - - - - - - - - - - -

*Uncle Dick, thank you for giving
my brother back to me.*

—Johnny's sister Lisa to family friend and
founder of Exodus, Dick Sattler

- - - - - - - - - - - - - - - - - - - - - - - - - - - - - - - - - - - - - - - - -

wish life could be simpler, uncomplicated. I wish falling in love could be effortless, like fate leading me by the hand toward the best person I've ever known.

But that isn't how life works.

*If wishes were horses beggars would ride in a buggy of pride,* Lizzy used to say when I was a child asking for too much, *and we'd all drown in a sea of manure.*

Looking at Adrianne as we stand by the coffee table, I have no idea who this woman is. It doesn't occur to me that I'm beginning another journey.

When I first saw her from across the room, all I thought was, *There's someone I might be able to help.*

I say hello and she says hello. She turns a little bit, then looks back.

*Have we met?* she asks.

*I'm not sure.*

She tilts her eyes toward the DogWatch logo on my shirt. *You installed our hidden dog fence, didn't you?*

*That must be it.*

*So you're a doggy ditch digger?*

*That's me; best doggy ditch digger around.*

I smile and then the meeting begins. It's common in AA to ask if there's anyone new to the program or to the meeting and have them introduce themselves. Adrianne raises her hand and says, *Hello, my name's Adrianne and I'm an alcoholic and an addict.*

The meeting responds with, *Hi, Adrianne.*

Then she says she's new to the meeting, but was in Al-Anon for a few years before her own sobriety. And that's it. The meeting moves along. At the end, I say goodbye and go work.

The next meeting I say hello and goodbye. I do the same at the next three. She's quiet, but focused. She starts sharing some of her story. Every so often a little more comes out. I watch her and there's something authentic about her. She's lean bodied and sparse when she speaks, but direct, sure of her story, and by her devotion to being an emotionally healthy person.

The bits and pieces of her childhood resonate with me. I knew life with an addict for a mother, but she hints at something harder, crueler about her experience.

Within a couple of weeks Adrianne asks my friend Jean to be her sponsor. She's moving forward with purpose, with intention. She's transforming from the shy woman I first met into a fuller person. I think about her, but it doesn't occur to me that there's a deeper meaning behind my thoughts.

Life's too complicated.

She's married.

I'm married.

I met my wife Carolyn in a pink cloud.

The compulsion to drink left me when I read my letter to Mom aloud to the group, but it didn't magically restore me. I still had to fight to overcome a lifetime of poor choices.

I owed the IRS for three years of back taxes, I was months behind on child support, my kids wouldn't have anything to do with me, I'd lost my driver's license for a year, my business was in receivership, gout and other health issues plagued me, my home was at threat of foreclosure, and my emotions flooded out.

The first affirmative step, and one that Pete helped with, was not setting conditions on my own sobriety. God gave me two ears and one mouth for a reason. I shut my mouth, opened my eyes and ears and listened. For the first time in my life I heard what people said and I trusted them enough to follow their advice.

As I worked the twelve AA steps I set out to rebuild my life. Sobriety, in and of itself, wasn't enough. I turned my life over to the ideal of progress, not perfection.

I learned, and I can't believe I'm even saying this, but I learned the value of honesty, the meaning of integrity, and the power of respect. I wasn't a perfect person, but I worked to be a better person.

I spoke with an accountant and told him I hadn't paid taxes in three years.

*If they haven't sent a notice or come after you, I would wait to see if they do,* he said.

*No. I'm going to pay them and I want you to help me figure it out.*

*Really?*

*Really.*

We created a financial plan that included back taxes, child support, and getting current with my mortgage. I reached out to the suppliers for my company and asked what it would take to get out of receivership. It was a huge, hard mountain to climb, but I worked from dawn 'til night to pull my business from the brink.

I couldn't do anything about my driver's license, but I avoided driving at all costs, only for work and AA. I'm not proud of this, and I did have a few close calls with the police, but work was key to healing.

And I learned to manage my emotions without alcohol. This is an ongoing act of personal growth, but one that allows me to enjoy friendships and life again.

The one broken piece of life I couldn't fix is my relationship with my kids. I reached out to them and their mother to make amends and ask their forgiveness, but I had caused a lot of pain.

As I worked the steps and ticked off the broken pieces of life, I was less anxious, more confident. People at meetings noticed and reached out to me, seeking help. I ran into an old friend from the Codasco days when I installed a hidden dog fence for her. She noted how well I looked. Before long she examined her own drinking and asked me for help.

Another woman told me I had the best smile she'd ever seen.

That's when it hit me. I don't think I'd smiled for a decade. Was I happy? Something must be wrong.

I called Barbara, my counselor at Exodus.

*What's up?* she asked.

*I feel great.*

*Good!*

*But this can't be right. I feel as if I'm floating and made of Teflon; everything just slides off me.*

*And, the problem?*

*I keep waiting for the other shoe to drop and everything to fall apart.*

*It's what we call the pink cloud. Your mind and body are free of alcohol and you're starting to get life right. It doesn't last forever, so enjoy it.*

*Am I done?*

*No. Look, if you think you've beaten it and you're done, I can tell you, you're not. Your own head and ego is the other shoe waiting to drop.*

In the back of my mind I remembered something Pete had said: *You're an egomaniac with an inferiority complex.* He was right. I had gone through life not listening and thinking I knew better, despite all evidence to the contrary.

*Stay out of your own way,* Barbara said. *Keep working the steps, rebuilding your life, and you'll be fine.*

I hung up the phone and felt a true sense of joy. I was proving myself worthy of Lizzy's love and Mrs. Tice's faith. When I saw life spread out before me, rather than pain and slow death, I now saw possibilities.

Carolyn walks into our morning meeting for the first time in early summer. She's a show-stopper for Pete. She's pretty and carries herself with an air of confidence. During the meeting she introduces herself and tells a bit of her story. It's obvious she's been sober for some time and is confident in her sobriety.

After the meeting Pete approaches her, but comes back with his tail between his legs.

*I guess leading with robbing a McDonalds wasn't the best approach,* he says.

*That's what you get for trying to thirteenth-step her.*

Some people use their confidence and status in AA to sleep with vulnerable newcomers. It's the lowest of the low, but I'm joking with Pete.

*Piss off,* he says.

Carolyn disappears, but comes back in late August. My head is still swirling in the pink cloud when she walks up to me and says, *Hi, what's your name?*

Someone told me that when you get sober you revert back to where you were when you started drinking. I don't think it's exactly true, but she looks at me with one eyebrow raised and I'm eighteen again.

I'm also less than a year into sobriety. I should know that dating with less than a year is a no-no. She has more than seven and is well aware of thirteenth stepping.

I should tell her no right then and there, but I don't. We date, break up, get back together, she's impressed I'm a Cella, break up again, get back together, then she wants to get married.

All my friends say, *No Johnny.* Barbara says, *No Johnny.* My family says, *No Johnny.* I ask her to marry me anyway.

There are few things more painful than marrying a woman no one wants you to have anything to do with.

It doesn't take long to learn what a dry drunk is. She stops going to meetings and becomes critical of everything I do and every choice I make. Nothing is good enough; she is angry and self-centered. She remains sober, but the fragments of her personality that drove her to drink never heal.

Tension builds and we stop sharing a bed. We stop socializing together. We stop being a married couple. I try encouraging her to seek help, to go back to AA, but she refuses. We sleep under one roof, but live different lives.

Like the fluttering wings of a butterfly causing havoc a continent away, I stop listening and think I know better and the pink cloud blows away. Some of the darkness comes back.

The night Adrianne calls for the first time, I'm lost in this marriage; I feel small and pathetic in the face of Carolyn's negativity and anger. It's obvious there are still lessons to learn. I need to say goodbye to my eighteen-year-old self completely. I'm doing my best to be the kind, open, thoughtful person I believe resides in my heart.

It's within this frame that Adrianne's sponsor Jean tells me she's going on vacation and asks if Adrianne can call me while she's away. I wonder if I'm too quick to say yes.

*Hi Johnny,* Adrianne says. Her voice is soft, tentative.

*What's wrong?*

*Well, this is when I call Jean.*

*Oh?*

*I think I need the continuity, you know, routines, regular check-ins, predictability; all that equals security, right?*

*Yes, of course.*

*Also, I relapsed last month and I don't want to get to the point where I'd put a pill in my mouth to make my heart feel better.*

*Heart?*

*To escape, emotionally, my soul.*

*I think the hardest part of all this is creating a calm life, free of triggers.*

*There's only so much I can do about that right now.*

I know the outlines of her story: Elaine and Herb taking her away from her parents, becoming addicted to pills, and the tension with her husband. But I don't know the full extent of it.

*I'm sorry for that, and I'm sorry to hear you relapsed. Are you safe tonight?*

If she says she needs someone I'm not sure what I would do. It might not be the best thing for a man to show up at her home, and it's discouraged in AA for men to sponsor women, and vice versa.

*No, I'm safe. He isn't here.*

She tells me that last Saturday her husband said he was going out for drinks with a colleague. This wasn't his normal routine, it felt out of character for him to do this, and it upset her. A friend suggested they go to a movie to get her mind off being left for the evening. After the movie, they talked for a bit and Adrianne was home by eleven.

Her husband wasn't home so she waited up for him. At two in the morning she called him, only to have him scream at her and give an excuse that felt like a lie. They fought the next day and then he left, saying he had to work.

*I worried that if I got too tired I'd have a lupus flare-up, so I was desperate to sleep. His Xanax was right near to me as I lay in bed, so I took one.*

*I'm sorry.*

*I went to my counselor that Monday and asked if that was a relapse and she said it was. I told her I believe he's trying to sabotage my sobriety.*

*Why do you think that?*

*I don't know, I guess because he left the pills right next to my bed. And it's just a feeling I get from him.*

*What did your counselor say?*

*She recommended a marriage counselor who's in recovery, too.*

*And?*

She pauses. *We've been through a lot of counseling and I'm not convinced it'll work.*

*I think you have to try.*

*I don't know.*

*It's worth a try if it means keeping your family together, isn't it?*

*I don't know.*

She describes what her marriage is like, the tension, anger, fights, how it's a trigger for her desire to get high, to escape. I listen, ears open, mind open, mouth closed.

*I know it's hard, Adrianne, but I've lost my kids. Drinking's a big part of that, but the divorce was hell on them.*

Adrianne's quiet for a moment. I'm not sure, but I think I've hit a sore spot. *I don't mean to say you'll lose your kids, but it'll be hard on them.*

*Are you married now?*

I feel my cheeks warm. *I'm probably not one to talk.*

*I'm sorry.*

*I've shared so much of my life in AA I don't think there's much you don't know, but my marriage is a challenge right now.*

*Sorry.*

*It's okay.*

*So, counseling's worth a try.*

*I think you have to be sure, don't you?*

*Yeah, I do.*

And that's it. We say goodnight and goodbye. Within my heart I feel a guilty pleasure and am happy she called, happy she'll probably call tomorrow night. I want her to keep calling, to hear her voice again and again.

The next morning I see her at meeting and a few inches of distance between us is gone. We say hello and spend a little more time chatting than normal. After the meeting, we linger by the coffee table talking.

That night she calls at the same time.

*Hi Johnny.* Her voice is soft, not so tentative.

*How are you?*

*We had another fight and he left, but I'm okay.*

*Do you want to talk about it?*

*Not tonight.* She pauses, like she's taking a breath. *Do you still find it hard not to drink?*

*I do, sometimes. Not all the time. It used to be all I ever thought about— you know, if things don't get better I'm gonna get drunk—but now I do this.*

*What's that?*

*Listen mostly, but talk with someone, try to help someone, if I can.*

*You're a good listener, I can tell.*

*I work on it. How about you?*

*I think about having a drink and the pills, but less than I used to. I thought maybe life would get easier being sober, and it has, but the problems that sent me running for my pillbox are still there.*

*I know. I had to learn how to do everything sober. One of the hardest was learning to cook on the grill without a beer in one hand and a spatula in the other.*

*I know!* She laughs. *I used to putter around the kitchen with a glass of wine in one hand and cooking dinner with the other. And you know? I was so bad, I went out and bought a colorful Art Nouveau pillbox.*

*I had beer cozies . . .*

*You didn't! That's so funny.*

*I know. The things you do.*

*I used to carry that pillbox everywhere and I miss it, not the pills, but having it with me, like a fashion accessory.*

I laugh and we continue talking like this for a little while more.

The next morning we talk a little longer before meeting starts. Afterward, we chat for nearly an hour.

She calls that night.

*I'm a woman of routine.*

*Oh, that's more than all right. I need routines too, and if something doesn't go right or how I want it, I can be impatient, I guess, or a bit of a control freak.*

*Tell me about it. I think I'm the most obsessive house cleaner I know. I need it to be a certain way, I need a certain order, to feel secure.*

*I remember you talking about cleaning the apartment you lived in with Elaine.*

*Yeah, I hoped she'd stop hitting me.*

*Control helps me feel a little less broken.*

*Maybe that's it.*

*All of us are broken, not put together right, like the Island of Misfit Toys, or something, and just need a little love.*

*I still feel broken.*

*Me too, but, you know, keep working on it.*

*I do, but after fights and everything, I just want everything to stop, and that scares me.*

*Why?*

*Because that's why I fell into the pills; to get everything to stop.*

*There's two things I heard recently I like. One is a George Carlin quote, I think, 'I got the monkey off my back, but the circus is still in town.'*

*I like that.*

*Another is from the tennis player Roger Federer; he was talking about an opponent and he said, 'He played like he was dead broke.'*

*I like that too. Goodnight, Johnny.*

*Goodnight, Adrianne.*

The next few days are the same. We talk and linger a little longer in the morning and then chat at night. Not for too long, but enough to get us through the night.

Jean comes back from her vacation and I expect that's about it for the nightly calls, but a few nights later Adrianne calls.

*Do you believe in God?* she asks.

*I do.*

*Why?*

*Because I've changed.*

*Me too.* Her voice fades into the phone.

*Are you religious?* she asks.

*I don't know. I heard someone say religion is man-made, but spirituality is God given. I like that. I like having a higher power.*

*I've heard that, too, and that God is everywhere and in everyone.*

*True, and that's why I work to be compassionate to people, though I'm far from perfect.*

*Yeah, me too.*

I pause to think for a moment. *I do have to remember to be careful to keep my balance.*

*Careful?*

*If I let anything come between my higher power and me, it becomes my new higher power, my new God.*

*How so?*

*Alcohol was my God for a long time. Work became my new God. Carolyn, too. By balance, I need to keep everything else, that isn't my higher power, in perspective, in balance.*

Adrianne's voice warms. *Change what we can, accept what we can't and know the difference.*

*Yeah, perfect.*

And this is how our friendship is born; conversations stretching through the evening, allowing the other in a little at a time at first, but then plunging into the interior of our lives.

She talks about her husband. I open up more about Carolyn. She tells me about her children, their victories and challenges, especially Frankie's health. She tells me about her mom and Dad and says that she's worried about her Dad. Most of the stories about her parents are funny, endearing: Jones Beach, the bakery each Saturday morning, the tree out back that came down during a hurricane, the optimist and the pessimist bickering into the night.

I tell her about growing up in Ladue and that I graduated (barely) from Codasco.

*You're a Ladue boy,* she says.

*Born and bred, someday dead.*

*What about the whole doggy ditch digger thing?*

*I own the company.*

Then I tell her some of my stories, one of which is Thanksgiving at Uncle Charles' house with the servants and private hunting blind.

*Wait, Charles Cella's your uncle?*

*He's my mother's brother, but my life is quite a bit different from his.*

*What do you mean?*

*Well, no huge inheritance. Mom's money's long gone.*

I tell her about Lizzy. She laughs at the image of Lizzy sticking her head out the kitchen door to spit tobacco juice. I feel her warmth when I describe coming home from a day in the woods and Lizzy saying, *John David, I knew it was you comin' cause I could see your blond hair bouncing in my direction.* And I feel her empathy as I describe Mom passed out on her couch in her urine-stained nightgown.

I tell her about my friend George and the day his brother called. *Johnny, I've heard how you've turned things around and George needs help, too,* he said.

*What did you do?* Adrianne asks.

*I called him right away and jumped down into the hole with him.*

*What happened?*

*He told me to piss off.*

*I'm sorry. Is he still drinking?*

*No, I kept at it and finally got through to him. We were talking the other day, and he doesn't usually get soft and mushy, he's a guy. But he said 'Thanks to you, Johnny, I have my life, my kids and my sanity.'*

*I'm happy for you, and him, too.*

*Me too.*

I'm nervous to reach out to her, but evening conversations quickly turn into meetings for coffee. At the first of these, she excuses herself from the table for a moment and my Ladue upbringing kicks in.

*Are you standing for me?* she asks.

I smile. *Politeness is an inexpensive way to make friends.*

*You're kind of a goob for a doggy ditch digger,* she says.

Coffees become lunch and occasional afternoon chats. We talk as friends about sobriety and the pressure put on us in our relationships. We share the banalities of life, our small defeats and victories, our joy and sadness.

I do my best to keep my ears and eyes open and mouth shut; be an active listener. I also want her to find a way to make her marriage work, but with time I start to see what she sees.

She calls, upset, on a warm July evening and says, *We had another big fight. I'm sorry.*

*He wanted to leave the house tonight and said he'd be out late, but I wanted us to spend the evening together as a family. I tried and tried, but nothing would keep him here.*

*He left?*

*He did. Right in front of the girls, he left.*

Adrianne struggles with her marriage and I feel lost in mine, unsure what to do. I want Carolyn to go back to AA, but I hate the fights. I tell her that her anger is hard for me. She says I'm just deflecting. I tell her I'm imperfect, but her anger isn't right. She says if I wasn't such a problem she wouldn't get angry.

And then there's our house.

Two years ago we purchased a new home. She took over decorating it, but the house is in the exact same state we bought it in.

*She hasn't done anything?*

*We've spent a lot of money, bought and returned furniture, looked at paint samples until we have a pile of them, but she can't decide what colors or furniture. I offer my thoughts but she laughs me off, saying I have no taste or a horrible eye for color. She says I have no sense whatsoever and would embarrass her.*

A couple of weeks later, around July Fourth, Carolyn says, *This house is pathetic. It's un-decoratable.* I have no idea what that means, but ask her what she wants.

*We need to design and build a new house,* she says.

I say okay and started looking for builders.

*You're doing what?* Adrianne asks.

*Looking for builders.*

*Do you want to build a new house?*

*I don't know.*

*Do you?*

*No, I don't.*

*Then tell her no.*

I chuckle and look away from Adrianne, *Yeah, that'd go over . . .*

In my mind I know I'm just scared of the conflict, of another hard fight.

*I spoke with Dina the other day,* Adrianne says.

*Yeah?*

*And told her about the things we talk about.*

*What'd she say?*

Adrianne smiles. *She said, "That's intimacy!"*

*Oh yeah.* I say avoiding her eyes. There's something lovely about her smile, her eyes, and it embarrasses me to think she could look into my eyes and read my mind.

*I asked why, and she said, 'That you're allowing yourself to be that vulnerable, that's intimacy.'*

*Is that okay?*

*I think so. We're friends, right?*

*Yeah, friends.*

For the first time I feel a twinge saying the word *friend* in relation to Adrianne. There is an ease, an intimacy, a comfort, a sense of belonging between us that's become more than *friend*. There's no name she or I have given it. It just is.

A few days later, Carolyn asks about the builders and why I haven't found one yet.

*I'm not building us a new house.* I have no idea where the words came from.

*What?!*

*No, and I mean no. I'm not going to do it.* My hands and head shake from nerves.

Our separate bedrooms are further apart than ever.

In mid-August, on a Friday afternoon, Adrianne calls. *Get this,* she says, *he said he needs to clear his head and he's going to a hotel for the weekend.*

*That doesn't sound good.*

*No, it doesn't.*

Adrianne's working through fear and insecurity toward clarity. I don't want to steer her or guide her. I do my best to listen, but I can't be dishonest either.

*I think you may be right, he's having an affair.*

There's a pause and I hear a leaden breath.

*I know,* she says.

*Have you asked him?*

*He gets pissed and says, 'Of course not.'*

*Do you think he's telling the truth?*

*No, I don't.*

*I don't think he is either. If it walks like a duck and quacks like a duck, it's a duck.*

*I'm scared.*

*I know.*

*It feels like there's too much to lose.*

The next week Adrianne tells me her husband is gone for a few days, for work.

*I called our marriage counselor and told him everything,* she says.

*What'd he say?*

*He said, 'We'll find out.'*

Adrianne calls two days later.

*He walked into the counselor's directly from the airport for a session and said, 'I'm done and I'm moving out.'*

*That's it?*

*That's it. He didn't even come home.*

*Is he having an affair?*

*He swears he isn't.*

It doesn't take long for the other woman to make her appearance.

As I well know, with divorce comes change. It's change I fear when I think about leaving Carolyn. It's change that I see as Adrianne begins the painful, if necessary, path of creating a new life. I fear instability and Adrianne does too, but she begins as she should: one day at a time, one step at a time.

One of the first steps is cleaning out her garage. Of course there are hundreds, thousands, limitless metaphors for this one simple step, but Adrianne is too direct for that. Security for her begins with a sense of order, a need to clear the detritus.

I agree to help.

Despite the depth of our friendship, I've never been to her home. She has two dogs, three girls, and a full life. The house is loud and chaotic, not like the quiet of my home and my separate existence from Carolyn.

At first, the task seems overwhelming, but Adrianne and I fall into a rhythm as we rummage through the possessions of her past life. We chat and laugh. She isn't critical; I don't watch every word, afraid she'll throw it back at me. I look at her and all I feel is warmth, but life is too complicated.

Frankie helps and I catch her watching me, observing how her mom and I interact. At one point her husband pulls up in the driveway. He eyes me, then speaks with Adrianne and leaves.

When we finish, Adrianne and I stand together in the driveway and chat. Our voices are low, soft. Adrianne's eyes gaze into mine and mine into hers. There's affection and a sense of connection in the way she's looking at me and without thinking, I kiss her forehead.

My face reddens. Her face reddens. Have I stepped too far?

*I have to go,* I say.

She follows me to my truck. Neither of us speaks. Her eyes look down at the pavement. I expect her to say perhaps we shouldn't see each other for a while, that I crossed a line, that she's not ready, that she's touched and cares for me too, but can't.

I open the door and turn to her.

*I'm sorry,* I say.

*For what?* Her eyes drift to mine. They are bright and wide, seeking.

*Kissing you.*

*It's okay.*

*And for falling in love with you.*

*I'm falling in love with you, too.*

I'm scared and can't believe I'm doing to Carolyn what I've done in every relationship, but I'm elated.

She reaches out to me and gently holds my hand.

*Will you wait for me?* she asks.

*Wait for you?*

*Please be patient. I need some time.*

*We'll have to be patient with each other. I've only got one more relationship in me.*

*Thank you.*

When I tell Carolyn it's over, she breaks down and says she didn't see it coming.

Ed's a tall man, about my dad's age, and an in-your-face, direct type of therapist. He wears glasses, but his eyes penetrate through the frames.

*You're lucky,* he says. *The person after you canceled, so we have two hours.*

This is my first appointment with him. I look around the room and think there really is an archetypical therapist office. A comfortable chair and couch set to one side of the room, a desk and a few bookshelves.

I sit in the corner of the couch, which is lower than the chair he's sitting in. He crosses his long legs. His height means he's above me, looking down through his glasses.

*So, why are you here?* he asks.

*I'm at the end of one relationship and the beginning of another, and I've spent my life doing this, marrying the wrong woman, cheating on her, leaving her and doing it again.*

*And you want to stop.*

*I've done this from my first relationship and right through sobriety. I don't want to hurt anyone again, so I need to surrender and reach out for help.*

*You've internalized AA pretty well,* he says, stretching his back. *We've got time, so start at the beginning and let me know what you've been doing.*

I begin at the beginning and become a babbling brook. Born into a party that never seemed to stop. Mom. Lizzy. Dad. Margaret. George. Cheating on Margaret. Marrying my first wife knowing I didn't love her. Drinking. Mary. Seeing my kids' faces as I leave the house to drink and sleep with Mary. Losing my marriage and then my kids. Near death. Mrs. Godfrey. Rehab. Sobriety. Pete. AA. Carolyn. Adrianne.

All of it.

A lifetime of adults hurting me, or me the adult hurting others.

A lifetime of bad decisions.

A lifetime of failing in the most basic ways with all of my most important relationships.

When I finish, Ed presses his fingers together, forming a chapel. His lips and eyes are stern. In the light of his gaze I feel small.

*Johnny, you may be many things, survivor among them, but that's about the most positive thing I can say. This is who you are: You're a liar; a cheater; an adulterer; an alcoholic; a terrible, hurtful father; a self-centered, egotistical boyfriend and husband; you will cause people great pain to avoid telling them the truth; in fact, most of your adult life is a story of causing others pain because you lack the will to do what's right.*

He shifts his legs. *Now, I'm going to tell you why you are these things.*

For the next half hour he backs up each of my failings with the evidence I've given him, the truth of my life. He is intense, matter of fact, forceful, and each word has a profound effect on me.

The litany is overwhelming and when he finishes I'm in tears and speechless.

*Go home and think about all of this and I'll see you next week.*

For the first time in my life, I sit with a candle and meditate.

I'm beaten and battered and enjoy time with Adrianne, but it's at arm's length. I don't know how to move forward and she's asked me to be patient, which is a welcome relief. We kiss lightly after dinner together, but that's as far as we go. She's still impressed that I stand for her each time I leave the table and she tells me she feels safe with me, secure.

These words feel kind and good, but I wonder if they are true. If she knew the truth I laid out for Ed, she might strip my emotions bare, as he did.

Sitting in Ed's office for our next meeting, I feel scared and vulnerable. He begins by saying *We've torn you down; now we build you back up.*

*I'm ready for the work.*

Near the end of the session Ed pauses, shifts his legs and says, *Johnny, there's something you need to do.*

*Yes?*

*You need to lay it all out for Adrianne.*

*All what?*

*She needs to know the man you've been in your past relationships.*

*I don't know.*

*What are you afraid of?*

*She'll leave me.*

*Maybe. Look, the only way for you to truly know her is for her to truly know you. She's seen the good man you can be, but there's a reason why you've left a trail of wreckage behind you. She needs to see it to believe it really is behind you.*

*But—*

*Johnny, we've just started, but you've come too far to live your life in constant fear and insecurity. There's a phrase in AA I'm sure you know well, "Let go and let God." This is an opportunity and you need to trust fate, not fear it.*

*I'm not sure.*

*Do it.*

*Okay.*

As I leave Ed's, I call Adrianne and ask her to come for dinner. I don't want to give myself a chance to chicken out.

When I ended things with Carolyn, I moved out of our house into a small, eight-hundred-dollars-per-month, crappily furnished apartment in Kirkwood. I don't like it and it embarrasses me when Adrianne visits.

As I pull dinner together my phone rings. It's Adrianne, checking in. This is the second or third call this afternoon. This is now the norm for her with me: an update, a quick story of how her day is, and then off.

As I clean and cook, I'm scared. I don't want her to leave me. I do love her.

I worry, *What if she isn't the right one? What if I'm projecting onto her what I want to see and just repeating my pattern?*

The anxiety of it dries my throat and tightens my muscles.

There's a knock on the door and Adrianne comes in. It's early evening in late summer, so the sky is a deep blue, the sun still bright. She's wearing a white, low-cut blouse and jeans. Her eyes are a dazzling hazel and her hair a soft chestnut that rolls in light waves to her shoulders. My heart beats faster whenever she's close and she's the most beautiful woman I've ever seen.

I give her cheek a gentle kiss. She smiles and I feel my cheeks redden.

I'd wanted to wait until after dinner, but I can't imagine sitting through a meal with the weight of what I have to tell her on my chest.

*We need to talk.*

Her gentle hazel eyes sadden. *Okay.*

We sit on the couch, turned to face each other.

*I spoke with my therapist today and he said I need to be honest with you about my past.*

She folds her arms across her belly. *Haven't I heard most of it already?*

*No. I haven't shared everything.*

*You're scaring me.*

*I'm sorry, but you need to know these things about me.*

*All right.*

I start with Margaret. I tell Adrianne that when Margaret and I met it was a wonderful relationship where we meant so much to each other that it's hard to put into words. Then one night, at a party, I slept with another girl. Then I did it again, and again.

Margaret found out and broke up with me, but I begged her to come back and she did.

I'd sleep with another girl and the cycle would repeat until she finally had enough and left me. I did the same with my next girlfriend and every subsequent girlfriend. It was an endless series of lies, egotistical and self-centered behavior mixed with escalating reliance on and addiction to alcohol.

I hated hurting these people and the guilt of it deepened my self-hatred. But I didn't stop. There are excuses—they were drinking affairs, mistakes, I felt guilty, never again—but the truth is I was a liar and a cheater. I was selfish, egocentric, mean, and hurtful. I liked the excitement of the whole deal, the danger and risk of it, even as I knew how destructive the affairs were.

I was also insecure, afraid, and damaged. I did to these girls and women what Mom did to me. I tore them down.

By the time I married my first wife, alcohol was in charge. I didn't love her, but I didn't care enough about her or myself to be honest. I'd lied and cheated, so what was one more lie? Dad called me *Unconscious* and he was right.

My first child and then my second child came, but becoming a father didn't dent the shell I'd built. All I wanted was to drink and with that I wouldn't say no to any woman. This is why Mary was the perfect affair. She was a drunk, I was a drunk.

I describe to Adrianne walking past my kids at age four and two to leave the house and then waving goodbye to them as I pulled out of the driveway to get drunk and sleep with Mary. I was close to my kids, I loved them as any parent would, but I tore them down. The sadness in their eyes is the most painful memory I have, because love wasn't enough to get me to stop.

I should have remembered what it was like when Mom dragged us to Florida and we saw bellhops carry her limp, inebriated body into the hotel. I should have known that what I was doing hurt. I've been through it. I've felt that fear, that loss and, in the simple, clear-eyed way of a child, wondered, *Why doesn't Mom love me enough to stop? Am I unlovable? Am I not worth the act of love it takes to not drink?*

During the divorce my wife accused me of sexually abusing the kids, which meant I couldn't see them. I was a horrible dad, but I didn't do that. It was a common tactic used by divorce attorneys in the early 1990s—she had sharks, like Mom had against Dad—and I was a test case. I passed a lie detector test and when subsequent information came to light it became clear the accusation was a lie. But it's part of my story and I can't erase it, nor do I want to hide from it.

After the divorce, Mary and I maintained a terror of a relationship. She was abusive and had affairs. I had affairs and turned my life over to drinking and making a mess of life, mine and others. Nine months before getting sober I went to a party and hooked up with the hostess, who was twenty. I was forty, and she'd gotten engaged that same day.

As I sank further into alcohol, I became an embarrassment and disappointment to my friends and family. After pushing a friend down, I was all but thrown from his party. I was uninvited to parties, not asked to be in weddings, to be a godfather, or to receive many of the other marks of love and friendship others take for granted.

Like my mom's relationships, mine faded as people decided they didn't want the tragic drunk I'd become in their home, at their party, with their kids, in their lives.

Now I tell Adrianne, *I know there's a higher power in my life because I've opened my eyes and ears to it and I have changed. I have my friends back and I'll spend the rest of my life begging for my kids' forgiveness.*

*And then there's Carolyn. I knew I should have said no to her. We broke up many times and I knew I didn't love her. Everyone in my life said I shouldn't marry her, but I asked her anyway.*

*Even in sobriety, I still needed to learn the hard lesson of listening and keeping my eyes open. I needed to learn all over again, like a second sobriety, to not let ego and self-centeredness run my life. Down that path is all the behaviors I want excised from my life. It's the source of the pain I've caused so many other people and the source of my self-hatred.*

*I've spent my life hating myself. After hearing all of this, I imagine you don't like me very much either, but I want you to know everything I've described is the person I was, not who I am.*

*Who I am now is the guy who will do anything to help anyone find sobriety. I'm the guy who has enough sense to realize what he's doing when he meets the woman of his dreams, and I'm reaching out for help so I can be the man of your dreams. I'm the guy who will try anything to improve himself, whether it's meditation, dancing, sweat lodges, needlepoint, learning guitar or a new language, but most importantly, being honest about who I was so I understand who I am now and who I want to be.*

*I'm also the guy who's drawn to you in a way I've never felt before.*

*I've seen you become so strong, no longer a victim to your circumstances. You're beautiful and kind and everything I could ever hope for in a woman. When I'm with you, you influence me in ways that are hard to describe, but I'm my best self and I feel at home, at peace, blessedly calm. There are no doubts, no nagging thoughts, no indecision, no fear or insecurity.*

*I love you and how I feel with you.*

*I love you enough to be this honest, this vulnerable. I love you enough to say all this knowing that you may walk out of here and never have anything to do with me again. I'm lovesick for you and you're sitting right next to me.*

*I'm not perfect, but I'll spend my life doing my best to honor you, to make you proud that I'm your man. I hope you feel the same, or at least see a way forward for us.*

I look at her, but she turns from me. Her lips are parted and her arms remain crossed. She's silent. Marigold evening sunlight suffuses through the apartment.

With each moment I lose hope. My mind runs through the words she'll say to leave me and how it'll feel to hear them.

I tilt my head down toward hers. *I think I've screwed it all up. I'm sorry.*

# Chapter Eleven

## ADRIANNE: LIFE ON LIFE'S TERMS

*There are women succeeding beyond*
*their wildest dreams because of their sobriety.*

—Mary Karr

Iridescent, marigold evening sunlight sweeps in through a window and warms my face. I turn my eyes from Johnny's and feel him waiting for me, watching me, wanting me to say something, but I don't know what to say.

Who is this man? Is he a projection, an illusion born from the fantasies and dreams of a damaged little girl?

Or, is he like me; flawed, broken, a work in progress; an authentic person, complicated and with no small number of contradictions?

Becoming his friend was effortless. It felt natural to like him, to trust him, to see him as brave and genuine. Love grew in our conversations, his courage and thoughtful attention, the small details of being near him, and then a rush that ran through my body when his lips touched my forehead.

A kiss that was such a gentle act of affection and kindness, it could only come from some true place within him.

*You told him you love him?* my friend Dina asked.

*I did.*

*That seems quick.*

*I know, but there's something different about him.*

*Enough to rush into a relationship?*

*No, I need time, so I asked him to wait for me.*

*What'd he say?*

*He said he would.*

*And is he?*

*Yes, like a gentleman.*

*Don't rush, okay?*

*I won't.*

*And for God's sake, don't kiss him because once you get going—*

*I won't.*

I haven't.

All that's passed between us is gentle and kind, loving and caring.

The burnt evening light darkens by degrees.

He turns a light on, but otherwise remains patient and quiet, waiting. My eyes focus on my hands, which lie clasped in my lap. I don't know what to say or how to start. I feel his tenderness and his fear, but I think he would sit quietly waiting for as long as I need.

*I appreciate your honesty.*

*Thank you.* His fingers fidget. *But?*

I turn to look into his eyes. There's pain, fear of loss, I suppose. Am I worth this effort?

*You've been honest, so I'll be honest.*

*I've never had an affair, at least not a physical affair. The closest I came was with a man named Boyd. In the late nineties, I had something of a political awakening and volunteered for a campaign. As I got more involved I found that this was something I was good at and realized that people appreciated my work.*

*This led to candidates for national office asking me to volunteer on their campaigns and then the state chair of the party asked me to liaise with the bigger donors. Things sort of snowballed from there and it felt good to do something important. I'd been in pharmaceutical sales, but this was different.*

*For a split second my husband liked what I was doing, but then he started hating it. He became jealous and complained that I was one of a few women doing this work. His jealousy turned to anger and out of fear I said no to new opportunities because I didn't want to deal with the backlash.*

*Then I thought if I kept him happy he wouldn't get mad and I could balance what I wanted to do with his needs. I had dinner ready, called him throughout the day to check in, cleaned the house constantly, and did anything I could think of to appease him.*

*The problem was, the more I danced around trying to keep him happy, the more controlling he got.*

*At about the same time, the back pain started and I had the first surgery and started using meds to manage the pain. We also started fighting more over finances and, well, everything became a constant battle.*

*But I didn't want to give up on the politics and was invited to the state convention, which I loved. I met so many people and for the first time in my life felt respected for who I am and what I can do. I also started talking with Boyd about life outside of politics. After the convention, we kept talking.*

*I didn't cross a line, or at least I didn't feel I had, but my husband started getting more and more jealous. Then I was elected as a delegate to the national convention and my husband asked if Boyd would be there. I said no, even though I knew he would be.*

*The day I left, my husband fell off the deep end. His jealousy was out of control and he couldn't believe I'd leave the family to go to an event where there'd be so many men.*

*Before I left, reporters interviewed me on TV about the convention. Somehow, a reporter found out about the custody battle and the story about how I'd been taken from Mom and Dad. Other reporters saw the story and asked about it as well. At first, it felt like opening an old wound, but their narratives focused on how I'd overcome the challenge of my early life to find a measure of success.*

*The first day of the convention, I met some of the most powerful politicians in the country and organizers asked me to take on a number of responsibilities. I'd become someone people trusted and respected. I was having fun and my ego was on a high I'd never experienced. That night, there was a dinner and Boyd was there. There were drinks and everyone was schmoozing and Boyd and I found each other and spent the evening flirting.*

*The next day I felt guilty for it and called my husband. He blew up and accused me of having an affair. I didn't, but I didn't feel comfortable, either. We fought and I hung up the phone. When I did that he went through my phone records and noticed a lot of calls to and from the group Boyd worked for. Most of it was just to prepare for the convention, but that didn't matter.*

*My phone wouldn't stop ringing and every time I answered it there was a fight. I went from the time of my life to feeling so guilty and nervous that I barely ate and started taking the pills with alcohol.*

*Our marriage was difficult before, but when I came home, it became impossible. Everything became impossible: politics, friends, everything. I let it all go out of fear.*

Johnny listens, his eyes soft, intent, pained.

*I felt like a child living with Elaine again. My life faded into the background and I watched others, wondering how their lives could be so normal. I wanted that so much, but never had any idea how to get it.*

I rub tears from my eyes with the back of my hand.

*I remember Elaine all but pulling me out of my hiding place the day she took me. I sobbed and pleaded for Mom and Dad, anybody, to help me. There wasn't anyone. The people who were supposed to keep me safe gave me to Elaine and Herb. Mom and Dad couldn't help me. I couldn't even help myself. I escaped, but Mom and Dad had to send me back.*

*Even after Elaine died, I was afraid. I manage it better now, but I'm still afraid.*

*I'm afraid of other people's anger. I'm afraid of divorce. I'm afraid to lose my kids. I'm afraid for Frankie. I'm in constant pain and lupus will forever be part of my life, which makes me wonder how anyone could find me attractive.*

*I'm afraid of my financial issues. We're broke, lying to everyone we know about money, creditors call every week, and we're going to speak with bankruptcy lawyers. How am I supposed to make it? What do I do?*

I pause and take a breath.

*Anyway, I'm telling you all of this because I want you to know, really know, that I'm a much stronger woman in sobriety than I've ever been, but I get overwhelmed sometimes and feel small and vulnerable.*

Johnny shifts his body a little. *But you're so much more than that. If you could see what I see, you'd know it's true.*

*Thank you. I'm also afraid of repeating my past and making the wrong choice for the wrong reasons, again.*

These words hit Johnny harder than I've meant.

*You mean me?* he asks.

*I married my husband despite many red flags because I mistook neediness and jealousy for attention and love. I mistook money for security and peace of mind. None of it was true.*

*I complained to girlfriends and tried to use them as therapists, but I wore them out. 'If you're so unhappy, just leave,' they'd say, but I couldn't. I was too afraid and believed I didn't have the power to change my life. I knew what I wanted, but had no idea how to get it . . . Sorry, I say that a lot.*

*No, it's okay,* Johnny says. *I've felt the same way for too long, too.*

*What do you mean?*

*Well, you know, why does everybody else get to be happy except me? What did I do that's so wrong?*

A sly smile crosses my lips. *Poor me, poor me, pour me a drink.*

Johnny smiles. *Right, right, egomaniacs with inferiority complexes.*

He's folded his legs on the couch near mine. I look at the knees of his jeans. There's dirt embedded into the fibers. I remember he's spent his day working, probably since sunrise, with just a break for our morning AA meeting.

I brush his knee and feel the grittiness of it on the tips of my fingers. I like this about him. That he lives out in the world; his mind and body connected to work. There's something attractive, a little sexy, about a tanned, dusty man.

I pull my hand away.

*Fear kept me in a failed marriage even after I knew he was having an affair. I mean, my God, I went to rehab so I wouldn't fail my kids, but also so I wouldn't be the cause of my marriage failing. I kept trying, but in the end, after everything, he was the one who left.*

*If there's one thing I've learned, I'm never giving my power, my life away to another man again.*

Johnny wipes his hand over his mouth. *We're done?*

Wisps of sandy blond hair fall across his forehead. I want to reach out and blend them.

*I think I'm strong enough to be on my own, but I know I'm stronger with you. I don't know who you were, but I feel like I know who you are.*

*When I hear you and see you, you're kind, sweet and authentic. I've seen you live what you say and be brave and honest with others, but especially with me. No one has ever been as honest with me as you just were. I don't mean to excuse what you've done or who you were, but I don't see a liar and cheat.*

*You kind of remind me of my dad. You crack me up and are so cute. You'll also try anything and never tell me I'm dumb for liking the things I like. You let me be authentically me.*

*And for so long I've lived life waiting for the other shoe to drop, even though I have no idea what it is. It's just that every time I turn around there's some bad thing happening. I guess it's more like waiting for a closet full of shoes to drop. It hasn't gone away; I still look over my shoulder and feel there's a lot to worry about, but when I feel it building into a panic, I talk with you and we work it through, and I'm able to let go.*

*You're the antithesis of every man I've ever been with. I feel safe and secure, and I like how that feels. I like who I am with you and I've been so proud to have your love. I want to see if it stays that way.*

*I'm still afraid, though, and feel like I'm jumping from a ledge into a deep unknown, but my heart says you're worth the risk, that I won't hit the ground because if you don't catch me, I'm strong enough to care for myself.*

*I also feel like I know what doesn't work. I've tried drugs, alcohol, sex, and everything else to fill the God-shaped hole in my heart and my life. I want to do something different. The path I want to be on is based on sobriety, my relationship with a higher power, and building a relationship from honesty and love. It's the only way left.*

*But Johnny, please be careful with me.*

He leans forward. *I will. I always will, I promise.*

*Be patient and let me move at my own pace. I'm here with you, it's what I want, but I'm not ready for all of it, not yet. Please be careful with me and please be patient.*

He reaches out and holds my hand. *I will. I promise.*

Like two toddlers taking their first awkward steps, we begin to build a relationship neither of us has ever experienced.

We are tentative around each other, but our conversations fall into the easy, natural pattern we'd created before what we now call *The Stare* (the moment our eyes connected in love and Johnny kissed my forehead) and *The Speech* (Johnny's explanation of his past). The first few days, I call him throughout the day until he recognizes it's out of insecurity and says I don't have to call so much, or even at all if I don't want.

Rather than the frown or red-faced anger I'm used to, his words come with a smile and he offers them as a kindness, not an admonition.

Johnny is as patient as he promised to be, and he continues to stand whenever I leave the room. We talk every night and when we can during the day. He honors my needs and excuses my anxieties. He listens and allows me to own my life and choices without complaint or dismissive explanations about why I'm wrong or how I could do better.

He asks about the girls and offers help, but doesn't push to insert himself into the world I inhabit with them. They know him, know he is a presence in my life, but they are never forced to contend with the new man. They can process the ongoing divorce of their parents without intrusion and I'm allowed the space, when I need it, to do the same.

I feel safe and cared for. I'm loved, truly loved, rather than scrutinized or judged. I no longer feel powerless.

Late summer slides into September and then October. An ease and comfort between us replaces our initial, awkward steps. He is still patient and allows a gentle kiss and soft *I love you* to be enough. He revels in the simplicity of it all and tells me we are doing a fine job of filling the God-sized hole that exists within us both.

My husband moved out of the house, but there are a number of his belongings tucked away here and there. Our divorce churns along, slow and methodical, but unstoppable.

By Halloween there is little daylight between Johnny and me. That night, we are alone at my house, and I know the time is right. We fumble like teenagers, but let go and let God.

He holds me in his arms and for the first time in a long time, the world has stopped. It no longer spins and I don't feel like a juggler with three-too-many balls in the air.

This is when my husband, unannounced and uninvited, opens the bedroom door. He stands staring at us, silent, expressionless, his widening eyes pulling at the features of his face. Neither Johnny nor I move. For endless seconds the three of us are still, looking at the other, unsure of what to do, what to expect. Without a word, he steps out of the room and closes the door.

*Are you okay?* Johnny asks.

*I don't know. Hold me.*

I curl into his arms.

We fall asleep like that and I have a dream, a vision of our future. I'm standing with Johnny and the girls are near us. There's no tension, no fear, no anxiety; just a bright, opalescent light and warmth.

My eyes open and Johnny is still holding me. I pat his arm and give it a gentle kiss. A tear drops onto his skin.

*Are you all right?* he says.

*I am. I really am.*

I feel his body near mine and I feel safe. I'm calm.

I close my eyes knowing that I can accept life on life's terms.

# AFTERWORD

# LIVING WITH THE PAINTING AND THE PIANO

> *There is no real ending.*
> *It's just the place where you stop the story.*
>
> —Frank Herbert

The end of Adrianne and Johnny's separate stories is where they merge and become our story together.

It's not a perfect happy ending because life isn't like that, but that's okay because we've learned to live life on life's terms.

After our Halloween visit from Adrianne's husband, he went out and called a number of people from our morning AA meeting. Not only was this an embarrassing theft of our chance to share our happiness with friends, it had the uncomfortable effect of announcing we'd broken an important AA rule. Adrianne was less than a year into her sobriety.

After a friend called to tell us the cat was out of the bag, we decided to do what we'd been practicing: absolute honesty. The next morning we stood before our friends, many of with whom we'd shared some of the most difficult details of our lives and, holding hands, we announced our relationship.

Rather than the tsk-tsking and finger wagging we'd sort of expected, people were happy for us. They'd seen us grow close and maybe on some spiritual level, they believed we were each getting the person we deserved.

Of course, we were both still married.

No matter the circumstances, divorce is a difficult process, but we supported each other with love and honesty and managed our way through. In a serendipitous coincidence, our divorces were finalized on the same day.

We also kept our promise to move slowly.

Neither of us wanted our relationship to add more trauma or drama into the girls' lives. Both of us have experienced more than our fair share of childhood traumas and understood how damaging it can be. We wanted to be careful to ensure that Sam, Alex and Frankie had the best shot at remembering their youth fondly and starting life on their own terms, not carrying lingering resentments.

Easing Johnny into their lives and creating a sense of family was difficult at first. Change, even when done respectfully, is difficult. However, with our new superpowers of love, honesty and communication, we developed strategies to ensure the girls felt valued, their feelings validated and respected.

After about a year we agreed the time was right to move into the same home. Johnny's divorce agreement allowed him to move back into his house and we decided this would become our home. Adrianne, the girls, a truckload of belongings, and three dogs—one of them a Saint Bernard—moved in. That first night, the Saint Bernard took down the mailbox and the girls had a gaggle of friends over. Chaos ensued.

Johnny, a man used to a quiet and organized home, found himself in the maelstrom of living with three teenage girls.

Over the year we crept toward becoming a family, Adrianne's Dad's health worsened. He kept his sense of humor and optimism throughout, but a month after Adrianne's first sobriety birthday he passed away. Her mom had died while Adrianne was pregnant with Frankie. It was and remains hard to live life without the two people who provided her childhood and life with so much love and unquestioned support.

And although Adrianne was never close to Herb, she maintained some contact with him. She came to view him as a hapless man, hobbled by his addiction and his frailties, but she recognized that in his own troubled way he loved his children. Like Adrianne, he wanted a normal contented life with the love of his family. He died in 2010. Bina was with him when he died.

Bina called to tell Adrianne Herb passed and the two spoke for a little while, but their relationship faded back into its on-again-off-again status, until a few months ago. Bina and Adrianne reconnected, spending an entire day talking, reminiscing and connecting in a way they'd never been able to do before. Adrianne hopes to continue talking.

Johnny has also worked at remaining close with his family. His father recovered from the crash and is now back to being the brash, opinionated elder patriarch of the family. Joshua has had his struggles in his life, probably the result of abuse from his mother as well as verbal and physical abuse from Dale, but Joshua and Johnny are very close. Lisa has also had to work through her wounds, but has come out the other on side and is also close with Johnny and Joshua. They all have maintained a commitment to be together every Thanksgiving.

Chandler also occupies a place in Johnny's heart and is as much a sister as a friend, which is attested to by her support and help during Johnny's Dad's recovery from the crash.

As Adrianne and Johnny's lives together progressed, more challenges arose but with our second sobriety, which began the night we opened fully to each other, we've learned the skills to manage through life. We know we don't have to act out or use anger. Instead, we resolve conflicts rather than struggle to win a fight or force our will on others. We know the meaning and substance of nonviolent communication.

Over time, big problems faded and conflicts became opportunities to build trust. At one point, a friend of Frankie's said she was in awe at how normal our lives seemed. In much the same way I used to seek out the homes of friends for refuge, she wanted to be around us as much as possible.

Imagine that. The word *normal* used to describe us. It may seem like such a small thing, but finding a sense of happiness and normalcy, to be bored and content, no more drama or pity parties, is our life goal.

When either of us tells our story, we are often asked why we were able to survive and thrive while Johnny's Mom and Adrianne's biological mother died unhappy and alone.

There are a few reasons but, first and foremost, we were able to reach out for and accept help from a program composed of people a lot like us. In Alcoholics Anonymous and our outpatient groups we found more than twelve steps to maintain sobriety. It was a place where we met and bonded with a cast of characters who would do anything for us, and we would do anything for them.

We all come to the program flawed and damaged, but with the support of similarly flawed people we work through a process of getting sober and then learning the tools to deal with our flaws. Like the Island of Misfit Toys, we are all misfits and we are all broken. When we are on our own, life doesn't work well for us, which leads to the need to escape into addiction. When we are together and learn the true meaning behind *let go and let God*, we are very powerful.

When you think about it, other than Alcoholics Anonymous where can you go for a dollar donation and be able to tell people all of your problems, knowing they will support you? It's therapy, it's an education in honesty and responsibility, and it's laughter and building a life where once there was addiction. AA certainly wasn't on our bucket list, but it sure worked out!

This knowledge, the tools and the chance to bond with people like us, is what fills the God-shaped hole in our bodies and lives that we filled for so long with drugs or alcohol. This is what separates us from our mothers. They didn't have people like those we met in AA. They didn't have any of what we've found, because they were never able to reach out for and accept help from others.

We believe our sobriety is a gift and that in some way, God chose us to receive this gift. If that's the case, it is our responsibility and honor to pass it on to others. We are committed to reaching out to people who are ready to acknowledge that they can't manage their addiction on their own.

To this end, we have sponsored numerous people seeking sobriety and have traveled the country sharing our story with anyone who will listen. We've spoken in rooms filled with hundreds of people and in church basements containing just a handful. We have spoken at places from Washington University to death row.

We both realize we are only one drink or one bad choice from losing everything. We see the truth of this almost every day, but not more powerfully than in prisons. The contrast between the St. Louis Country Club and a maximum security prison couldn't be starker, but with addiction as fuel, the distance isn't as much as one might think.

For Johnny, looking into the eyes of these men is like looking into a mirror. Alcohol brought him to a deep and dark place where one poor choice could have irreparably altered the course of his and others' lives. *There but for the grace of God go I.*

As much as our lives of service are for the people we hope to help, we serve for our own benefit as well. Staying true to the course of sobriety requires diligence. Each experience with those suffering through the slow suicide of addiction or its consequences brings us one step closer to our higher power and one step further away from the oblivion of addiction and the traumas of our childhoods.

We are blessed. We know this. We are blessed to have found each other in this large world. We are blessed to be alive. We are blessed to be sober. And we are blessed to have the lives we have. We are blessed to know how to manage our lives when things go wrong. And we are blessed to have broken the cycle of addiction and death begun by our mothers.

Johnny will never forget one of the last things his therapist Ed said as they prepared to finish their work together. *Johnny, you're not just a survivor. You've gone beyond being a survivor. You are onto something much deeper, much better.*

The day Johnny wrote the letter to his mother and read it to his outpatient group, and then again at his mother's grave, the overwhelming compulsion and desire to drink faded from his body. This also marked the moment he began to forgive his mother and let go of his anger.

Adrianne had a similar experience. With Johnny, she returned to the apartment building in Brooklyn where she had lived with Elaine and Herb. In her hands she held a letter she'd written to Elaine, which she burned on the sidewalk in front of the building. Before this moment, she'd long since learned to live with the enduring pain and anger from Elaine. After this moment, she began to let go of that pain and anger and move forward. Her life is a vision fulfilled of possibility, hope and love.

A few years after we moved in together, we realized there was something left to do.

For nearly forty years the piano that had graced Johnny's childhood family room was kept in storage. It was now time to bring it from its confinement.

A few days before Thanksgiving, we brought the thing into our home and eased it into our family room. We removed the protective pads and wrapping to reveal the olive-colored antique piano with its stenciled fluted Grecian vases linked by ivy and ornamental ivy.

The sight of it stopped Johnny in his tracks. He hadn't seen the piano since his parents announced their intention to divorce. It is the object that links him to his childhood memories of his mother drinking to the point of incontinence. He heard Uncle Bobby playing his perverse rendition of *The Little Drummer Boy* for friends and family. He smelled the alcohol- and cigarette-soaked breath of his mother and father, their family and friends. He was back standing in the corner, watching, as the adults of his childhood became louder and louder and he was lost in it all.

Johnny walked from the room and for the next two days avoided the piano as much as he could.

On Thanksgiving Day, his father, Celeste, Joshua, and Lisa arrived with Lisa's family. With Johnny, they walked into the family room. They hadn't seen the piano for forty years. There wasn't a sound.

It was clear that the piano connected them to their past. So many of those people were gone, lost to alcohol or to the effects of punishing their bodies with drink and cigarettes. As Johnny stood with them, he began to see that a piece of him was among those lost people. He was no longer the scared, lonely boy of his childhood or the tragic, drunk adult he'd been.

The piano marked a deep contrast between the person of his past and the person of his current and future life. It could be as much a reminder of his journey to the light, as it was of his life within the darkness.

Soon after the piano returned to Johnny's life, the painting of Adrianne's childhood returned as well.

As we hung it in our front hall, Adrianne's childhood memories came to her. Many were pleasant and revolved around her mom and dad sitting together in their Long Island home after dinner. He read the newspaper while she knitted or sewed.

Adrianne remembered laying her head in her mom's lap and looking up at the image of the older woman needlepointing a soft, white length of fabric as a young girl watched. Both gazed tenderly at a small, framed circle of fabric in the woman's hands. Her mother had painted this scene before Adrianne came into her life. As a little girl, she'd felt it play out night after night, only to be broken by the appearance of Elaine and Herb.

Adrianne's memory shifted to being told that Elaine and Herb wanted her back, then that the judge has ordered it so. Her last memory of the painting was from when she was hiding behind the chair she and her mother used to curl up in. She was sobbing, *I don't want to go, I don't want to go.*

Love is the stronger memory. Today, Adrianne adores the painting. It brings back only the happy memories of her childhood, the time before life became difficult and painful, where the love of a little girl for her mom and dad could never be broken, and it never was.

We both understand that as much as any object could, the painting and the piano represent our two unique, yet parallel and braided journeys to become the people we are now.

In the AA *Big Book* it says, *The promises will be fulfilled, sometimes quickly, sometimes slowly, but they will always materialize if you work for them.*

One day, about a year ago, Johnny's daughter called and asked to visit. For the first time in twenty years, she came to his home, our home. She and Johnny chatted and we all had lunch together. It was nice and we thought the visit went well, but we had no idea.

Of all the painful losses, for Johnny losing his relationship with his children was the most painful. There were untrue accusations during his divorce from his son and daughter's mother, but even after the accusations were proven to be untrue, his drinking and dishonesty had caused too much damage.

Since his earliest days as a sober person, Johnny had sought to reconnect with his children and gain their forgiveness. Until his daughter's visit, this seemed more hope than possibility.

Adrianne pointed out that during lunch Johnny told his daughter over and over again he wanted to see her again and asked when he could. He understood he wasn't living in the moment, but was already on to the next chance to see his daughter. He texted to apologize and she replied that it was okay.

A couple of hours later she texted to ask if the two of them could have dinner. Johnny was over the moon and said yes, of course.

They met at a restaurant. His daughter noted they hadn't been alone together in twenty-one years. It was a sad truth that Johnny acknowledged, but it led to an opportunity for her to ask why and receive honest, heartfelt answers. He didn't sugarcoat a thing and was hard on his past behavior. He told her of his vision of seeing her and her brother standing in the dining room at age two and four waving goodbye as he went out to drink and continue his affair.

For two-and-a-half hours they talked this way, truthfully and from the heart. When they were done, they hugged and promised to stay in touch. Johnny got into his car and tears poured from his eyes.

Since then, there have been other dinners, other conversations, and a lot of time remembering to be in the present, enjoying what is happening right now and thanking God for the life you have and the person you've become.

Today our lives are good. The girls made it through high school and are now off at college. Johnny sold his doggy ditch digging business and with a little luck we were able to buy a beautiful condo on the coast of Florida. Our balcony overlooks the ocean and it's like a dream come true for us both.

We remain involved with AA and continue to do everything we can to help anyone in need. We miss the morning meeting where we met, but we've found a wonderful AA meeting here. We continue to sponsor people and share our stories when we can. Adrianne also volunteers at Hartman House, which is a halfway home for men transitioning from rehabilitation into a sustainable recovery plan.

Unfortunately, Adrianne deals with near continuous pain from her lupus and spinal issues. She wakes up each morning in pain and goes through a routine to get ready for the day, but she has the tools to manage it so that it's part of her life, but it isn't her life.

And we love our home on the beach.

As Adrianne told a friend, *I've always wanted to live on the ocean and it sounds so corny, but I have a great life. I really do. I feel so at peace and haven't felt like this since I was a little girl.*

It was while watching the sunrise over the ocean that we decided to write a book, as a roadmap of sorts to anyone feeling overwhelmed by life.

We lived in such darkness and were so lost that we believe that if we can find our way to the light, then anyone can. We are blessed, but it's a blessing available to anyone willing to reach out for help and take the journey.

Johnny remembers when he reached out for help from his kitchen floor, shaking and vomiting. He wasn't looking for a spiritual partner, just for some way to stop the shaking and to not die.

On the night of his sixteenth AA birthday, Johnny had a dream. He was back on Oakleigh Lane in the living room with the piano. His mother was sitting on their couch dressed as only a socialite could dress and asked, *How has your life turned out? Have you accomplished what you set out to do?*

He woke with tears in his eyes knowing, *I am slowly becoming the man I think you would have wanted me to become. Thank you for my life. I know you did the best you could.*

# ACKNOWLEDGMENTS

First of all we want to thank our higher power whom we refer to as God, as well as our AA groups, outpatient/therapy groups and all our counselors along the way.

We wish to thank our families, without their help, willingness and understanding this book would not have been possible.

A big shout out to James for his creativity, insight, friendship and compassion for our vision. Laurie for her endless devotion, Lawna for her cover design idea and Pat for perfecting our work. Our team at HCI Books: Kim, Christine, and Taklima.

Without our friends this journey would not have been possible. We won't mention by name, but you know who you are and we can't thank you enough for your encouragement, interest and participation.

# ABOUT THE AUTHORS

Award-winning authors *John Lipscomb* and *Adrianne Lugo* reside in South Florida. When not touring and speaking about their book and lives, they sponsor and help others in their local recovery community. Please visit their website at *www.paintingpiano.com* for more information or speaking opportunities.

## Final Thought

We want to thank you from the bottom of our hearts for purchasing our book. Our hope is that you found it to be hopeful, informative, and inspirational. From day one, we have said that if this book helps just one person then it is worth it!